M·A·T·H STARTERS!

5- to 10-Minute Activities That Make Kids Think, Grades 6-12

JUDITH A. MUSCHLA · GARY ROBERT MUSCHLA

THE CENTER FOR APPLIED RESEARCH IN EDUCATION
West Nyack, New York 10994

Library of Congress Cataloging-in-Publication Data

Muschla, Judith A.
    Math starters! : 5- to 10-minute activities that make kids think,
grades 6 – 12 / Judith Muschla & Gary R. Muschla.
        p.   cm.
    ISBN 0-87628-566-3
    1. Mathematics—Study and teaching (Elementary)   2. Mathematics—Study and
teaching (Secondary)   I. Muschla, Gary Robert.
II. Title.
QA135.5.M85   1998   98-28657
510`.71′2—dc21   CIP

Production Editor: Mariann Hutlak
Compositor: Publications Development Company of Texas

© 1999 by The Center for Applied Research in Education

All rights reserved.

Permission is given for individual educators to reproduce the activity sheets and
problems for classroom use. Reproduction of these materials for an entire school
system is strictly forbidden.

Many of the illustrations are reproductions from the Dover Clip Art and Dover
Pictorial Series.

For Erin

Printed in the United States of America

10   9   8   7   6   5

ISBN 0-87628-566-3

ATTENTION: CORPORATIONS AND SCHOOLS

The Center for Applied Research and Education books are available at quantity discounts with bulk purchase for educational, business, or sales promo-
tional use. For information, please write to: Prentice Hall Career & Personal
Development Special Sales, 240 Frisch Court, Paramus, NJ 07652. Please
supply: title of book, ISBN number, quantity, how the book will be used, date
needed.

**THE CENTER FOR APPLIED RESEARCH
IN EDUCATION**
West Nyack, NY 10994

On the World Wide Web at http://www.phdirect.com

ABOUT THE AUTHORS

Gary Robert Muschla received his B.A. and M.A.T. from Trenton State College and teaches at Appleby School in Spotswood, New Jersey. He has spent many of his 23 years in the classroom teaching mathematics at the elementary level. He has also taught reading and writing and has conducted writing workshops for teachers and students. A successful freelance writer, editor, and ghostwriter, he is a member of the Authors Guild and the National Writers Association.

Mr. Muschla has authored other resources for teachers, including: *Writing Resource Activities Kit* (The Center for Applied Research in Education, 1989), *The Writing Teacher's Book of Lists* (Prentice Hall, 1991), *Writing Workshop Survival Kit* (The Center, 1993), *English Teacher's Great Books Activities Kit* (The Center, 1994), and *Reading Workshop Survival Kit* (The Center, 1997).

Judith Muschla received her B.A. in Mathematics from Douglass College at Rutgers University and is certified K–12. She has taught mathematics in South River, New Jersey for the last 23 years. At South River High School she has taught math at various levels, ranging from basic skills through Algebra II. She has also taught at South River Middle School. While there, in her capacity as a Team Leader, she helped revise the mathematics curriculum to reflect the standards of the NCTM, coordinated interdisciplinary units, and conducted mathematics workshops for teachers and parents. She was a recipient of the 1990–1991 Governor's Teacher Recognition Program Award in New Jersey.

Math Starters! 5- to 10-Minute Activities to Make Kids Think, Grades 6–12 is the third book Gary and Judith Muschla have co-authored. They have also written *The Math Teacher's Book of Lists* (Prentice Hall, 1995) and *Hands-on Math Projects with Real-Life Applications* (The Center, 1996).

ACKNOWLEDGMENTS

We would like to extend our thanks to James Pope, principal at South River High School, William Skowronski, principal at Appleby School, our supervisors, and colleagues for their encouragement and support.

Our thanks to Geraldine Misiewicz, math supervisor at South River High School, for her suggestions and comments regarding many of the problems that appear in this book.

Thanks also to Michelle Philpott, a colleague at Appleby School, who offered countless helpful suggestions on just about every part of the manuscript.

We appreciate the efforts of Sonia Helton, Professor of Education at the University of South Florida, whose recommendations helped us to focus many of the topics of this book.

Most special thanks to Susan Kolwicz, our editor, whose insight and guidance helped us once again to fashion a book from its conception into its final shape.

We also appreciate the efforts of Mariann Hutlak, our production editor, who took the pages of our manuscript and guided them through the process of becoming a book.

And, of course, we'd like to thank our students, who never fail to make our days challenging and rewarding.

ABOUT MATHEMATICS INSTRUCTION

Mathematics has always been important, but never more than today. A solid understanding of math skills is becoming increasingly critical in the modern world's fast-paced, information-based economy.

To meet the demands of preparing students for success, math curriculums around the country have expanded. Along with providing instruction in mathematics, the math class of today must offer an environment in which students can work individually and in cooperative groups on meaningful, real-life problems, share ideas, use technology, and realize the great importance of mathematics in their lives. Most math teachers these days worry that there is not enough time for them to teach all the skills their students need, but extending the length of time math is taught is seldom an option when several subjects demand equal attention. Teachers need to make the very most of the class time they have.

Using a math-starter problem can help you achieve this goal. Providing students with a problem as they enter the classroom encourages them to focus their minds on math immediately. Because they will help you to fill every class with meaningful, productive activities, math starters will enable you to improve the amount and quality of learning that goes on in your classes.

We trust that this book will support you in your efforts. We'd like to extend our best wishes to you in your teaching.

Gary and Judith Muschla

How to Use This Resource

Math Starters! 5- to 10-Minute Activities to Make Kids Think is divided into two parts. Part One, "Making Math Starters a Part of Your Program," offers suggestions that will help you to effectively implement math-starter problems in your classes. Part Two, "Math Starters," contains over 650 problems, organized in broad topics and labeled for level of difficulty.

We suggest that you read through Part One before using the problems with your students. This section of the book provides information for incorporating math starters in your teaching routines. It also offers ideas for classroom management, tips on how to organize cooperative groups for math starters that are specifically designed for group work, and provides various methods for evaluation. Included in this section are reproducibles that may be handed out to students. For example, "Problem-solving Strategies" and "Rules for Working in Teams on Math Starters" provide guidance that will support the efforts of your students as they work on the math starters in this book. Overall, this section will help you to implement math starters effectively.

Part Two is divided into six sections:

- Section 1, "Whole Numbers: Theory and Operations," has 86 problems. This section includes a variety of problems on number theory, such as types of numbers, basic operations, greatest common factors, multiples, and rules for divisibility.

- Section 2, "Fractions, Decimals, and Percents," contains 122 problems. Included in this section are numerous problems on operations with fractions, decimals, percents, ratios, and proportions.

- Section 3, "Measurement," contains 76 problems that include operations with measurement in the English and metric systems, time, temperature, and other types of measures.

- Section 4, "Geometry," has 130 problems that cover the basics of geometry up through and including concepts and skills taught in high school. Some topics include angles, polygons, parallelism, congruence, similarity, right triangles, circles, perimeter, area, and volume.

- Section 5, "Algebra," has 128 problems, including topics taught in pre-algebra and extending to those topics taught in a high school algebra class. Just some of the topics include expressions, integers, linear equations and inequalities, graphing, monomials and polynomials, quadratic equations, factoring, and imaginary numbers.

- Section 6, "Potpourri," contains 112 problems. This section includes numerous problems on topics as varied as data analysis, probability, fractals, codes, symmetry, vectors, matrices, and networks.

Each problem stands alone, and is numbered according to the section. For example, problem 1–76, "Greatest Common Factor," is the 76th problem in Section 1. Problem 4–33, "Classifying Triangles by the Measures of Their Angles," is the 33rd problem in Section 4, while 5–1, "Simplifying Expressions: Without Exponents," is the first problem in Section 5. Background information and any necessary diagrams or figures are included with the problems.

The titles of the problems focus on the skill or topic the problems address. Thus, the table of contents doubles as a skills/topic list. For example, if you are teaching quadrilaterals, you would simply turn to Section 4, "Geometry," in the contents and skim down to problem 4–64, "Identifying Types of Quadrilaterals." You may decide to use this problem to introduce new skills or reinforce skills you've already taught.

The skills in each section generally follow a sequence common to the typical math curriculum, from basic to more complex. Problems are also identified with one, two, or three stars: one star (∗) indicates a basic problem, two stars (∗∗) identify a problem that is somewhat more difficult, and three stars (∗∗∗) denote a problem that is challenging. Often two, three, or more problems will address a specific skill with increasing degree of difficulty. Problems designed for group work are designated with a **G**. Always read problems before you assign them to determine if they are appropriate for the abilities of your students.

Because mathematics is not an isolated subject, many of the problems in this book use information or situations from other areas, for example, literature, science, geography, or history. This helps to generate interest and broaden the scope of your math instruction.

You will find that many of the problems in this book are ideal for use with calculators. Whether to use calculators or not, however, is a decision you must make, depending upon your preferences and teaching situation.

"Answer Keys," contains the answers to the problems. The answer keys are arranged according to section. While most of the problems have only one answer, some have multiple answers, or answers may vary based upon the reasoning of the students. Some problems require written explanations. In such cases, you should accept any answer that students can justify.

We suggest that you use this book as a resource, selecting the math starters that best enhance your program. Beginning each class with a math starter will help you to make the most effective use of your class time.

CONTENTS

Section 3   MEASUREMENT 91

PART ONE

Making Math Starters a Part of Your Program

The first few minutes of any class are critical. Classes in which students begin working from the start are usually more successful than those in which the first few minutes are lost "getting settled." This is especially true of math classes where there always seems to be too much to learn in too little time. Just losing five minutes at the beginning of class each day adds up to 25 minutes per week, or about a full period every two weeks. For the typical school year, that's 20 periods (or about 20 days of math instruction and learning). When cast in this context, five minutes per day is significant.

While there are many ways you can start your math classes, one of the most efficient and effective is with a "starter" problem. Referred to by a variety of names—including do-nows, openings, beginnings, and anticipatory sets—math starters (the term we like because a math starter *starts* the class) can help you get your students working from the moment they sit down.

THE VALUE OF MATH STARTERS

A math starter is a problem that students begin working on right after they step into your class. The problem is designed to take 5 to 10 minutes, which includes going over the answer and conducting any discussion that may be necessary.

Math starters are valuable in several ways. They provide students with a reason to come into class ready to work. Being presented with a problem upon their arrival encourages students to focus immediately on math. The problems may be used to review prior skills, supplement current instruction, or challenge students with new material. When used as a review, math starters can help keep skills sharp and foster in students feelings of success and achievement. When used to supplement current studies, the problems can provide different perspectives or applications of the skills and concepts students are learning. When used to introduce new material, the problems can challenge students by extending their learning horizons.

Utilizing math starters at the beginning of class supports classroom management. While students are solving the problem, you may take attendance, hand back papers, check homework, or circulate around the room observing your students' work. These few minutes are valuable because they allow you to interact individually with your students. It's a time when you may note students' strengths and weaknesses, help them to master a new skill, or offer encouragement, praise, or a helpful suggestion. Rather than always being in front of the class, you will become a part of the class.

STARTING CLASS WITH A MATH STARTER

You and your students will benefit the most from the math starters in this resource if you use the problems regularly at the very beginning of class. On the first day of school, as you explain your goals, expectations, and the requirements of your class, tell students that they will be expected to complete a math starter upon their arrival to class each day. (Of course, you may prefer not to use a math starter on days of quizzes, tests, or special projects.)

You may wish to begin this first class with a math starter, perhaps a review of skills students learned last year. This is a good way to demonstrate the idea and procedure of completing math starters. Be sure to explain the purpose of math starters, why they are valuable for students, and how you will assess them. (See "Evaluation" at the end of Part One.)

You may present math starters via copies or an overhead projector. Either way is practical and efficient; select the one that better suits your teaching style.

- If you prefer to use copies, you may distribute them once students are in their seats, or you may put them on the corner of your desk or another accessible location so that students may take a copy of the problem as soon as they enter the classroom. Students should then go to their seats and start working. This method has several advantages: (1) Students get their work upon arriving at class; (2) they are encouraged to sit down and begin working, thus reducing talking and "fooling" around; and (3) class time is used most efficiently. They may solve the problems right on the sheet, reducing the amount of paper the class uses, or you may prefer that they maintain a math-starter notebook for their work. See "Purpose and Value of a Math-starter Notebook," which follows.

  Instead of having students pick up the problems as they enter class, you may distribute them after all your students have arrived. This method is ideal if you need to have everyone's attention before the class starts working. As you are handing out copies of the problems, you can give any directions, special instructions, or hints that you feel are necessary.

- Using an overhead projector to present math starters eliminates the need for copies. Have the projector ready and show the problem as soon as students are in their seats. While they may do their work on single sheets of paper, we recommend that students maintain a math-starter notebook that will contain all of their work on math starters.

Whichever method you select to present math starters, it is important to set and maintain a classroom atmosphere that supports learning. Students must be made to realize the importance of beginning work as soon as they come to class. They should work in a serious manner, and take pride in their progress in learning math. The atmosphere that is established while they work on math starters will extend into the rest of the class.

PURPOSE AND VALUE OF A MATH-STARTER NOTEBOOK

An excellent way to enhance the importance of math starters, as well as provide a place in which problems can be saved for future reference, is a math-starter notebook. This notebook will become a type of journal in which students work out math-starter problems, offer written explanations of solutions when necessary, and keep notes on the problems they solve. You may also encourage them to write down any thoughts, questions, concerns, or ponderings they may have about math. Using a math-starter notebook in this manner can eliminate the need for a separate math journal. In time, the notebook will become a storehouse of students' work and ideas regarding their impressions of math as well as cast light on their progress.

While spiral notebooks or composition books are best for a math-starter notebook, a section of a binder or even looseleaf pages stapled together may serve well. Instruct your students to put their names on their notebooks. If they fill one, they should number successive notebooks in order. Students should always date their work and include the number of the problem.

We recommend that you review the notebooks periodically. You may collect them every few weeks, or check some from each class two to three times per week. Such a schedule makes your workload more manageable, yet enables you to monitor the progress of your students. While we don't recommend that you score each problem, you may wish to assign a point value for problems completed so that students realize they are accountable for their work. (See "Evaluation" later in Part One.) As you review the work of your students, you may write notes, comments, or suggestions, encouraging them to respond. You will probably be surprised at how many students will write back and establish a dialogue with you.

Since it's likely many of your students will not have had to maintain math-starter notebooks before, it's important that you explain how the notebooks will be used and what will be required. You might wish to distribute copies of "Math-starter Notebook Guidelines" and review the ideas with your students.

THE VALUE OF WRITTEN EXPLANATIONS

The importance of writing in math classes has been made clear through various studies in recent years and should be a part of every math program. Writing offers

Math-starter Notebook Guidelines

1. Use a standard spiral notebook or a composition book for your math-starter notebook.

2. Put your name and class number on your notebook. If you fill one notebook, number each additional notebook successively.

3. Bring your math-starter notebook to class each day.

4. Use your math-starter notebook only for math class. Don't use it for other subjects.

5. Start each problem on a new page. This will give you plenty of room for work.

6. Keep your work in order. Date and label your work. For example: Nov. 2, 1998, Problem #2–7.

7. Be aware that I will check your math-starter notebooks periodically. I may offer comments and suggestions about your work. If you want, write brief notes to me in your notebook, and I will respond to you. We can carry on a dialogue about your progress in math.

8. While I will respect the privacy of your work and ideas, remember that if I read something in your notebook that I feel endangers you or someone else, I must report it.

9. Periodically review your math-starter notebook and see how you are progressing in your learning of math.

10. Take some of your best work and share it with others. Discuss some of your ideas about math with others.

© 1999 by The Center for Applied Research in Education

students a way to analyze and share their thoughts about math in a formalized manner. Clear, effective writing requires students to think through their ideas, connect what they are learning to what they know about the real world, and communicate their conclusions and opinions to others. The math-starter notebook is a place where students may solve problems and provide written explanations of their work.

Whenever possible, encourage your students to share their ideas about math—its purpose, methods, applications, and value—through writing. Make writing an important and respected part of your program.

COOPERATIVE PROBLEM-SOLVING USING MATH STARTERS

In the real world, many jobs require that people work together to solve problems. While projects, group reports, and other special activities focus on cooperation, you can offer your students a taste of cooperative problem-solving with math starters designed for group work.

Working in teams offers many potential benefits to students. Along with fostering discussion and inquiry, cooperation provides a learning situation in which students can acquire considerable social skills. In small groups, where everyone has a role and must contribute, it is easier for students to take an active part in learning. As the team works together on the same problem, many students, even those who may feel intimidated speaking before the entire class, are more willing to share their thoughts. Moreover, ideas are usually debated quickly, resulting in fast feedback. As students work on solving a problem, several tasks may be involved. Strategies that might lead to a solution must be considered, mathematics must be applied correctly, solutions must be checked, and a method through which to share the team's results must be determined.

The math starters in this resource designed for group work may require 10 to 15 minutes of class time: 5 to 10 minutes to solve the problem and 5 minutes for discussing the solution. Although the problems obviously aren't so complex as those you'd find with major group projects, the math-starter cooperative problems here will promote critical thinking, foster cooperation, and build student confidence. Done periodically, they can provide a nice change to the class's routines, yet still support your objectives and program.

ORGANIZING TEAMS FOR PROBLEM-SOLVING

The best math teams are organized randomly. Groups of three to five work well for math starters designed for cooperative problem-solving. Less than three becomes no group if someone is absent, while more than five will be unwieldy. Since the problems are designed to take up no more than 10 to 15 minutes of class time, they are not complex enough to sustain the efforts of large groups.

Because the time allotted for math starters is limited, you should design your groups so that members sit close to each other. For example, if the four members of Group One sit in the first two seats of the first two rows, it is easy for them to come to class and push their desks together. This reduces the disruption of moving a lot of furniture or having students change seats.

Teams should be changed regularly, certainly after working together for three or four problems. Reorganizing your teams allows students to interact with many different personalities throughout the year, exposing them to varying viewpoints, dispositions, and abilities. They will be gaining valuable experience for coping with the real world. When rearranging your teams, it's not necessary to change everyone. As long as you change half of the members of the group, you will have provided it with a new "team" personality. When changing teams, it's often best to change students' seats as well to keep the shuffle of furniture under control. See "How to Set Up Teams for Cooperative Math Starters," which follows.

Since it's possible that at least some of your students have never worked in cooperative teams (or their experience is limited), you should explain the purpose of teamwork, your expectations, and the procedures students should follow. To help your teams work efficiently, consider assigning members specific tasks, such as leader, recorder, time monitor, checker, and presenter. Distribute copies of "Rules for Working in Teams on Math Starters" and review the information with your students.

You will likely need to train students in the methods for working together effectively, model appropriate behavior, and sit in on your teams and remind them of the proper procedures often, particularly in the beginning of the year. As students gain experience, they will be able to assume more responsibility for the team's work and you will be able to fade more to the background.

HOW TO SET UP TEAMS FOR COOPERATIVE MATH STARTERS

Working together in cooperative teams offers students a stimulating way to learn math. The following suggestions can help you to organize teams to solve challenging math starters.

- For solving math starters designed for cooperative groups, teams of three to five work best for middle and high school students.
- While you should organize your teams randomly, you should be sure to mix abilities, genders, personalities, and ethnicities.
- Always reserve the right to "readjust" teams. Some students, even when picked randomly, won't work well together. Other students should be kept apart. One disruptive group can disrupt the entire class.
- Set up teams so that team members sit close to each other. This reduces the need for moving desks, chairs, or students.
- Reorganize your teams regularly. This enables students to work with others and fosters cooperation with a variety of personalities.
- When you rearrange your teams, move students' seats.
- Make sure students understand what is expected of them. Model appropriate behavior and remind students of the proper procedures.
- Consider assigning specific roles to promote the efficiency of the teams, such as:
  - *Team Leader* to keep the team focused on finding a solution to the problem
  - *Recorder* to write down the team's progress and solutions

Rules for Working in Teams on Math Starters

By following the suggestions below, you and your team will work more efficiently.

1. As soon as you come to class, organize your group and be ready to work.

2. Be willing to work with other members of your team.

3. Be willing to share your ideas with others.

4. Carefully think about your ideas before presenting them to others.

5. After you are done speaking, let others speak.

6. Listen carefully and politely when others are speaking.

7. Ask questions when you don't understand something or haven't heard something clearly.

8. Remember to speak softly so as not to disturb other groups.

9. Strive to keep the discussion on finding the solution to the problem.

10. Remember that you are responsible for your behavior. You must keep your emotions under control and speak calmly.

© 1999 by The Center for Applied Research in Education

—*Monitor* to keep track of time and be responsible for any materials the team uses

—*Checker* to review the team's work, checking for accuracy

—*Presenter* to share the team's solutions with the class

Note: For small groups, students may assume multiple roles.

THE VALUE OF SHARING AND DISCUSSION

The importance of sharing and discussing the solutions to math problems cannot be overemphasized. After students have completed a math starter, the answer should be provided and explained. For problems that may have several solutions, the different solutions should be discussed and analyzed. Only when students understand how problems are solved can they master mathematical skills and concepts.

Whenever students present solutions to the class, encourage them to explain how they arrived at their answer. What operations did they use? What steps did they follow? What key words in the problem helped them to identify exactly what they needed to find? They should share successful strategies they used, as well as strategies they might have considered and then rejected. As information about the concepts, methods, and applications of math are discussed, students gain understanding and insight.

While you should encourage questions, don't allow students to interrupt a speaker when he or she is describing how an answer to a problem was found. Wait until the presentation is made, and then permit questions. Use the questions to review specific methods or skills, or expand the scope of learning. Never permit negative comments or sarcasm, for these can quickly erode the confidence and desire of some students to share their ideas.

USING PROBLEM-SOLVING STRATEGIES

Many of the math starters in this resource will require students to use problem-solving and critical-thinking skills as well as computation. Since the types of skills needed to solve the problems vary, you should familiarize your students with various strategies they can use as necessary. (Be sure not to assign problems that include skills your students haven't been taught as this will lead only to frustration.) Explain that strategies are simply methods or procedures that can be used individually or with other methods to solve problems. Note that some problems may be solved in many ways, using different strategies, and that the best strategy for solving a particular problem is often the one that works best for the person solving the problem.

To give students an idea of some of the more common problem-solving strategies, you may wish to distribute copies of "Problem-solving Strategies." Review and discuss the various strategies with your students, emphasizing that some strategies will work better than others for solving specific problems. Suggest that students keep this handout in their binders or folders so that they may refer to it as needed.

© 1999 by The Center for Applied Research in Education

Name _____ Date _____ Section _____

Problem-solving Strategies

There are many ways to solve math problems. Before you can solve any problem, you must understand the problem and what you are asked to find. Use the first three steps below to clarify your understanding.

1. Read the problem carefully. If necessary, reread the problem several times so that you understand it.

2. Study the problem for "hidden" questions.

3. Identify the information you need to solve the problem. Because some problems contain more information than you need, eliminate unnecessary facts.

Now you are ready to formulate a plan to solve the problem. The following strategies may be helpful.

1. Carefully study any charts, tables, graphs, or illustrations included with the problem. It is essential that you understand them. For some problems you may find it helpful to construct a table or chart of facts. This will help you to see your data clearly.

2. Look for connections, relationships, patterns, or causes and effects. Look for order and sequence.

3. Organize your facts. Writing information in the form of a list can show patterns, associations, and relationships you might otherwise miss.

4. Divide the problem into parts, working on one part at a time. Breaking down a big problem into smaller parts can make it easier to manage.

5. Use trial and error, which is also called guess and check. Try a strategy or method and see if you can solve the problem. Keep trying different plans until one works.

6. Look at the problem in different ways. Assume you have found a solution, then work backwards to try to see how you might have found it.

7. Estimate your way to a solution. Round off numbers. Working with whole numbers instead of fractions or decimals can make it easier to see relationships between numbers and help you to find a solution.

8. Draw or sketch a model. This can help you to visualize a problem, which can lead to a solution.

After you have formulated a plan (or several plans), solve the problem.

When you feel you have found a solution, call on common sense. Some answers obviously can't be right. Discard these. Double-check your work, be certain you have used all of the necessary facts, and check your calculations.

Throughout the year as your students are working on problems, point out the use of various strategies and when they might be applied. Encourage your students to try different strategies and become proficient with them.

EVALUATION

To ensure accountability, evaluate the work your students do on math starters. Unless students feel that their work is being evaluated, many, unfortunately, will not put in the effort necessary that will help them to benefit from the skills presented in the problems. There are several ways you can evaluate the progress of your students without burdening yourself with a significant increase to your workload. Some of the best methods through which to evaluate students' work for math starters include:

- Checklists
- Point systems
- Quizzes that include math starters
- Review of students' math-starter notebooks
- Student participation
- Inclusion of math starters in student portfolios

Whichever method, or methods, you choose, be sure it is consistent with the grading policy of your school or department. Also be sure to explain to your students how your evaluation of math starters will affect their grades. Only when students know what is required of them can they hope to satisfy your expectations.

Checklists

A checklist provides a relatively easy way to evaluate the work of your students. As students are working on a math starter, you may circulate around the room with a checklist that contains the names of the students in class, observing and noting their progress. An easy way to do this is to use a page in your record book. A check for *acceptable* work and a minus for *unacceptable* may be used to record progress. You should determine what you want "acceptable" to mean. It may mean no more than that the student worked on the problem diligently, or it may require that the student found the correct answer. Likewise, you must decide what "unacceptable" means. Using checklists to chart daily progress will enable you to accumulate an impressive record of your students' achievements throughout the marking period. The data on the checklist can become a part of your students' classwork or class participation grade. The checklist is a simple but effective means of evaluation.

Point Systems

Some teachers prefer to utilize a point system for evaluation. To set up a point system, you would assign a specific value for the successful completion of a certain number of math starters.

For example, if you assign 30 problems during a marking period, students may earn 10 points toward their grade by completing all 30 correctly. Completing 15 correctly may earn 5 points. Completing 5 may result in 2.5 points. (The rest of their grade may come from quizzes, tests, class participation, and homework.)

A practical way to keep track of the progress of your students is to collect the problems upon completion each day, then look through them the following day as students are working on the next problem. This will help you to keep abreast of the ongoing work, yet not burden you with more papers to look through at home.

Quizzes that Include Math Starters

An easy way to monitor and evaluate your students' work on math starters is to include a few math starters that students have done on quizzes or tests that you give. This will help to ensure that students take seriously the work they do on math starters. An option here is to give students periodic quizzes that are based entirely on math starters that they have already done, using the same or similar problems. If you require students to maintain math-starter notebooks, they can use their notebooks to study prior to the quiz or test. This also encourages students to keep math-starter notebooks accurate and up to date.

Review of Math-starter Notebooks

If you require students to maintain math-starter notebooks, you may collect them periodically and review their work. You may wish to assign grades to the overall quality of the notebooks, or assign point values that can be incorporated with students' classwork grades. An excellent notebook, for instance, might earn 10 points, an average one may earn 5, and one of poor quality may earn 2.

Student Participation

Some teachers prefer to evaluate the efforts of their students through participation. This may involve having students put solutions to problems on the board or an overhead projector, or explain their solutions to the class. While you should note students who consistently volunteer, you should also select students randomly to share their answers and solutions. Random selection helps to ensure that everyone does the work and is prepared to participate. The participation efforts of your students during work on math starters may be incorporated with their overall classroom participation grade.

Portfolios

If your students are required to maintain math portfolios, they may wish to include examples of the work they do on math starters with their portfolios. Selecting three to five problems per marking period that they feel best represents their work on math starters can be a nice addition to a general math portfolio. If the portfolios are used in evaluation, the math starters can be an important part of that assessment.

A FINAL WORD

Math starters offer you a practical and effective way to begin your math classes. They help get your students working as soon as they enter the room, reducing the amount of time lost in getting prepared to work. Math starters encourage students to come to class ready to begin, and help ensure that the greatest portion of class time is spent learning math.

PART TWO

Math Starters

Section 1

WHOLE NUMBERS:
THEORY AND OPERATIONS

1–1   Natural Numbers   ☆

Natural numbers were likely the first numbers used by ancient people. They are represented by the set of numbers {1, 2, 3, 4, . . . }. The three dots mean that the numbers continue in the same pattern without ending. Natural numbers are used in virtually all aspects of life.

Problem: Write at least three common or well-known phrases in which a natural number, or numbers, is used. *Example:* A cat has *nine* lives. Be ready to share your answers with the class.

1–2   Natural Numbers   ☆

Many Olympic events consist of several contests. These events are often denoted by a prefix that represents a numeral, followed by *-athlon,* which means contest.

Problem: Use your knowledge of prefixes and the Olympics to state the number of contests in the events listed below. List as many of the contests of these events as you can.

biathlon _____

pentathlon _____

heptathlon _____

decathlon _____

1–3   Natural Numbers   ☆

Only two people know the secret ingredient of Coca-Cola®. When these people travel, they take separate planes in case of a fatal accident. Others know the secret ingredient only as a code name, written as a formula.

Problem: Use the clues below to find the code name of Coca-Cola®'s secret ingredient.

It is one more than the sum of the first three natural numbers, followed by the 24th letter of the alphabet.

1-4 Natural Numbers ★★

Natural numbers, also known as the counting numbers, are represented by the set of numbers {1, 2, 3, 4, . . . }.

Problem: Answer the questions below:

1. The sum of the first two natural numbers = _____.
2. The sum of the first three natural numbers = _____.
3. The sum of the first four natural numbers = _____.
4. The sum of the first five natural numbers = _____.
5. The sum of the first six natural numbers = _____.

Explain the pattern of the sums.

1-5 Whole Numbers ★

Some words suggest a particular number or imply a certain number without actually stating it. Some examples include individual (1), couple (2), and trio (3).

Problem: List at least five more words that imply numbers.

1-6 Whole Numbers ★

Whole numbers are the set of the natural numbers and zero, represented by the set of numbers {0, 1, 2, 3, 4, . . . }.

Problem: Sometimes a pattern that involves letters is actually a numerical pattern in disguise. Find the next three letters in the pattern below. (*Hint:* Think of the set of whole numbers.)

Z, O, T, T, F, F

1-7   Whole Numbers   ✭ G

Whole numbers are the set of natural numbers and 0. Although 0 represents *nothing,* it is extremely important to us.

Problem: Speculate what would happen if we didn't have 0 in our number system. What would come after 9? How could we calculate large numbers? How would this change our lives? Be ready to discuss your conclusions.

1-8   Whole Numbers   ✭✭

The *whole numbers* are the set of numbers {0, 1, 2, 3, 4, . . . }. Another way to describe this set is the union of the natural numbers and 0.

Problem: Answer the questions below.

1. The sum of the first two whole numbers = _____.
2. The sum of the first three whole numbers = _____.
3. The sum of the first four whole numbers = _____.
4. The sum of the first five whole numbers = _____.
5. The sum of the first six whole numbers = _____.

Explain the pattern of the sums.

1-9   Numerical Operations   ✭

The word *compute* comes from the Latin word *computare,* which means a "notched tally stick." Basic computation involves addition, subtraction, multiplication, and division. While computation requires an understanding of numerical facts, it doesn't require creative thinking.

Problem: Explain why or why not the name "computer" is a fitting name for today's personal computers. Support your explanation with examples and facts.

1-10 Numerical Operations ☆ G

When you read a word problem in math, sometimes a key word, or words, suggest certain operations. For example, words such as *sum* and *combined* mean addition. *Minus* or *how much more than* means subtraction.

Problem: Create a list of words or phrases that may suggest mathematical operations.

1-11 Adding Whole Numbers ☆

Although addition problems can be performed quickly with a calculator, calculators may not always be handy when numbers need to be added. Thus, the ability to add numbers remains an important skill.

Problem: Of the four problems below, which are correct?

(a) $\begin{array}{r} 4,659 \\ + 4,979 \\ \hline 9,738 \end{array}$ (b) $\begin{array}{r} 1,863 \\ + 5,683 \\ \hline 7,546 \end{array}$ (c) $\begin{array}{r} 1,359 \\ + 4,055 \\ \hline 5,314 \end{array}$ (d) $\begin{array}{r} 58,614 \\ + 38,821 \\ \hline 97,435 \end{array}$

1-12 Adding Whole Numbers ☆

If you add two 2-digit numbers, the sum may be a 2-digit number or it may be a 3-digit number. The answer depends on the numbers you are adding. Note the following examples:

$$\begin{array}{r} 24 \\ + 36 \\ \hline 60 \end{array} \qquad \begin{array}{r} 85 \\ + 71 \\ \hline 156 \end{array}$$

Problem: If you add two 2-digit numbers, what is the smallest sum possible? What is the largest sum possible? (You may repeat digits in the problem.)

1–13 Adding Whole Numbers ★★

The smallest sum of adding two 2-digit numbers is 20 (the sum of 10 + 10). The largest sum is 198 (the sum of 99 + 99). In these problems, the same digits are used more than once.

Problem: If you do not use any digit more than once in the problem, what is the smallest sum of two 2-digit numbers? What is the largest?

1–14 Adding Whole Numbers ★★

471 is an example of a 3-digit number. Each of the numbers, 4, 7, 1, is called a *digit*. The word *digit* was taken from the Latin word *digitus,* meaning finger, because in ancient times fingers were used for calculations.

Problem: Add two 3-digit numbers to get a 3-digit sum using each of the numbers 1 through 9 only once.

1–15 Adding Whole Numbers ★★

The word *addition* comes from the Latin word *addere,* which means "to put together." Addition is the process by which numbers are put together to obtain a sum.

Problem: Add, or "put together," two 2-digit numbers to get the smallest possible sum if different digits must be used in the problem and the sum. What is the largest possible sum? (Remember that no digit may be used more than once anywhere in the problem or the sum.)

1-16   Subtracting Whole Numbers   ☆

Probably the trickiest skill to master in subtraction is regrouping, or borrowing. Once the steps to regrouping are mastered, subtraction is easy.

Problem: In the four problems below, find and correct the mistakes in regrouping.

(a)   5,703
− 2,845
———
3,168

(b)   9,800
− 5,678
———
4,232

(c)   3,864
− 1,584
———
2,388

(d)   2,932
− 1,863
———
1,161

1-17   Subtracting Whole Numbers   ☆

When people make mistakes in subtraction, more often than not their mistakes are in regrouping (borrowing). Being careful to regroup reduces mistakes.

Problem: Imagine that you are teaching the skill of regrouping to a young student. Write an explanation of how regrouping is done. Include an example to clarify your explanation.

1-18   Subtracting Whole Numbers   ☆

Many of the mistakes people make in subtraction are because of carelessness. These mistakes can be avoided by carefully working out each problem.

Problem: Find and correct the mistakes in the four problems below. (Some might be correct.)

(a)   4,786
− 2,809
———
1,977

(b)   8,205
− 6,593
———
1,712

(c)   10,795
− 8,876
———
1,929

(d)   543,792
− 468,386
————
75,416

| 1–19 | **Subtracting Whole Numbers** ✮ |

A solid understanding of subtraction is a basic math skill.

Problem: Find the missing digits to complete the problems below.

(a)   ☐,☐63
      − 3,9☐9
        2,83☐

(b)   71,☐4☐
      − 4,8☐6
        6☐,270

| 1–20 | **Subtracting Whole Numbers** ✮✮ |

A popular event at many field days is a tug-of-war. To balance the teams, the number of students on each side of the rope should be equal.

Problem: If the number of students on one side of the rope is 54, and the number of students on the other side is 36, how many students must be moved?

| 1–21 | **Multiplying Whole Numbers** ✮ |

The word *multiplication* comes from the Latin words *multi* and *plicare*. *Multi* means many and *plicare* means fold. Multiplication, therefore, means repeated addition of numbers to obtain a solution. For example, rather than adding 318 29 times, you can simply multiply 318×29. The steps necessary for all multiplication problems are the same. The answer to a multiplication problem is called a *product*.

Problem: Multiply 318×29. Then write an explanation describing the steps you followed to find the product.

1-22 Multiplying Whole Numbers ☆

Accuracy in multiplication is a math skill of which to be proud.

Problem: Each of the problems below has a mistake. Find the mistake and correct the problem.

(a)
```
   296
 × 48
  2368
 1284
15,208
```

(b)
```
   183
 × 79
  1647
 1281
14,557
```

(c)
```
 1,586
 × 34
  6364
 4758
53,944
```

(d)
```
 2,087
 × 63
  6261
12442
130,681
```

1-23 Multiplying Whole Numbers ☆

Knowing multiplication facts will help you to avoid mistakes in multiplication.

Problem: Find the missing digits to complete the problems below.

(a)
```
    4□8
  × 9□
  1314
  3□4□
 □0,□34
```

(b)
```
    5,□□3
  × □07
   3□2□1
  2□01□0
 2,8□0,7□1
```

1-24 Multiplying Whole Numbers ☆

Practice in multiplication is never wasted time.

Problem: Write a multiplication problem with a 6-digit number multiplied by a 4-digit number. On the back of the paper on which you wrote your problem, work out your problem and check that the product is correct. When you are done, exchange your problem (without showing its answer) for the problem of another student. Solve each other's problems and check your products to be sure they are correct.

1–25   Multiplying Whole Numbers   ★★

Before multiplication was developed, people had a hard time calculating large numbers. Even though calculators perform much of the multiplying we do these days, a good understanding of multiplication facts is fundamental to computation.

Problem: Using the boxes below—one box for each of the numbers 1, 2, 3, 4, 5—write a multiplication problem that gives the largest product. You may use each number only once.

1–26   Multiplying Whole Numbers   ★★

In the multiplication problem $159 \times 48 = 7{,}632$, each of the digits 1 through 9 is used only once.

Problem: Create another problem by filling each box below with a number from 1 through 9. Each number can be used only once.

1–27   Multiplying Whole Numbers   ★★ G

The place of a digit in a multiplication problem can alter the product significantly.

Problem: Use the digits 3, 4, 8, 7, 2 to create a multiplication problem that gives the largest product. Each digit may be used only once. Be ready to explain what strategies you used to get your answer.

1-28 Dividing Whole Numbers ✮

Division is the mathematical operation of finding how many times a number, called the *divisor,* is contained in another number, known as the *dividend.* The product is called the *quotient.* Division is a basic skill in mathematics.

Problem: Which of the following have correct quotients?

(a) $37\overline{)1,833}$ 49R20

(b) $49\overline{)2,506}$ 51R7

(c) $32\overline{)2,820}$ 88R4

(d) $53\overline{)3,803}$ 714R40

1-29 Dividing Whole Numbers ✮

Like all forms of computation, accuracy in division is important.

Problem: Find and correct the mistakes in the following problems.

(a)
```
        597R2
   76)45,380
      380
      738
      684
      540
      532
        2
```

(b)
```
       91R52
   56)51,408
      504
      108
       56
       52
```

1-30 Dividing Whole Numbers ✮

Division is much like learning to ride a bicycle. Once you master the steps, you won't forget them.

Problem: In a paragraph, explain the steps of long division.

1-31   Dividing Whole Numbers ☆

It is easy to check the answers to division problems. Simply multiply the quotient by the divisor and add any remainder. If the answer you find equals the dividend, your problem is correct.

Problem: Check the quotients to the division problems below by multiplying. If a quotient is incorrect, correct it.

(a) $75\overline{)3{,}487}$ 46R27

(b) $84\overline{)6{,}792}$ 80R22

(c) $67\overline{)92{,}465}$ 1,390R5

1-32   Dividing Whole Numbers ☆☆

Some division problems can yield "interesting" quotients.

Problem: Divide and find the quotients to the following problems. Then explain the pattern in each quotient.

(a) $74\overline{)91{,}390}$ (b) $57\overline{)78{,}033}$ (c) $36\overline{)145{,}440}$ (d) $63\overline{)614{,}439}$

1-33   Dividing Whole Numbers ☆☆

Sports can be great fun for both players and spectators. Setting up teams and finding sponsors, however, may be a problem.

Problem: There are 112 students who signed up to play basketball in a recreation league. They have 14 sponsors. How many teams of 11 players each can be formed?

1–34   Whole Numbers: Multi-step Problem   ✮

The seven seas are referred to in songs as well as in literature. In the past mariners used the expression "the seven seas" to refer to all the oceans of the world: The North and South Atlantics, the North and South Pacifics, and the Indian, the Arctic, and the Antarctic Oceans.

Problem: Express the number 7 by using seven different 1-digit numbers.

1–35   Whole Numbers: Multi-step Problem   ✮

A centurion was an officer in the Roman army. Each centurion led a unit of 100 men.

At the height of the Roman Empire, the army consisted of 175 legions. The number of soldiers per legion varied from 4,000 to 6,000 men. Each legion was divided into groups of 100, led by a centurion.

Problem: At the height of the Empire, about how many centurions were in the Roman army?

1–36   Whole Numbers: Multi-step Problem   ✮✮

An old English children's rhyme goes like this:

"As I was going to St. Ives,
I met a man with seven wives,
Every wife had seven sacks,
Every sack had seven cats,
Every cat had seven kits."

Problem: How many people and animals were going to St. Ives?

1–37 Whole Numbers: Multi-step Problem ★★ G

In professional football, scoring is based on 6 points for a touchdown, 1 point for an extra point after a touchdown, 2 points for a conversion after a touchdown, 2 points for a safety, and 3 points for a field goal.

Problem: List any number less than 50 that is impossible for a team to score.

1–38 Estimation with Compatible Numbers ★

Compatible numbers are numbers that are easy to compute mentally. They are often used to estimate answers.

Consider this example. The sophomore class made a profit of $372.70 at its annual car wash. The students washed 198 cars. About how much profit did they make per car?

This answer could be easily estimated by using the compatible numbers of 400 (dollars) and 200 (cars). It is much easier to compute 400 ÷ 200 = 2 than $372.70 ÷ 198.

Problem: Write a word problem in which compatible numbers could be used to estimate the answer.

1–39 Rounding Whole Numbers ★

Attendance at free events is often estimated because there is no accurate way of determining the exact number of people who show up.

Problem: A magazine article reported that 16,000 people attended a free concert in the park. What number(s) below *cannot* be rounded to 16,000?

(a) 15,500   (b) 15,400   (c) 16,500   (d) 16,499   (e) 15,499

1-40 Prime Numbers ☆

Prime numbers are natural numbers that have only two factors: 1 and the number.

Problem: List the prime numbers between 1 and 50.

1-41 Prime Numbers ☆

Because prime numbers have only two factors—1 and the number itself—understanding factors is helpful to understand prime numbers.

Problem: Write an explanation of why 1 is *not* a prime number.

1-42 Prime Numbers ☆☆

In 1742 Christian Goldbach made two conjectures. Although no one has ever been able to prove that either of them is always true, no one has ever found a case in which either of them is false.

Goldbach's conjectures follow:

Every even number greater than 2 can be written as the sum of two prime numbers. For example: 8 = 5 + 3.

Every odd number greater than 7 is the sum of three prime numbers. For example: 17 = 7 + 7 + 3.

Problem: Keeping Goldbach's conjectures in mind, write the numbers from 10 to 15 as the sum of two or three prime numbers.

1–43   Prime Numbers   ★★

Triskaidekaphobia is the unnatural fear of a certain number.

Problem: To determine this number, use the following clues. Prove your answer by showing the math.

It is a prime number less than 20.

The sum of its digits is twice the first prime number.

1–44   Prime Numbers   ★★

We see the American flag every day at school, sporting events, and buildings.

Problem: Use the clues below to determine numbers related to the flag.

The number of red stripes is the fourth prime number.

The number of white stripes is the sixth prime number minus the number of red stripes.

The total number of stars equals the square of the number of red stripes plus 1.

1–45   Prime Numbers   ★★

The 21st century lasts from January 1, 2001 through (and including) December 31, 2100.

Problem: What is the last year of the 21st century that is a prime number?

1-46 Relatively Prime Numbers ★★

Relatively prime numbers have no factors in common except for the number 1. For example, 5 and 18 are relatively prime numbers because they have no common factor other than 1. Another example of relatively prime numbers is 12 and 49.

Problem: Give an example of two other numbers that are relatively prime.

1-47 Symmetric Primes ★★★

Symmetric primes are two prime numbers that are the same distance from a given number on a number line. For example, 3 and 7 are symmetric primes of 5 because each number is two units away from 5 on the number line. Another example is 3 and 13, which are symmetric primes of 8.

Problem: List the symmetric primes of 10. Do you think all natural numbers have at least one pair of symmetric primes? Explain your answer and provide some examples.

1-48 Twin Primes ★★

Twin primes are prime numbers that differ by 2. The first pair of twin primes is 3 and 5. The next pair is 5 and 7.

Problem: List the next four pairs of twin primes.

1-49 Emirps ★★

An *emirp* is a prime number that remains a prime when its digits are reversed. The word *emirp* is *prime* spelled backwards. For example, 13 is an emirp because it is a prime number as 13, and it is also a prime when reversed as 31.

Problem: List three emirps (other than 13 and 31) that are less than 100.

1-50 Emirps ★★ G

Emirps are special prime numbers. When the digits of an emirp are reversed, the number is a prime. 17 is an emirp, because both 17 and 71 (the digits of 17 reversed) are prime numbers.

Problem: Find the 12 emirps between 100 and 200.

1-51 Place Value with Whole Numbers ★

A French mathematician in the 15th century called 0 "a figure causing confusion and difficulty."

Problem: Do you agree or disagree with this quote? Write an explanation of your answer.

1–52   Place Value with Whole Numbers   ★★

A 3-digit number appears on the back of a 5-dollar bill, on the hedges to the left of the Jefferson Memorial steps in the pattern of the shading.

Problem: Determine this 3-digit number by using these clues.

All three digits are different prime numbers.

The sum of the hundreds and tens digit is 10.

The sum of the tens digit and units digit is 9.

1–53   Place Value with Whole Numbers   ★★

Baron Karl von Drais, inventor of a 2-wheel vehicle in the 19th century, is called the "father of the bicycle."

Problem: Use the following clues to determine the year in which he completed his invention.

The tens digit is the same as the thousands digit.

The sum of the digits is 16.

(Remember that the Baron invented his 2-wheeler in the 19th century.)

1–54   Place Value with Whole Numbers   ★★

Roger Bannister was the first person to run the mile in less than four minutes. His time was 3:59.4 This occurred at a meet in Oxford, England on May 6.

Problem: Use the clues below to determine the year Bannister broke the 4-minute barrier for the mile.

The sum of the thousands and hundreds digit is 10.

The sum of the tens and units digit is one less than 10.

The units digit is one less than the tens digit.

1–55 Place Value with Whole Numbers ★★

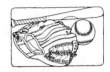

Most baseball fans know that Jackie Robinson was the first African-American baseball player to appear in a major league game. Robinson began playing in the big leagues with the National League's Brooklyn Dodgers in 1947.

Lawrence Eugene (Larry) Doby was the first African-American baseball player to appear in an American League game.

Problem: To find out the year Larry Doby first played in the American League, use the clues below.

This year was in the 20th century.

The sum of the digits of this year is 21.

The tens digit is 3 less than the units digit.

1–56 Composite Numbers ★

A *composite number* is a natural number that has more than two factors. 6 is a composite number because its factors are 1, 2, 3, and 6.

Problem: List the composite numbers that are greater than 9 and less than 21. Then state the number of factors of each composite number you have listed.

1–57 Composite Numbers ★★

Some numbers may be members of various sets. For example, 5 is a member of the set of natural numbers and prime numbers. 8 is a member of the set of natural numbers and composite numbers.

Problem: Do you agree or disagree with the statement below? Explain your answer.

Every natural number is either prime or composite.

1–58   **Perfect Squares**   ☆

A *perfect square* is a product of a natural number times itself. An example of a perfect square is 16, the result of 4×4. Another is 25, the result of 5×5.

Problem: List the perfect squares starting with 1 and ending with 100.

1–59   **Perfect Squares**   ☆☆

A *perfect square* is the product of a natural number times itself. Some examples are 1, 4, 9, 16, . . .

Problem: Explain why the product of two different prime numbers can never be a perfect square.

1–60   **Perfect Squares**   ☆☆

To find a perfect square, multiply a number by itself. For example: $6 \times 6 = 36$. Conversely, the square root of a perfect square is always a whole number. For example: $\sqrt{36} = 6$.

There is another way to find a perfect square. Take four consecutive numbers, find their product, and add 1. For example, $2 \times 3 \times 4 \times 5 + 1 = 121$. The answer 121 is a perfect square because $\sqrt{121} = 11$.

Problem: Use the method above to find a perfect square using any group of four consecutive numbers greater than 2 and less than 10.

1-61   Perfect Squares   ★★

Sometimes the sum of two perfect squares can equal another perfect square. For example: 9 + 16 = 25. Another example: 25 + 144 = 169. All of these numbers are perfect squares.

Problem: There is another pair of numbers between 1 and 100 (other than 9 and 16 in the example above) whose sum is a perfect square. Find this other pair.

1-62   Perfect Squares   ★★

Dice are used in several board games to determine the number of spaces a player moves around the board.

Problem: If you toss two dice, how many sums are perfect squares? What are the perfect squares and which numbers on the dice result in them?

1-63   Deficient Numbers   ★

The ancient Greeks considered a number to be *deficient* if the sum of its factors, excluding the number itself, is less than the number. 8 is a deficient number because the sum of its factors (1 + 2 + 4) = 7. (Remember, the number 8 cannot be used as a factor of itself.)

Problem: Which of the following are deficient numbers?

(a) 36   (b) 40   (c) 41   (d) 50

1-64 Perfect Numbers ☆

According to the ancient Greeks, a *perfect number* is a number that equals the sum of its factors, excluding itself. For example, 6 is a perfect number because the sum of the factors $1 + 2 + 3 = 6$. (Remember, the sum of the factors does not include the number itself.)

Problem: Which of the following are perfect numbers?

(a) 24   (b) 28   (c) 32   (d) 44

1-65 Abundant Numbers ☆

The ancient Greeks defined an *abundant number* as a number whose factors, excluding the number itself, add up to a sum that is more than the number. 12 is an abundant number because the sum of its factors $1 + 2 + 3 + 4 + 6 = 16$. (Remember, 12 is excluded as a factor.)

Problem: Between 45 and 50 there is one abundant number. What is it? Show the sum of its factors.

1-66 Deficient, Abundant, and Perfect Numbers ☆☆ G

The ancient Greeks enjoyed mathematics and classified all natural numbers as *deficient, abundant,* or *perfect.* To do this they found the sum of the factors of a number but did not include the number in the sum.

They determined the categories like this:

If the sum of the factors (excluding the number itself) is less than the number, then the number is deficient.

If the sum of the factors (excluding the number itself) is greater than the number, then the number is abundant.

If the sum of the factors (excluding the number itself) is equal to the number, then the number is perfect.

Problem: Of the numbers 1 through 20, classify each as deficient, abundant, or perfect.

1–67 Divisibility by 2, 4, and 8 ✯

Understanding divisibility is useful in several mathematical applications. The divisibility tests for 2, 4, and 8 are listed below.

A natural number is divisible by:

2   if the last digit is even.

4   if the number formed by the last two digits is divisible by 4.

8   if the last number formed by the last three digits is divisible by 8.

Problem: Using the divisibility rules above, what numbers below are divisible by 2? by 4? by 8?

(a) 1,326   (b) 3,174   (c) 7,368   (d) 17,208

1–68 Divisibility by 3, 6, 9, and 12 ✯

Although a calculator can be used to test for divisibility, sometimes you may need to use divisibility tests. The divisibility tests for 3, 6, 9, and 12 are listed below.

A natural number is divisible by:

3   if the sum of the digits of the number is divisible by 3.

6   if the number is divisible by 2 and 3.

9   if the sum of the digits is divisible by 9.

12   if the number is divisible by 3 and 4.

Problem: Using the divisibility rules above, what numbers below are divisible by 3? by 6? by 9? by 12?

(a) 102   (b) 153   (c) 1,755   (d) 4,644

1-69   Divisibility by 5 and 10   ☆

The tests for divisibility for 5 and 10 only require you to look at the last digit of the number.

A number is divisible by 5 if it ends in a 5 or 0.

A number is divisible by 10 if it ends in 0.

Problem: Complete the sentences below with the number 5 or 10.

If a number is divisible by ——————, then it is always divisible by ——————.

If a number is divisible by ——————, then it may be divisible by ——————.

Give an example to show that your statement is correct.

1-70   Divisibility by 7   ☆

The test for divisibility by 7 is sometimes eliminated from lists of divisibility tests. The test has three steps, and in some cases it is easier to simply divide by 7.

To determine if a number is divisible by 7, do the following:

Drop the units digit.

Subtract two times the units digit from the remaining number.

If the difference can be divided by 7, the number is divisible by 7.

Problem: Use the test to determine if each number below is divisible by 7. Do you think it is easier to divide by 7 or use the test? Explain your reasoning.

(a) 237   (b) 256   (c) 455   (d) 623

1-71 Divisibility by 11 ★★

Testing divisibility by 11 has several steps. If you wish to impress your friends, you might ask them to give you a number and you can determine if it is divisible by 11.

To test if a number is divisible by 11:

Add every other digit, starting with the first digit.

Add every other digit, starting with the second digit.

Subtract the smaller sum from the larger.

If the difference is divisible by 11, then the original number is divisible by 11.

Here is an example. To see if 101,706 is divisible by 11, do the following:

Add: $1 + 1 + 0 = 2$

Add: $0 + 7 + 6 = 13$

Subtract: $13 - 2 = 11$.

11 is divisible by 11, therefore 101,706 is divisible by 11

Problem: Which of the numbers below is divisible by 11?

(a) 3,386　　　　(b) 4,477　　　　(c) 87,846　　　　(d) 106,195

1-72 Divisibility ★

The rearrangement of numbers and operations with them often leads to astonishing results. Consider the following steps.

Take any number and rearrange the digits in any order. Of the two numbers you now have, subtract the smaller from the larger. The difference will always be divisible by 9.

Problem: Choose three other examples to illustrate the above steps. Be sure to include your work.

1-73 Divisibility ★

"Buddy" was the first Seeing Eye Dog in America. He was brought to the United States from Switzerland by his owner Morris Frank.

Problem: Use the clues below to determine the year Buddy came to the United States.

The thousands digit and the tens digit are consecutive numbers.

The hundreds digit is one more than the units digit.

The year is divisible by 4.

1-74 Factors ☆

Some people feel it is strange that our number system is based upon 10, while other items are grouped by 12, such as 12 eggs in a dozen, 12 months in a year, or 12 signs in the zodiac.

When it comes to pricing, 12 is a much more practical number because it has more factors than 10. The factors of 12 are 1, 2, 3, 4, 6, and 12, while the factors for 10 are 1, 2, 5, and 10. Because of this, commercial items are counted in multiples of 12. For example:

12 items = 1 dozen

12 dozen = 1 gross

12 gross = 1 great gross

Problem: How many dozen items are in a great gross? How many items are in a great gross?

1-75 Factors ☆

Joe Teacher is thrilled when he receives his class list of students. He likes to break his class into groups with an equal number of students in each group. When he sees the number of students, he knows he can have groups of 2, 3, 4, 6, 8, and 12.

Problem: How many students are in his class?

1-76 Greatest Common Factor ☆

The *greatest common factor,* or GCF, of two numbers is the largest number that is a factor of both numbers. For example, the factors of 12 are 1, 2, 3, 4, 6, and 12. The factors of 32 are 1, 2, 4, 8, 16, and 32. Therefore, the GCF of 12 and 32 is 4.

Problem: The last number in each column below may or may not be the greatest common factor of the two numbers above it. Circle the one(s) that is incorrect. Then find the GCF for the incorrect problem(s).

(a)	20	(b)	15	(c)	24	(d)	20
	30		18		36		9
GCF =	5	GCF =	3	GCF =	12	GCF =	1

1–77   Greatest Common Factor   ★★

Over 2,000 years ago, Euclid developed an algorithm, or method, that he used to find the greatest common factor, or GCF, of two numbers. Euclid's algorithm is still used today. Following are the steps of Euclid's algorithm:

1. Divide the larger number by the smaller.
2. Divide the divisor in step 1 by the remainder in step 1.
3. Repeat step 2 until there is no remainder.
4. The last divisor is the GCF of the original numbers.

Problem: Using Euclid's algorithm, find the GCF of 208 and 464.

1–78   Multiples   ★

A *multiple* of a number is the product of the number times a natural number. For example, the multiples of 4 are 4, 8, 12, 16, 20, . . .

Harvard University was established in the 17th century. You can use your knowledge of multiples to find the year Harvard was established.

Problem: Use the clues below to determine the year.

The last two digits, written in order, are a perfect square.

The units digit is a multiple of the tens digit.

1–79   Multiples   ★

Joe Money ran short of cash. He deposited a check for $200 in his checking account but never carries his checkbook. He never carries much cash either.

He needs to purchase a CD for $16.99 and a gift certificate for $25. Seeing an automatic teller machine (ATM), he decides to access some cash. The amount he can enter in the ATM has to be a multiple of 20.

Problem: How much money should Joe withdraw so that he will have enough for these two purchases?

1–80 Multiples ☆

The Great Wall of China, begun in 220 B.C. and completed in 204 B.C., is one of the world's architectural wonders.

Problem: Use the clues below to determine the length in miles of the Great Wall.

The length is a 4-digit number.

All digits are multiples of 2.

The tens digit is four times the thousands digit.

The hundreds and units digit are the same and each is twice the thousands digit.

1–81 Multiples ☆

Dimples are not only on some people's cheeks, but on golf balls as well. The impressions on golf balls are also called dimples.

Problem: Use the clues below to determine the number of dimples on a golf ball.

The hundreds and the tens digits are the same prime number.

All digits are multiples of 3.

The sum of the digits is 12.

1–82 Least Common Multiple ☆

The *least common multiple,* or LCM, of two numbers is the smallest number that is a multiple of both numbers. For example:

The multiples of 6 are 6, 12, 18, 24, . . .

The multiples of 8 are 8, 16, 24, 32, . . .

The least common multiple of 6 and 8 is 24, because 24 is the smallest number that appears in both sets.

Problem: 12 is the least common multiple of one of the two pairs of numbers listed below. For which pair of numbers is 12 the least common multiple?

(a) 12	(b) 3	(c) 6	(d) 18
18	15	12	36

1-83 Least Common Multiples ★★

A common way of finding the least common multiple of two numbers is to make lists of multiples and find the smallest number that appears in both lists. There is also a simple formula you can use.

$$LCM = Product \div GCF$$

Note that in this equation LCM stands for least common multiple, the Product is the result of the two numbers being multiplied together, and GCF stands for greatest common factor.

Here is an example of how this equation works.

The LCM of 20 and 30 can be found by $20 \times 30 \div 10$. (10 is the GCF.) The LCM of 20 and 30 is 60.

Problem: Find the LCM of each pair of numbers by dividing the product of the numbers by their GCF.

(a) 15 and 20   (b) 10 and 50   (c) 21 and 63   (d) 17 and 29

1-84 Symbols ★

Calculators use an array to display all digits from 0 to 9, depending upon which parts are lit. An array for a one-digit number is pictured to the right.

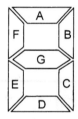

Problem: State which parts are lit to display the numbers 0 to 9.

1-85 Symbols ★

Symbols are often used in mathematics and real life. Two common symbols are < and >.

< is read as "is less than."

> is read as "is greater than."

Problem: Write an explanation why the fast-forward symbol on a VCR resembles the "greater than" symbol and the rewind resembles the "less than."

1–86 A Quotation Applicable to Mathematics ☆

Hypathia of Alexandria (370–415) was the first woman mathematician about whom we know many details. Along with her pursuits in mathematics, Hypathia was also a writer, teacher, scientist, and astronomer when it was unusual for women to receive an education. By all counts, she was a remarkable woman and true trendsetter of her times.

Hypathia received much of her passion for learning from her father, Theon, who was a noted writer and thinker. Although at the time Christians believed that math and science were heresy, Theon is credited with keeping mathematical and scientific thought alive through tireless inquiry and discussion.

Problem: Explain these words said by Theon to Hypathia: "Reserve your right to think, for even to think wrongly is better than not to think at all."

Section 2

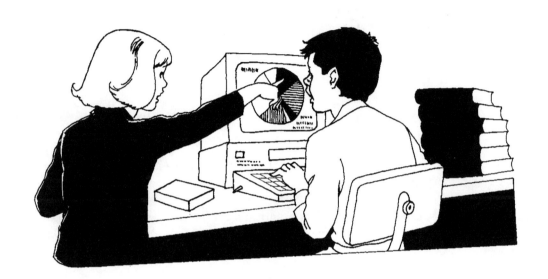

FRACTIONS, DECIMALS, AND PERCENTS

2–1   Fractions ☆

The word *fraction* is derived from the Latin word *fractus,* which means to break. Two other words we use with fractions, *numerator* and *denominator,* also come from Latin words. Numerator comes from *numeros,* meaning number, and denominator comes from *denominare,* meaning name.

Problem: Using $\frac{3}{5}$, explain the words *fraction, numerator,* and *denominator.*

2–2   Fractions ☆

A *solidus* is the slash sometimes used with fractions instead of a horizontal bar. $3/4$ is a fraction written with a solidus.

Problem: Explain why some people find the solidus confusing and prefer to use the horizontal bar when working with fractions.

2–3   Equivalent Fractions ☆

When a whole number is multiplied by 1, the product is the original number. Sometimes, when a fraction is multiplied by 1, the product is equal to the fraction but it is expressed in a different form.

Here is an example.

$$\frac{4}{4} = 1$$
$$\frac{5}{6} \times 1 = \frac{5}{6}$$
$$\frac{5}{6} \times \frac{4}{4} = \frac{20}{24}, \text{ which is equivalent to } \frac{5}{6}$$

Problem: Find the missing numerator or denominator by writing equivalent fractions for the problems below.

(a) $\frac{5}{8} = \frac{}{24}$ (b) $\frac{3}{4} = \frac{27}{}$ (c) $\frac{2}{3} = \frac{8}{}$ (d) $\frac{7}{22} = \frac{}{132}$

2–4   Equivalent Fractions   ☆

Equivalent fractions have the same value when expressed in the simplest form. For example, $\frac{1}{4}, \frac{2}{8}, \frac{3}{12}$, and $\frac{4}{16}$ are all equivalent. $\frac{1}{4}$ is the fraction that is in simplest form.

Problem: Which of the following equals $\frac{3}{7}$?

   (a) $\frac{9}{63}$ (b) $\frac{9}{10}$ (c) $\frac{21}{49}$ (d) $\frac{9}{21}$

2–5   Simplifying Fractions   ☆

Simplifying a fraction often makes the fraction easier to work with. A large numerator or denominator sometimes "hides" the value of a fraction.

Problem: Of the fractions listed below, which are simplified? Simplify the rest.

$\frac{21}{49}$ $\frac{13}{14}$ $\frac{29}{37}$ $\frac{15}{21}$ $\frac{19}{38}$ $\frac{47}{63}$ $\frac{12}{18}$ $\frac{2}{9}$ $\frac{10}{45}$

2–6   Simplifying Fractions   ☆☆

A Venn diagram may be used to show the way certain groups of numbers are related. It consists of two or more circles that overlap. The numbers in the portion that overlaps are in both groups.

Problem: Place each fraction below in the appropriate part of the Venn diagram.

$\frac{20}{21}$ $\frac{63}{81}$ $\frac{21}{27}$ $\frac{9}{11}$ $\frac{3}{14}$ $\frac{7}{9}$ $\frac{77}{99}$

Fractions
Equivalent
to $\frac{14}{18}$

Fractions
That Can't
Be Simplified

2–7 Writing Improper Fractions as Mixed Numbers ☆

An *improper fraction* is a fraction in which the numerator is equal to or greater than the denominator. All improper fractions can be expressed as a mixed number or a whole number. Simply divide the numerator by the denominator and write the remainder (if there is one) over the denominator.

Problem: Which of the following are expressed correctly as a mixed number? (Be sure to simplify.)

(a) $\frac{32}{7} = 4\frac{3}{7}$ (b) $\frac{76}{8} = 9\frac{1}{2}$ (c) $\frac{367}{100} = 3\frac{67}{100}$ (d) $\frac{41}{9} = 4\frac{5}{9}$

2–8 Writing Mixed Numbers as Improper Fractions ☆

To convert a mixed number to a fraction, multiply the denominator by the whole number, add the numerator, and write the sum over the denominator.
For example, $7\frac{3}{4} = \frac{31}{4}$

Problem: Write the numerator in each fraction below.

(a) $9\frac{1}{4} = \frac{}{4}$ (b) $13\frac{2}{5} = \frac{}{5}$ (c) $5\frac{7}{8} = \frac{}{8}$ (d) $6\frac{4}{9} = \frac{}{9}$

2–9 Comparing Fractions ☆

Sometimes scores on tests or quizzes may be expressed as a fraction, placing the number of problems correct over the number of problems on the test or quiz.

Problem: Manuel had two math quizzes this marking period. On the first quiz he got 24 out of 30 questions correct. On the next quiz he got 15 out of 20 correct. On which quiz did he receive the higher score? Explain your answer.

2–10   Comparing Fractions   ☆

It is easy to compare fractions if the denominators are the same. Just look at the numerators. The larger numerator represents the larger fraction. For example: $\frac{3}{4} > \frac{1}{4}$.

To compare fractions that have different denominators, you must first find common denominators, write equivalent fractions, then compare the numerators.

Problem: The signs >, <, and = are used to compare the fractions below. Some are wrong. Find and correct the incorrect signs.

(a) $\frac{5}{8} < \frac{4}{7}$ (b) $\frac{3}{5} > \frac{11}{15}$ (c) $\frac{7}{9} = \frac{35}{45}$ (d) $\frac{6}{7} > \frac{8}{9}$

2–11   Ordering Fractions   ☆☆

You must compare fractions before putting them in order.

Problem: At least one of the fractions below is out of order. Circle the fraction(s) that is placed incorrectly. Write equivalent fractions to support your answer.

$$\frac{2}{3}, \frac{3}{5}, \frac{2}{5}, \frac{21}{25}, \frac{33}{75}$$

2–12   Adding Fractions   ☆

When you are adding fractions with like denominators, you add the numerators and simplify if necessary. When you add fractions with unlike denominators, you must find common denominators first, write equivalent fractions, then add the numerators, and simplify.

Problem: Complete the addition problems below.

(a) $\frac{3}{7} = \frac{}{35}$

$+\frac{4}{5} = \frac{28}{}$

$\overline{}$

$\frac{}{35} = 1\frac{}{35}$

(b) $\frac{5}{6} = \frac{10}{}$

$+\frac{3}{4} = \frac{9}{}$

$\overline{}$

$\frac{19}{} =$

| 2–13 | **Adding Fractions** ☆ |

In some communities special routes are designed for people who wish to walk or jog. On many of these routes, distances are marked for those who would like to keep track of how far they have gone.

Problem: José is starting a running program. He plans to alternate walking and running for a total of two miles today. As his endurance increases, he hopes to gradually walk less and run more. If he walks $\frac{1}{2}$ mile, runs $\frac{1}{4}$ mile, walks $\frac{3}{4}$ mile, runs $\frac{1}{4}$ mile, and walks $\frac{1}{8}$ mile, what is his total distance?

| 2–14 | **Adding Mixed Numbers** ☆ |

If you are not careful, it is easy to make errors when adding fractions.

Problem: The two problems below have at least one error each. Find the errors and correct the problems.

(a) $8\frac{7}{12} = 8\frac{7}{12}$
$\underline{+\ 6\ \frac{3}{4}\ = 6\frac{7}{12}}$
$14\frac{14}{12} = 14\frac{1}{6}$

(b) $7\frac{5}{6} = 7\frac{15}{18}$
$\underline{+\ 2\frac{1}{9} = 2\frac{3}{18}}$
$9\frac{18}{18} = 10$

| 2–15 | **Adding Mixed Numbers** ☆ |

Adding mixed numbers requires several steps. You must find the least common denominator, write equivalent fractions, add, and simplify. Since it is possible to make a mistake in any of these steps, accuracy is very important.

Problem: Which of the four problems below are correct? Correct the ones that are wrong.

(a) $3\frac{2}{7}$
$\underline{+2\frac{3}{8}}$
$5\frac{37}{56}$

(b) $7\frac{3}{10}$
$\underline{+5\frac{3}{4}}$
$12\frac{1}{20}$

(c) $5\frac{2}{5}$
$\underline{+8\frac{4}{15}}$
$13\frac{2}{3}$

(d) $6\frac{5}{8}$
$\underline{+2\frac{7}{12}}$
$9\frac{1}{6}$

2–16 Subtracting Fractions ✩

Finding the least common denominator may be one of the hardest steps in subtracting fractions with unlike denominators.

Problem: Find the least common denominator for the subtraction problems below. Then complete the problems.

(a) $\dfrac{2}{9}$
  $-\dfrac{1}{6}$

(b) $\dfrac{4}{5}$
  $-\dfrac{2}{3}$

(c) $\dfrac{2}{3}$
  $-\dfrac{4}{7}$

(d) $\dfrac{7}{8}$
  $-\dfrac{9}{20}$

2–17 Subtracting Fractions ✩✩

Good cooks follow recipes carefully. Since many recipes call for fractional portions of ingredients, a solid understanding of fractions is helpful in cooking.

Problem: 4 tablespoons of butter equal $\frac{1}{4}$ cup. $5\frac{1}{3}$ tablespoons equal $\frac{1}{3}$ cup. How much larger is $5\frac{1}{3}$ tablespoons of butter than 4 tablespoons? Express your answer in terms of cups.

2–18 Subtracting Mixed Numbers ✩

When subtracting mixed numbers with unlike denominators, you must first find common denominators.

Problem: Which of the following are correct? Find and correct the mistakes in the problems that have a wrong answer.

(a) $17\frac{2}{3}$
  $-4\frac{5}{12}$
  _____
  $11\frac{1}{3}$

(b) $12\frac{2}{3}$
  $-3\frac{2}{15}$
  _____
  $9\frac{8}{15}$

(c) $9\frac{2}{5}$
  $-1\frac{1}{4}$
  _____
  $8\frac{3}{20}$

(d) $7\frac{4}{5}$
  $-3\frac{3}{10}$
  _____
  $4\frac{1}{10}$

2–19   Subtracting Mixed Numbers   ★★

Regrouping is necessary for subtracting some mixed numbers from others.

Problem: Write an explanation of the process of regrouping for subtracting mixed numbers. Provide an example to clarify your explanation.

2–20   Subtracting Mixed Numbers   ★★

Regrouping in the subtraction of mixed numbers requires several steps.

Problem: Complete the problems below. Each requires regrouping.

(a) $\begin{aligned} 14\tfrac{2}{} &= 13\tfrac{}{9} \\ -\ 7\tfrac{2}{} &= 7\tfrac{6}{} \\ \hline &6\tfrac{5}{9} \end{aligned}$

(b) $\begin{aligned} 7^{} &= 6\tfrac{8}{} \\ -\ 4\tfrac{7}{} &= 4\tfrac{3}{} \\ \hline &2\tfrac{7}{} \end{aligned}$

2–21   Subtracting Mixed Numbers   ★★

Subtracting mixed numbers requires careful, accurate work.

Problem: Create problems that will result in the answers given below. At least one of the problems you create should require regrouping.

(a) $8\frac{4}{9}$ (b) $3\frac{5}{12}$

| 2–22 | **Subtracting Mixed Numbers**   ✮✮ |

Sometimes it can be more difficult to create a good math problem than it is to solve one.

Problem: Create a word problem that requires students to subtract mixed numbers to find the answer. After writing your problem, exchange it for the problem written by another student. Try to solve each other's problems. Then check the work.

| 2–23 | **Subtracting Mixed Numbers**   ✮✮ |

A good understanding of fractions is useful in many real-life problems.

Problem: Eddie is helping his father panel the family room. As they are working with the trim, Eddie's father notes that the final piece of trim is $6\frac{1}{2}$ feet long. The last section of wall they need to trim is $4\frac{3}{4}$ feet. There are also a few other small sections where they could use any trim that is left over. How much trim will they have left after completing the last section of wall?

| 2–24 | **Multiplying Fractions**   ✮ |

Gardening and planting provide enjoyment and relaxation for many people. Sometimes a sound understanding of fractions comes in handy.

Problem: Erin needs $\frac{1}{4}$ pound of peat moss for each juniper she plants. How many pounds of peat moss are required for 20 junipers?

2–25   Multiplying Fractions   ✩ G

When multiplying fractions, you must multiply numerators times numerators and denominators times denominators.

Problem: Using the digits 2, 3, 5, and 7, form two fractions that have the largest product. (*Hint:* Improper fractions may be used.)

2–26   Multiplying Fractions   ✩✩

At Elmville Middle School, students take a unit test at the end of each math unit. Three tests are taken each quarter, and the test average counts $\frac{1}{3}$ of the quarterly average. There are no midterm or final exams.

Problem: One test is what part of the quarterly grade? One test is what part of the end-of-the-year average?

2–27   Multiplying Fractions   ✩✩

Grandpa's a great guy but his love for math puzzles is sometimes a bit much. Occasionally he also gets a little mixed up.

He said that he would give his grandson Billy $200. But there were some conditions, as follows:

1. Half of the $200 could be spent on anything.

2. Half of what was left must be saved.

3. Half of what was left after saving must be used on clothing.

4. Half of what was left after buying clothes must be used to buy books.

5. Half of what was then left must be spent at the movies.

According to Grandpa, after all of his conditions are met, $10 will be left over.

Problem: Is Grandpa right? Explain your answer.

2–28 Multiplying Fractions ★★

"Reduced calorie" on a food label means that the product has at least $\frac{1}{3}$ fewer calories than the product normally would have.

Problem: A bottle of salad dressing has a total of 90 calories per serving, including 80 fat calories per serving. Another bottle of the same brand and flavor is advertised as having $\frac{1}{3}$ less fat. It has a total of 45 calories per serving, including 35 fat calories per serving. Could this also be advertised as "reduced calorie"? Explain your answer.

2–29 Multiplying Fractions and Mixed Numbers ★

Multiplying fractions and mixed numbers is a basic skill in mathematics.

Problem: Which problems below have correct answers? Correct the ones that have the wrong answers.

(a) $\frac{4}{9} \times \frac{3}{8} = \frac{1}{18}$ (b) $20 \times \frac{1}{8} = 2\frac{1}{2}$ (c) $\frac{5}{9} \times 3\frac{3}{10} = 1\frac{17}{18}$

2–30 Multiplying Mixed Numbers ★

Being able to solve problems quickly and efficiently is an advantage when taking tests. You can improve your problem-solving speed and efficiency through practice.

Problem: Which of the following problems equals 12? Show the work.

(a) $2\frac{1}{4} \times 5\frac{1}{3}$ (b) $2\frac{3}{7} \times 4\frac{2}{3}$ (c) $1\frac{5}{6} \times 6\frac{3}{4}$

2–31 Multiplying Mixed Numbers ★★

Estimation is an important skill when working with fractions, just as it is with whole numbers.

Problem: Estimate the answer to the problem below. Explain how you arrived at your answer.

$$2\frac{3}{4} \times 4\frac{1}{3}$$

2–32 Multiplying Mixed Numbers ★★ G

Usually students are asked to solve problems to find answers. In the problem below, you are asked to find a problem that results in the answer.

Problem: Create a problem in which two mixed numbers multiplied together equal $7\frac{2}{3}$. Write an explanation of what strategy you used.

2–33 Dividing Fractions ★

For the holidays, some people make special family recipes and package the food as gifts.

Problem: Sue plans to use a recipe that yields 15 pounds of fudge. She intends to wrap the fudge she makes in $\frac{3}{4}$-pound boxes and give one box to each of her friends and relatives for gifts. How many gifts will she have?

2–34 Dividing Fractions ⋆⋆ G

When dividing fractions, it is important to rewrite the problem using the reciprocal. For example: $\frac{3}{4} \div \frac{1}{5} = \frac{3}{4} \times \frac{5}{1} = \frac{15}{4} = 3\frac{3}{4}$

Problem: Using the digits 2, 7, 9, and 11, create a division problem for fractions that results in the smallest quotient.

2–35 Dividing Fractions and Mixed Numbers ⋆

When you divide mixed numbers, remember to convert the mixed numbers to improper fractions, use the reciprocal of the divisor, then multiply.

Problem: Which of the following have the correct answer? Find the correct answer of those that are incorrect.

(a) $4\frac{1}{3} \div \frac{5}{6} = 3\frac{11}{18}$ (b) $4 \div 1\frac{1}{7} = 3\frac{1}{2}$ (c) $3\frac{3}{4} \div 1\frac{2}{3} = 3\frac{3}{4}$

2–36 Dividing Fractions and Mixed Numbers ⋆⋆

Creating problems can sometimes be as hard as solving them.

Problem: Create a word problem for dividing fractions and mixed numbers. Exchange the problem you created for the problem created by another student. Solve each other's problems.

2-37   Fractions: Multi-step Problem   ☆

Fractions are especially important in building, whether it is a new structure, a renovation, or a simple installation.

Problem: Wanza is installing a shelf to hold some items in his room. Brackets that are $\frac{1}{4}$-inch thick are to be fastened through a $\frac{1}{2}$-inch sheetrock wall and extend at least $1\frac{1}{2}$ inches into wooden supports behind the wall. He only has 2-inch nails with which to secure the brackets. Are the nails long enough? What are the shortest nails he can use?

2-38   Fractions: Multi-step Problem   ☆☆

Taxi fares depend upon the distance that is traveled. Fares may also vary according to the city and number of passengers.

Problem: Tony's Taxi charges $3 for the first mile and $1 for each additional half mile (or fraction thereof). If the taxi ride is $5\frac{1}{4}$ miles, what is the fare?

2-39   Decimals   ☆

Simon Stevin (1548–1620), a Flemish mathematician, first used decimals in *La Disme,* which was published in 1585. He used a circle to represent a decimal point instead of the "period" used today. The word *dime* is taken from the title of Stevin's book.

Problem: Write an explanation about how the word "dime" could be taken from a work dealing with decimals.

2-40   Ordering Decimals   ☆

Many libraries use the Dewey Decimal System to classify their books. Following are the ten main classifications of the Dewey Decimal System.

000   Generalities
100   Philosophy and Psychology
200   Religion
300   Social Sciences
400   Language
500   Natural Sciences and Mathematics
600   Technology (Applied Science)
700   The Arts
800   Literature and Rhetoric
900   Geography and History

Each class is further broken down into tenths, hundredths, thousandths and so on. Books are arranged by numbers and ordered from lowest to highest. The first three letters of the author's name appear under the number.

Problem: Below are call numbers for books in a library. Two are out of order. Which are they and where do they belong?

510	513.0212	510.2	510.212	510.03	510.3
Wor	Hop	Han	Bur	Gib	Jam

2-41   Ordering Decimals   ☆

Some countries are very small. The world's ten smallest countries and their area (in square miles) are listed below.

Nauru, 8.2   Liechtenstein, 61.0   Monaco, .7   Macao, 6.2

Tuvalu, 10   Bermuda, 20.6   Antigua, 108   Gibraltar, 2.5

Vatican City, .17   San Marino, 23

Problem: List the countries in order from smallest to largest according to their area.

| 2–42 | **Ordering Decimals** ☆ |

The first person to swim across the English Channel was Matthew Webb in 1875. Webb's time was 21.25 hours. The second, third, and fourth people and their times were Thomas Burgess, 22.583 hours; Henry Sullivan, 26.83 hours; and Enrico Tiraboschi, 16.55 hours.

Problem: Arrange the times of these four people in order from the greatest to the least.

| 2–43 | **Place Value with Decimals** ☆☆ |

The Great Pyramid in Giza, Egypt was constructed about 2580 B.C.

Problem: To find the height of the Great Pyramid in meters, use the clues below.

The tenths digit is 4 more than the hundreds digit.

The tenths digit is the only prime number in this decimal.

The tens digit is 4 times the hundreds digit.

The units digit is 1 more than the tenths digit.

| 2–44 | **Writing Fractions as Decimals** ☆ |

A *decimal fraction* is a rational number written as units, tenths, hundredths, thousandths, and so on.
For example, $\frac{2}{5}$ equals 0.4 in decimal notation. $\frac{3}{4}$ equals 0.75 in decimal notation.

Problem: List 3 fractions and express them as decimal fractions.

2–45 Writing Fractions as Decimals ★

At service stations, pumps measure gasoline in increments of thousandths of gallons.

Problem: What will the pump read after pumping $18\frac{1}{8}$ gallons?

2–46 Writing Decimals as Fractions ★

Reading decimals using place value can help you write fractions.
For example:

.1 is one-tenth or $\frac{1}{10}$

.25 is twenty-five hundredths or $\frac{25}{100}$ or $\frac{1}{4}$

3.61 is three and sixty-one hundredths or $3\frac{61}{100}$

Problem: Express each decimal below as a fraction or mixed number. Simplify.

   (a) 2.6   (b) .75   (c) 14.95   (d) 1.004

2–47 Writing Decimals as Fractions ★★

A *mixed decimal* consists of an integer and a proper fraction. $.3\frac{1}{3}$, $.87\frac{1}{2}$, and $.66\frac{2}{3}$ are examples of mixed decimals.

To express a mixed decimal as a fraction, look at the number to the right of the decimal point. If there is one digit to the right, multiply the mixed decimal by $\frac{1}{10}$; if there are two digits to the right, multiply the mixed decimal by $\frac{1}{100}$, and so on. For example:

$$.3\frac{1}{3} = 3\frac{1}{3} \times \frac{1}{10} = \frac{10}{3} \times \frac{1}{10} = \frac{1}{3}$$

Problem: Each decimal on the left can be written as a fraction on the right. Match each decimal with its equivalent fraction.

$$.1\frac{1}{9} \qquad\qquad \frac{1}{3}$$
$$.6\frac{1}{3} \qquad\qquad \frac{1}{9}$$
$$.7\frac{1}{7} \qquad\qquad \frac{5}{6}$$
$$.33\frac{1}{3} \qquad\qquad \frac{5}{7}$$
$$.83\frac{1}{3} \qquad\qquad \frac{19}{30}$$

2-48   Repeating Decimals   ★

Repeating decimals are nonterminating decimals in which a number or a group of numbers repeats infinitely.

For example: $\frac{1}{3} = .\overline{3}$ and $\frac{1}{6} = .1\overline{6}$

Problem: Listed below are some fractions whose numerators are 1. (These are called unit fractions.) Which fractions below are repeating decimals?

$$\frac{1}{2}, \frac{1}{4}, \frac{1}{5}, \frac{1}{7}, \frac{1}{8}, \frac{1}{9}, \frac{1}{10}, \frac{1}{11}$$

2-49   Repeating Decimals   ★★

Repeating decimals do not end. Instead, a number or group of numbers repeats. A *unit fraction* is a fraction whose numerator is 1. Some unit fractions repeat; some do not.

Problem: The fractions $\frac{1}{3}, \frac{1}{6}, \frac{1}{7}, \frac{1}{9}, \frac{1}{11}, \frac{1}{12}, \frac{1}{13}, \frac{1}{14}$, and $\frac{1}{15}$ are unit fractions whose decimal equivalents repeat. Write each of these as a repeating decimal.

2-50   Comparing Fractions and Decimals   ★★

Drill bits are used to drill a hole in wood or other solid materials. The sizes of drill bits are often measured in fractions, using increments of 64ths of an inch.

Problem: Joe wants to drill a hole that is large enough to allow a .425-inch diameter wire to pass through as tightly as possible. Which of the following drill bits should he use? (The diameters of the bits are given in inches.)

(a) $\frac{13}{32}$ (b) $\frac{7}{16}$ (c) $\frac{15}{32}$ (d) $\frac{3}{8}$

2–51 Estimating with Decimals ☆

Estimating may be used to get an approximate answer or to see if an answer is reasonable.

Problem: Maria is ordering lunch at a fast-food restaurant. She estimates her bill as she is ordering. (All costs include sales tax.) Following are her estimates for lunch.

Soda, $1.25; estimate, $1.00

Hamburger Special, $3.49; estimate $3.00

Ice cream, $0.99; estimate $1.00

Maria has only $5.00. Does she have enough money according to her estimate? Does she really have enough? Write an explanation of your answer.

2–52 Rounding Decimals ☆

Rounding decimals is useful when you wish to be "reasonably" accurate but not exact. To round to the nearest whole number, tenths, hundredths, thousandths, and so on, look at the number to the right of the place you are rounding.

- If the number to the right is 5 or more, increase the number in the place you are rounding by 1.
- If the number to the right of the place you wish to round is less than 5, omit all the numbers to the right of the place you are rounding and leave the number of the place as it is.

Problem: Make a simple chart and round each of the numbers below to the nearest whole number, tenth, hundredth, and thousandth.

(a) 0.9375   (b) 2.7638   (c) 3.05882   (d) 0.4444

2–53   Rounding Decimals   ☆

Merchants and store owners are reluctant to round prices down. As a result, in pricing, the rules for rounding are changed slightly.

If canned goods are priced 3 for $1.00, the price of one can is $.333 . . . . If you follow the rules for rounding, the price would be $.33. However, because there is a digit (other than 0) to the right of the hundredths place, you would actually pay $.34. Rather than rounding down, the price is rounded up.

Problem: Determine how much you would pay for one item if the prices were:

(a) 2 for $1.99   (b) 2 for $3.00

(c) 3 for $2.00   (d) 8 for $5.00

2–54   Adding Decimals   ☆

When adding decimals, it is necessary to line up the decimal points in the numbers that are added. This will help you to keep each digit in its proper column.

Problem: Add the following:

(a) 27.3 + 5.65   (b) 52.0 + 1.345 + 0.54

(c) .657 + 2.3 + 86.389   (d) 5.678 + 3 + 19.487

2–55   Adding Decimals   ☆

Cash registers in most supermarkets are actually computer terminals. As a cashier rings up an order, the information is entered in the store's computer and the computer instantly records the information on an itemized cash register receipt.

Problem: Mary purchases the following items:

potato chips for $1.79

candy bar for $0.59

orange juice for $2.29

toothpaste for $2.79

milk for $1.29

How much does Mary have to pay for these items?

2-56 Subtracting Decimals ☆

To subtract decimals accurately, you must first line up decimal points so that digits are in their correct columns. (Remember to regroup when necessary.)

Problem: Subtract the following:

(a) $1.867 - .947$

(b) $356.2 - 4.7826$

(c) $6 - 2.49$

(d) $0.09348 - 0.058$

2-57 Subtracting Decimals ☆

Whether you are working as a cashier and must give the proper change to customers, or you are a consumer who receives change after making a purchase, being able to quickly count change is a valuable skill.

Problem: Determine the change in the fewest bills and coins as in the example.

Example: Purchase price, $13.95

Amount paid, $15.00

Change, $1.05 (one dollar bill, nickel)

Purchase Price	Amount Paid	Change
$15.89	$20.00	
$ 2.59	$ 5.00	
$23.35	$30.35	
$47.63	$60.03	

2-58 Subtracting Decimals ☆☆

Decimals are used in our everyday experiences. Money, measurements, scores and records in sports, even grade-point averages in school are all based on decimals.

Problem: Create a word problem that involves subtracting decimals. Exchange your problem for the problem of another student and solve each other's problem.

2–59 Multiplying Decimals ☆

It is easy to overlook a decimal point when multiplying decimals, but decimal points can make a big difference in your answer. Would you rather have $1000 or $10.00?

Problem: Each product below is correct; however, a decimal point is missing in one or both factors. Place the decimal points where they belong in the factors. (You may need to add place holders.) Is there more than one way to do this? Explain your reasoning.

(a) $36 \times 54 = 194.4$

(b) $78 \times 21 = .1638$

(c) $324 \times 65 = 2,106$

(d) $7 \times 3 = 0.00021$

2–60 Multiplying Decimals ☆

When multiplying decimals, pay close attention to your multiplication facts as well as your decimal point.

Problem: Which of the problems below are correct? Correct those that are wrong.

(a) 0.256	(b) 0.54	(c) 7.024	(d) 34.7
× 0.56	× 2.4	× 0.86	× 6.7
0.14386	0.1296	6.0464	232.49

2–61 Multiplying Decimals ☆☆ G

You may find that some problems in math may be solved by using various strategies.

Problem: Using decimals, create a multiplication problem that results in the answer of 2,564.38. Explain how you arrived at your answer.

2-62 ▌ Dividing Decimals ☆

A divisor must always be expressed as a whole number. This is very important when dividing by decimals.

Problem: Explain why a divisor must be expressed as a whole number.

2-63 ▌ Dividing Decimals ☆☆

When dividing by a decimal, it is often necessary to multiply a divisor by 10, 100, 1000, or so on, to express the divisor as a whole number.

Problem: Solve the problem below, then write an explanation of how you found the quotient.

$$.31\overline{)210.8}$$

2-64 ▌ Dividing Decimals ☆☆

Dividing decimals correctly requires careful work.

Problem: Which, if any, of the problems below are correct? Correct the problems that are wrong.

(a) $0.91\overline{)6.825}$ → 7.8 (b) $7.6\overline{)0.56468}$ → 0.743 (c) $0.006\overline{)0.5154}$ → 8.59 (d) $0.36\overline{)0.00306}$ → 0.085

2-65 Dividing Decimals ⋆⋆

To compute gas mileage, divide the number of miles driven by the number of gallons of gasoline used.

Problem: Sergio drove 300.5 miles on 14.8 gallons of gasoline. What was Sergio's mileage? Round your answer to the nearest mile per gallon.

2-66 Decimals: Multi-step Problem ⋆⋆

Everyone's body is different; however, the average of this uniqueness leads to some interesting facts.

The average length of the six longest bones in the human body are listed below.

Femur (upper leg), 19.88 inches

Tibia (lower inner leg), 16.94 inches

Fibula (outer lower leg), 15.94 inches

Humerus (upper arm), 14.35 inches

Ulna (inner lower arm), 11.10 inches

Radius (outer lower arm), 10.4 inches

Problem: Find the average length of the human arm, and the average length of the human leg. Which is longer, the average length of the human leg or arm?

2-67 Decimals: Multi-step Problem ⋆⋆

A unit price (or unit rate) is the amount charged per unit. A unit may be a single item, a measurement such as an ounce or pint, or some other quantity, depending on the product.

You can compare the cost of similar items by comparing unit prices. A lower unit price is the better buy.

Problem: A 35-ounce box of cereal sells for $6.49. A 20-ounce box of the same cereal sells for $3.99. Which is the better buy?

2–68 Decimals: Multi-step Problem ★★

Some companies pay employees time and a half for overtime. Usually overtime means time worked after 8 hours per day or time worked after 40 hours per week. Time and a half means 1.5 times the hourly wage.

Problem: A local restaurant pays cashiers $6.40 per hour, with time and a half for overtime. (This restaurant pays overtime for any hours more than 40 worked per week.) Casey worked 43.5 hours last week. How much money did Casey earn?

2–69 Decimals: Multi-step Problem ★★

Many people use coupons to save money when they shop. Most coupons may be used only for a specific brand or size of products.

Problem: Eat Rite Supermarket is having a "buy one get one free" sale on the 20-ounce box of Toasties cereal. One box sells for $3.99. Samantha has a coupon that is worth $0.75 off the 35-ounce box of Toasties. This box normally sells for $6.49. Which is the better buy? Explain your answer.

2–70 Decimals: Multi-step Problem ★★

Most people like pizza. Plain pies usually come with just cheese and tomato sauce, but most pizza shops will let you order extra toppings—for an additional cost.

Problem: Vinny's Pizza sells a 10-inch pizza for $8.49. The plain pie comes with tomato sauce and cheese. A special combination of any three additional toppings is $2.00 extra. If a fourth, fifth, or sixth topping is selected, the cost is $0.45 per topping. What is the cost of a 10-inch pizza with anchovies, onions, pepper, and pepperoni?

2–71   Decimals: Multi-step Problem   ★★

Electricians often charge a set amount for each hour they work, plus a service charge. The service charge doesn't vary and is charged regardless of how long a job takes.

Problem: How much would an electrician charge for doing $4\frac{1}{2}$ hours of work if the rate is $25 per hour, plus a service charge of $45?

2–72   Decimals: Multi-step Problem   ★★

Long-distance phone calls are based on the rates, the calling point, and the time the call was made.

Problem: A 15-minute long-distance call is calculated in the following manner:

Up to and including the first 10 minutes, the cost is $0.09 per minute.

Each additional minute is $0.03.

Find the total cost of this call.

2–73   Decimals: Multi-step Problem   ★★

An operator-assisted long-distance phone call is a call in which an operator "assists," or helps, a person complete the call. Such calls are usually more expensive than calls the caller completes her- or himself.

Problem: Dana was told that an operator-assisted call costs 1.5 times the cost of a direct-dial call to the same city. Find the cost of the direct-dial call if the operator-assisted call costs $5.45. Round your answer to the nearest cent.

2–74 Decimals: Multi-step Problem ★★

An odometer records the number of miles a car has traveled. Some people like to record the distance they travel, especially for long trips.

Problem: When the Santos family left for Florida, the odometer on their car read 8765.2 miles. When they arrived in Florida, the odometer read 9382.7 miles. While they were in Florida, they drove 18.6 miles. They returned home on the same roads they used for driving to Florida. What did the odometer of their car read upon their return?

2–75 Decimals: Multi-step Problem ★★

An *expression* is a group of numbers and operations. To simplify an expression means to find its value.

Mathematicians agree on steps for simplifying expressions with more than one operation.

1. Perform all multiplication and division from left to right.

2. Perform all addition and subtraction from left to right.

Problem: Using the steps stated above, simplify the following expression.

$$3.8 + 6.4 \div .2 - 1.8 \times 2.6 - 3.2 \div .8$$

2–76 Decimals: Multi-step Problem ★★★

Sometimes groups of numbers and operations are enclosed within grouping symbols such as parentheses. The steps for simplifying these expressions are listed below.

1. Numbers in parentheses must be computed first.

2. Multiply or divide in order from left to right.

3. Add or subtract from left to right.

Problem: Simplify the expression below.

$$6.2 \times 0.03 + (4.6 + 5.6) \div (2 + 3.1) - 2.06$$

2-77 | Decimals: Multi-step Problem ★★★

The word *parentheses* is taken from the Greek word *parentithenai,* which means putting in beside. When used in mathematics, parentheses permit you to put a number or numbers beside other numbers. In number sentences, any operations within parentheses are always computed first.

Problem: Place the decimals 1.7, 2.4, 3.8, 5.2, and 13.68 in the blanks below so that the number sentence equals 7.24.

$$\underline{\hspace{1cm}} \div \underline{\hspace{1cm}} + \underline{\hspace{1cm}} \times (\underline{\hspace{1cm}} - \underline{\hspace{1cm}}) = 7.24$$

2-78 | Decimals: Multi-step Problem ★★★ G

Teamwork can make even the toughest problems less difficult.

Problem: Create four problems that result in the answer 31.59. One problem should be addition, one should be subtraction, one should be multiplication, and the last one should be division. Be ready to explain the strategies you used.

2-79 | Ratio ★

A *ratio* is a comparison of two numbers. A ratio that compares the number 4 with the number 5 can be written in three ways.

- As a fraction, $\frac{4}{5}$
- With the word "to," 4 to 5
- With a colon, 4:5

Problem: Use three different ways to express the ratio of the number of days school is in session this month with the number of days in the month.

2–80   Ratio   ★★

The Statue of Liberty in New York Harbor was a welcome sight for many European immigrants. Being one of the largest statues in the world, its size makes it an impressive object from quite some distance away.

Following are some measurements of the Statue of Liberty:

From the bottom of the pedestal to the tip of the torch, the Statue is 151 feet, 1 inch.

The length of the right arm is 42 feet.

The length of the hand is 16 feet, 5 inches.

The length of the index finger is 8 feet.

Problem: What is the ratio of the Statue of Liberty's height to the length of the right arm? What is the ratio of the length of the Statue's right arm to the length of the hand? What is the ratio of the length of the Statue's hand to its index finger? (You may round off the lengths to the nearest foot.)

2–81   Ratio   ★★

Sterling silver is an alloy. (An alloy is a mixture of two or more metals.) It is $\frac{37}{40}$ pure silver and $\frac{3}{40}$ copper.

Problem: What is the ratio of copper to silver in sterling silver? Express your answer in simplest form. Explain how you arrived at your answer.

2–82   Ratio   ★★

In model railroading, two frequently used scales are the *O* scale and the *HO* scale.

The ratio of the *O*-scale model to the full-size railroad is 1 inch to 48 inches.

The ratio of the *HO*-scale model to the full-size railroad is 1 inch to 87 inches.

Problem: Which is the larger scale? Explain your answer.

2–83 | Proportions ☆

A *proportion* is a statement that two ratios are equal.

Cross products are used to determine which statements are proportions. If the cross products are equal, then the statement is a proportion.

For example: $\frac{3}{5} = \frac{12}{20}$. Since each cross product, 3×20 and 5×12, equals 60, the statement is a proportion.

Problem: Identify the number sentences below that are *not* proportions. Rewrite them by changing one number so that the statement is a proportion.

(a) $\frac{2}{3} = \frac{14}{21}$ (b) $\frac{5}{7} = \frac{25}{49}$ (c) $\frac{3}{8} = \frac{24}{64}$ (d) $\frac{10}{9} = \frac{30}{3}$

2–84 | Proportions ☆☆

Since a proportion is a statement about the equality of ratios, some surprising patterns may emerge.

Problem: Find the missing value in each problem below. Then explain the pattern.

(a) $\frac{6}{} = \frac{2}{7}$ (b) $\frac{6}{} = \frac{3}{7}$ (c) $\frac{6}{} = \frac{6}{7}$ (d) $\frac{6}{} = \frac{12}{7}$

2–85 | Proportions ☆☆

Along with nutritional information, a serving size is carefully defined on a food product's label. Many people believe that a serving is a quantity, or helping, that can be eaten in one sitting. If a person asks for seconds, these people feel that this is a second serving. Depending on the amount of the serving size, it may actually be a third, fourth, or more.

Problem: According to the label on a box of pretzels, a serving is about 1 ounce, or 12 pretzels. 110 calories are contained in each serving. Pete ate 30 pretzels while he watched his favorite TV show. About how many calories did he consume?

2-86 Proportions ★★

The word *proportion* is taken from the Greek word *proportione,* which means "for its own share."

Problem: Explain why a proportionate amount is a quantity that has its own share.

2-87 Proportions ★★

A stack of recyclable newspaper 36 inches high will save one tree. The number of trees saved by recycling is directly proportional to the height of a stack of recyclable newspapers.

Problem: Write and solve a proportion to find out about how many trees are saved if a stack of newspapers 14 feet high is recycled. (*Hint:* Remember to change feet to inches.)

2-88 Proportions ★★

The *O* scale is a scale used to build model trains. The ratio of the *O*-scale model to the actual train is 1 inch to 48 inches.

Problem: If the length of a railroad car is 80 feet, find the length of the scale model.

2-89 Proportions ★★

Model trains are often built according to the *O* scale. The ratio of the *O*-scale model to the actual train is 1 inch to 48 inches.

Problem: Accessories for model trains are available in various sizes. Could a 5-inch tree be used with an *O*-scale train? Explain your answer.

2-90 Proportions ★★

A printing press that prints money can print 8,000 sheets of 32 bills every hour.

Problem: If five-dollar bills are printed, what is the value of the money printed during an 8-hour shift?

2-91 Proportions ★★★

Road maps always contain a scale. Places are located on the map and the scale can be used to determine the actual distance between different places.

Problem: The scale on a map is $\frac{1}{2}$ inch = 15 miles. If two towns, Jackson and Lincoln, are 50 miles apart, how far apart are they on the map? Washington is 20 miles from Jackson. According to the scale, how far is Washington from Lincoln? Write an explanation of your answer.

2–92   Percents   ☆

The word *percent* means the number of parts in or to a hundred, which represents a *whole*. Thus, 100% means 1, 200% means 2, 300% means 3, and so on.

Problem: Miss Stern's first period class had 100% attendance on the day she planned to show an exciting math movie. Before the movie began, Miss Stern had 200% attendance. How could this be?

2–93   Percents   ☆☆

The Earth's surface is covered by water and land, but the area of water and land are not equal.

Problem: Imagine a map of the world. Estimate what percent of the Earth's surface is land. Then list the largest and smallest continents. (*Hint:* The surface of the Earth is about 3 parts water and 1 part land.)

2–94   Percents   ☆☆

Fred's Fix-it is having a sale on various auto services.

20% off tune-ups

50% off oil changes

20% off the cost of rotating tires

20% off the cost of wheel alignments

Wanting to draw in big crowds, Fred displays the following sign: "110% Off Auto Services."

Problem: Fred may know how to repair cars, but he doesn't know his math. What must Fred fix on his sign? Explain your answer.

2-95   Percents ★★

Nutritionists think in terms of percentages when they recommend daily amounts of calories. They often express their recommendations in ranges.

For example, most nutritionists agree that protein should be between 10% and 15% of your daily calories, fats should be between 10% and 30%, and complex carbohydrates should be between 55% and 70%.

Problem: Why doesn't the sum of the percentages at the low end of the range equal 100%? Why doesn't the sum of the percentages at the high end of the range equal 100%? Explain your answers.

2-96   Equivalencies ★

Fractions, decimals, and percents can be expressed as each other. Charts are an easy way to do this.

Problem: Express each word as a fraction, decimal, and percent.

Word	Fraction	Decimal	Percent
one-tenth			
three-fourths			
one-half			
one-eighth			
two-fifths			
one			

2-97 Equivalencies ☆

Percents, fractions, and decimals are related, and may be expressed in various ways.

Problem: Complete the chart below and explain the pattern.

Fraction	Decimal	Percent
$\frac{1}{8}$	.125	12.5%
$\frac{2}{8} = \frac{1}{4}$		
$\frac{3}{8}$		
$\frac{4}{8} = \frac{1}{2}$		
$\frac{5}{8}$		
$\frac{6}{8} = \frac{3}{4}$		
$\frac{7}{8}$		

2-98 Equivalencies ☆☆

Fraction, decimal, and percent equivalencies are often expressed in a table that has equivalent values written on the same line.

Problem: In the table below, one value on each line is incorrect. Find the incorrect value and correct it.

Fraction	Decimal	Percent
$\frac{2}{3}$	$.\overline{6}$	66%
$\frac{3}{57}$	.375	37.5%
$\frac{1}{10}$	.1	1%
$\frac{3}{8}$	$.83\frac{1}{3}$	$83.\overline{3}\%$
$\frac{5}{9}$	.55	$55\frac{5}{9}\%$

2–99   Equivalencies   ★★

Many stores run discount ads that say 10%, 20%, 30%, and 50% off the regular price.

Problem: Why are these the most common discounts? Why do you think stores sometimes include $33\frac{1}{3}$% off? Explain your answer.

2–100   Equivalencies   ★★★

Fractions such as $\frac{1}{3}, \frac{1}{6}, \frac{1}{9}$, and $\frac{1}{12}$ can be expressed as repeating decimals. If they are written as a percent, the percent is a mixed number.

Problem: Do you think all fractions whose denominators are multiples of 3 are repeating decimals? Explain your answer. Give examples (or counter examples) of the fraction, decimal, and percent equivalencies.

2–101   Finding the Percent of a Number   ★

The proportion below may be used to find the percent of numbers.

$$\frac{Part}{Base} = \frac{Percent}{100}$$

For example, in the expression 20% of 80, the Part equals n (which is the number to be found), the Base (which is always after the word "of") is 80, and 20% is written as 20 over 100, as noted below.

$$\frac{n}{80} = \frac{20}{100}$$

$$n = 16$$

Problem: Each problem below can be solved by using the proportion above. Write the proportion and solve it.

(a) What is 40% of 238?

(b) What is 34% of 240?

(c) What is 110% of 150?

(d) What is 68% of 100?

2-102 Finding the Percent of a Number ✭

Everybody likes shortcuts. Here is one for finding the percent of a number. Simply change the percent to an equivalent decimal and multiply, as in the example.

$$65\% \text{ of } 354 = .65 \times 354 = 230.1$$

Problem: Which of the problems below are correct? Correct those that have wrong answers.

(a) 78% of 6,284 = 4,801.52

(b) 39% of 756 = 294.04

(c) 230% of 348 = 80.04

(d) 68.5% of 125 = 85.625

2-103 Finding the Percent of a Number ✭

Labels on multi-vitamin bottles provide information about the different vitamins (and their amounts) contained in each tablet. These amounts are usually noted in milligrams. Also listed is the percentage each vitamin provides of the U.S. Recommended Daily Allowance (RDA). The RDA is the amount of each vitamin that the average person should have each day.

Problem: A vitamin tablet provides 200% of the RDA for vitamin B-2. The U.S. RDA is 1.7 milligrams. Find the amount of vitamin B-2 in the tablet.

2-104 Finding the Percent of a Number ✭

Items are often grouped together. A group of 20 items is called a *score*.

Problem: Calculate 60% of the number of items in a score. Your answer will be a number that is a common grouping today. What is the grouping?

2–105 Finding the Percent of a Number ✮✮

If you are like most people, you like money. You've also probably already learned that it's easier to spend money than it is to acquire it. To help themselves plan how to spend their money, many people set up a budget.

Problem: Assume that you have developed the following monthly budget to help you spend and save your money. You have decided that the money you earn from your allowance and chores will be spent as noted below:

25% will go to savings

20% may be spent on recreation and entertainment

15% may be spent on extras for lunch

30% may be spent on clothing

10% will be set aside for miscellaneous expenses

Assuming that you earned $96.50 last month from your allowance and chores, how much money would you put in each category listed above? Round your answer to the nearest dollar.

2–106 Finding the Percent of a Number ✮✮

When Mary and her friend Liz had to find the percent of numbers for homework, the first problem was 84% of 540. Mary multiplied .84 × 540 and got the answer 453.6. She didn't think it could be right, because her answer was less than 540. She called Liz for help. Liz told her the answer was correct, but Mary wondered how the product could be smaller than 540.

Problem: How would you explain to Mary that she was, in fact, right?

2-107 Finding What Percent a Number Is of Another Number ☆

To find what percent a number is of another, use the following proportion:

$$\frac{Part}{Base} = \frac{Percent}{100}$$

For example, to find what percent of 125 is 60, set up your proportion as noted below and solve for n.

$$\frac{60}{125} = \frac{n}{100}$$

$$125n = 6000$$

$$n = 48$$

The number sentence is then written as 48% of 125 is 60.

Problem: Solve each proportion below, and then translate it into a number sentence.

(a) $\frac{28}{70} = \frac{n}{100}$ (b) $\frac{22}{60} = \frac{n}{100}$ (c) $\frac{14}{7} = \frac{n}{100}$ (d) $\frac{9}{1800} = \frac{n}{100}$

2-108 Finding What Percent a Number Is of Another Number ☆☆

The typical 30-minute sitcom (situation comedy) on TV is not 30 minutes long. Within that half-hour period are several commercials.

Problem: Muhammad taped a rerun of his favorite episode of a 30-minute sitcom. He taped the opening credits and theme song, the show, and then the closing credits. He did not tape any commercials. His tape of the show ran 22 minutes. What percent of the total air time for this sitcom was spent on advertising? (Round your answer to the nearest tenth.)

2-109 Finding What Percent a Number Is of Another Number ☆☆

Sugar can give your body quick energy. It is a simple nutrient that can enter your bloodstream and feed your cells more easily than many other nutrients. Unfortunately, your body converts excess sugar and stores it as fat.

The average American consumes about 36 teaspoons of sugar each day. Much of this sugar is found in processed foods. Dietitians often refer to it as "hidden" sugar because people don't realize it is there. For example, one 12-ounce can of soda (non-diet) contains about 9 teaspoons of sugar.

Problem: Assume you are an average person. What percent of your daily sugar intake is found in a 12-ounce can of non-diet soda?

2–110   Finding What Percent a Number Is of Another Number   ✯✯✯

Of the zodiac's 12 signs illustrated below, four represent people, seven represent animals, and one represents neither people nor animals.

Problem: What percent of the signs represents animals? What percent represents people? What percent represents neither people nor animals?

2–111 Finding a Number When a Percent of It Is Known ⋆⋆

$\frac{Part}{Base} = \frac{Percent}{100}$ is a proportion that can be used to solve problems like the following: 12% of what number is 15? In this proportion, 15 is the Part, the Base is n since we don't know this number, and 12, as the percent, is written over 100.

The proportion is set up like this: $\frac{15}{n} = \frac{12}{100}$. You would then solve for n.

Problem: Each problem below is written with two proportions. Choose the correct proportion and solve it.

(a) 24 is 30% of what number? $\qquad \frac{24}{n} = \frac{30}{100} \qquad\qquad \frac{n}{24} = \frac{30}{100}$

(b) 5% of what number is 6? $\qquad \frac{6}{100} = \frac{5}{n} \qquad\qquad \frac{6}{n} = \frac{5}{100}$

(c) 42 is 150% of what number? $\qquad \frac{42}{n} = \frac{150}{100} \qquad\qquad \frac{n}{42} = \frac{150}{100}$

2–112 Finding a Number When a Percent of It Is Known ⋆⋆⋆

Tennis is a game that may be played with singles or doubles. To accommodate four players (doubles), the size of the court is widened. A singles tennis court is 75% as wide as a doubles tennis court.

Problem: A singles tennis court is 27 feet wide. How wide is the doubles court?

2–113 Finding a Number When a Percent of It Is Known ⋆⋆⋆

In their goal to remain healthy, many people try to eat foods with fewer calories. Keeping track of their caloric intake, however, may not be easy.

Problem: The label on a package of light ice cream claims that the ice cream has 30% fewer calories than regular ice cream. If $\frac{1}{2}$ cup of this light ice cream contains 110 calories, about how many calories are in a $\frac{1}{2}$ cup of regular ice cream?

2–114 | The Three Types of Percentage Problems ★★

The proportion $\dfrac{Part}{Base} = \dfrac{Percent}{100}$ can be used to solve three types of percentage problems. Care is needed to substitute numbers correctly in the proportion.

Problem: Pair each question below with the correct proportion. Then solve the proportion. (One proportion will not match any of the questions.)

(a) Sue typed 56 pages, 7 of which were double-spaced. What percent of the pages were single-spaced?

(b) 7% of the 56 students in the algebra classes have an "A" average for the marking period. About how many students is this?

(c) The PTA has 56 members, which is only 7% of the total the PTA wishes to enroll. What is the enrollment goal?

$$\frac{7}{100} = \frac{n}{56} \qquad \frac{7}{100} = \frac{56}{n} \qquad \frac{n}{100} = \frac{7}{56} \qquad \frac{n}{100} = \frac{49}{56}$$

2–115 | Percents: Multi-step Problem ★

At a Dollar-Day Sale everything in the designated section of the store is priced at a dollar or in multiples of a dollar.

Problem: Mary and José went shopping at a store holding a Dollar-Day Sale. The cost of the items they decided to buy was $5. They had to pay sales tax of 6%.

José figured that he could multiply $5 by .06 to get $.30, then add this to the $5 to get the total cost. Mary said to multiply $5 by 1.06 to arrive at the total cost. Who is correct? What do you think is the best way to solve the problem?

2–116 | Percents: Multi-step Problem ★★

A *successive discount* is a discount after a previous discount has been made. Successive discounts can lead to big savings.

Problem: The price of a jacket is reduced 40%. For one day only the reduced price is reduced another 10%. Is this the same as a 50% discount? Provide an example to support your answer.

2–117   Percents: Multi-step Problem   ★★

Buying things on sale is a great way to save money. It is important that you watch circulars and commercials to be aware of bargains.

Problem: A compact disc (CD) is marked 30% off the original price. The sale price is $12.60. Assuming there is no sales tax, find the original price of the CD.

2–118   Percents: Multi-step Problem   ★★★

A "tip" is a gratuity, or a payment for good service. People commonly tip waiters and waitresses, hairdressers, bellhops, and cab drivers. In most cases a tip of 15%, before sales tax is added, is acceptable.

Problem: Three people went to lunch together. The bill came to $23.91, plus a 6% sales tax. They decided to leave a 15% tip and divide the cost of lunch equally, each paying the same amount. How much would each person pay for lunch, including the tip? Round the answer to the nearest cent.

2–119   Percents: Multi-step Problem   ★★★

If an investment increases at approximately the same rate each year, a rule called the Rule of 72 may be used to estimate how many years it will take for the original amount of money invested to double. This assumes that the money is left in the investment and additional money is not added, except through the investment's growth.

The Rule of 72 does not take into account fluctuations or frequent compounding, but it is useful for a general estimate. To use this rule, simply divide 72 by 100 times the interest rate of the investment.

For example, if $1,000 is invested at an interest rate of 6%, divide 72 by 6 (6% × 100 = 6.) Since 72 divided by 6 equals 12, it would take 12 years for the $1,000 to double, assuming that the money is left in the account.

Problem: $6,000 is invested in a plan that pays an interest rate of 10.5%. Use the Rule of 72 to estimate how long it would take for the money to double, assuming the money is left in the account and the interest rate remains constant.

2–120 Percent of Increase ★★

Memorabilia are the kinds of things that everybody once had, but few can find years later. Because they are hard to find, such items may become worth much more money than they originally cost.

For example, past issues of *TV Guide* dating to the 1950s and 1960s sold for as little as $0.15 per copy. Today these copies may fetch as much as $7 to $9 from collectors.

Problem: Assuming an issue of *TV Guide* that once sold for $0.15 now sells for $7, what is the percent of increase?

2–121 Percent of Decrease ★★

Henry Ford worked to produce an inexpensive, universal car. When introduced in 1908, his Model T retailed for $850, but by 1924—because of mass production—it was selling for $290.

Problem: Find the percent of decrease. Round your answer to the nearest percent.

2–122 Quotation about Mathematics ★★

Albert Einstein was a brilliant German physicist who fit the stereotype of an absent-minded professor. Although it was said that he could not remember his phone number—he explained that if he needed it, he could always look it up in the phone book—he was the man who developed the Theory of Relativity, which has led to profound discoveries about our universe.

Problem: Explain these words of Albert Einstein: "Do not worry about your difficulties in mathematics. I assure you mine are still greater."

Section 3

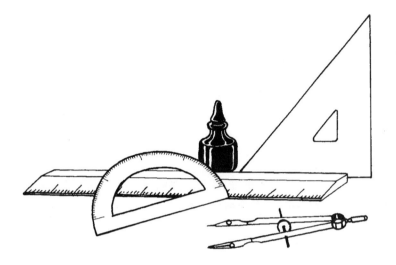

MEASUREMENT

3–1   Linear Measurement: English System   ☆

In building plans the ′ mark denotes feet and the ″ denotes inches.
For example, 16′6″ means 16 feet, 6 inches.

Problem: What is another way to write 16′6″ using only feet? How could you write 16′6″ in inches?

3–2   Linear Measurement: English System   ☆

In the English system, inches, feet, and yards are common measurements for length.

12 inches (in.) = 1 foot (ft.)

3 feet (ft.) = 1 yard (yd.)

A length is often simplified by expressing it in terms of the largest possible value, using whole numbers for the units of length. For example: 19 in. = 1 ft. 7 in.

Problem: The units are missing from the simplified measurements below. Fill in the proper units.

(a) 7 ft. = 2 _____ 1 _____

(b) 37 in. = 1 _____ 1 _____

(c) 170 ft. = 56 _____ 2 _____

(d) 6 ft. 15 in. = 2 _____ 1 _____ 3 _____

(e) 10 yd. 14 ft. 15 in. = 15 _____ 3 _____

3–3   Linear Measurement: English System   ☆

The word *mile* comes from the Latin *mille passum* which means 1,000 paces. During the days of the Roman Empire, a Roman pace was the distance covered by two strides.

Problem: How many strides were in a Roman "mile"? Is this an accurate measurement? Write an explanation of your answer.

| 3–4 | **Linear Measurement: English System** ★★ |

Charles Sherwood Stratton (1838–1883) was an entertainer best known as Tom Thumb. In 1863 he married Lavinia Warren, who, like himself, was a dwarf. George W. Morrison, known as Commodore Nutt, was the best man at the wedding.

Problem: Use the following clues to find the height in inches of Tom Thumb, his wife Lavinia, and Commodore Nutt.

Tom Thumb's height was 6 to the second power.

Commodore Nutt's height was 4 more than the sum of the first 5 odd digits.

Lavinia's height was 2 to the fifth power.

| 3–5 | **Linear Measurement: English System** ★★ |

An average adult flea can jump 200 times the length of its own body. An adult flea is about 0.1 inch long.

Problem: About how many feet can the average adult flea jump? If you were able to jump 200 times your height, about how many yards would you be able to jump?

| 3–6 | **Linear Measurement: English System** ★★ |

King Kong was a giant "Hollywood" gorilla that starred in a 1933 movie classic of the same name. The climax of the movie occurred when Kong climbed the Empire State Building and was shot down by airplanes.

Problem: Use the clues below to determine the length of King Kong's arm, leg, ear, chest, nose, and height.

The distance around his chest is 10 feet more than his height.

His nose is $\frac{1}{25}$ the length of his height.

His ear is $\frac{1}{2}$ the length of his nose.

His leg is 15 times the length of his ear.

His arm is 2 feet less than half of his height.

His face is 7 feet long. This is $3\frac{1}{2}$ times the length of his nose.

3–7 Linear Measurement: English System ⋆⋆ G

Did you know that altitude affects a baseball game? Because gravity pulls air molecules toward the surface of the Earth, air molecules are packed more densely near sea level. The higher in altitude you go, the less dense the air molecules become. At higher elevations, a moving baseball faces less resistance from the air. An increase of only 275 feet in elevation adds about 2 feet to the distance an average homerun will travel.

Problem: What implications might this have for baseball teams? (Include various aspects of the game such as hitting, pitching, and fielding.)

3–8 Linear Measurement: English System—Using a Formula ⋆

Lightning is an electrical discharge in the atmosphere that travels between clouds or between clouds and the ground. Thunder is caused by the rapid expansion of air molecules as they are heated by the lightning. These events occur almost at the same time, but because light travels much faster than sound, you may hear the thunder several seconds after the flash of lightning.

The difference in time between lightning and thunder can be used to determine about how far away the lightning occurred. Use the following formula: d = 0.2t.

In this formula, *d* is the distance in miles from the lightning, and *t* is the time in seconds that passed between the time the lightning was observed and the thunder was heard.

Problem: If you hear thunder 15 seconds after you see lightning, about how far away was the lightning?

3–9 Linear Measurement: English System—Operations and Conversions ⋆

Denominate numbers are numbers whose unit represents a unit of measurement. 7 feet, 9 yards, and 6 inches are examples of denominate numbers.

You can add, subtract, multiply, or divide denominate numbers, but you must always regroup first.

Problem: Match each problem below with its correct solution.

(a) 2 ft. 8 in.
　　+ 1 ft. 10 in.

(b) 4 yd. 2 ft.
　　− 1 ft. 6 in.

(c) 1 yd. 3 in.
　　　　　× 4

(d) 3)7yd. 2ft.

Solutions:

4 yd. 6 in.　　　　　2 yd. 1 ft. 8 in.　　　　4 yd. 1 ft.　　　　1 yd. 1 ft. 6 in.

3–10 Linear Measurement: Metric System ☆

A common metric prefix is *kilo,* which means 1,000. A kilometer equals 1,000 meters.

Problem: Ronnie uses an exercise journal to record the number of meters he runs every day. He runs 10,000 meters in the morning and 17,500 meters after dinner. Last week he followed this schedule every day except for the weekend. How many kilometers did Ronnie run last week?

3–11 Linear Measurement: Metric System ☆☆

Most countries in the world use the metric system of measurement. Every unit of the metric system is based on 10 times the unit before it, as noted below.

10 millimeters (mm) = 1 centimeter (cm)

10 centimeters = 1 decimeter (dm)

10 decimeters = 1 meter (m)

10 meters = 1 decameter (dam) or dekameter (dkm)

10 decameters = 1 hectometer (hm)

10 hectometers = 1 kilometer (km)

Problem: The numbers in the problems on the left of the equal sign are correct, but some decimal points and/or zeroes are incorrect in the numbers to the right of the equal sign. Correct the decimal points and zeroes.

(a) 2 m = 20 cm			(b) 3.4 cm = 0.34 mm			(c) 6 cm = 0.6 mm

(d) 15 mm = 0.15 cm			(e) 0.78 m = 78 mm			(f) 9,300 m = 93 km

3–12 Linear Measurement: Metric System ☆☆

In the metric system, the meter is the standard unit for the measurement of length. Each meter is divided into 10 decimeters (dm). Each decimeter is divided into 10 centimeters (cm). Each centimeter is divided into 10 millimeters (mm).

For example, 6 cm 7 mm can be written as 6.7 cm or 67 mm.

Problem: Write each length below in two ways.

(a) 8.3 cm			(b) 3 cm 6 mm			(c) 92 mm			(d) 2.5 cm

3–13 | Linear Measurement: Metric System ★★

When most people think of dinosaurs, they think of huge, frightening creatures. However, not all dinosaurs were big. The compsognathus, for example, was only a little bigger than a chicken, and was about only 600 mm in length. The largest complete dinosaur skeleton in a museum collection is a brachiosaur. It measures 12.5 m from the soles of its feet to its head.

Problem: Convert the length of the compsognathus and brachiosaur to centimeters. The length of the brachiosaur is about how many times the length of the compsognathus?

3–14 | Linear Measurement: Metric System—Using a Formula ★

An anthropologist is an individual who studies the physical, social, and cultural development of humans. Sometimes math can play an important role in an anthropologist's work. For example, an anthropologist can use formulas to estimate the height of a man or woman if he or she knows the length of certain bones. The two formulas below are based on the length of the humerus, the bone from the elbow to the shoulder.

To estimate the height of a *man,* in centimeters, anthropologists can use the formula:

$$H = 2.89L + 70.64$$

To estimate the height of a *woman,* in centimeters, anthropologists can use the formula:

$$H = 2.75L + 71.48$$

In these formulas H stands for the height in centimeters, and L stands for the length of the humerus in centimeters.

Problem: If a 43-centimeter humerus was uncovered in an ancient city, about how tall would the person be if the bone was a man's? About how tall would the person be if the bone belonged to a woman?

3-15 Linear Measurement: Metric System—Using a Formula ★

Sonar is an acronym for sound navigation and ranging. A sonar system emits sound waves to locate objects underwater. When the sound waves strike an object, they are reflected back and detected.

The following formula can be used to determine the distance of objects detected by sonar:

$$d = \frac{ts}{2}$$

In this formula d is the distance of the object, t is the time it takes for the sound waves to strike the object and return, and s is the speed of sound.

Problem: Determine the distance to an underwater object if the speed of sound is 1,531 meters per second, and it takes sound waves 30 seconds to strike the object and return. Express your answer in kilometers.

3-16 Linear Measurement: Metric System—Using a Formula ★★

The length of the spiral track on a typical compact disc (CD) is 5,838,437.5 millimeters. The playing time of the typical compact disc is 74 minutes. The following formula can be used to find the speed that the CD spins in millimeters per second:

$$r = \frac{d}{t}$$

In this formula r equals the rate in millimeters per second, t equals the time in seconds, and d is the distance in millimeters.

Problem: About how fast does the typical CD spin?

3–17   Linear Measurement: English System and Metric System   ★★

Below are some approximations to help you compare units of length of the English system with units of length of the metric system.

1 inch (in.) ≈ 2.54 centimeters (cm)

1 foot (ft.) ≈ 30 centimeters

1 centimeter ≈ 0.375 inches

1 meter (m) ≈ 39.37 inches

Problem: The largest flag in the United States measures 64 by 125 meters. It is kept in the White House and displayed every June 14, which is Flag Day. Approximate the dimensions of this flag in feet.

3–18   Linear Measurement: Obsolete Units   ★ G

The word *fathom* can be traced to a Middle English word, *fadme,* meaning the distance a person can estimate with outstretched arms. It was used by sailors to measure the depth of water on which their ship sailed.

Problem: Starting with your arms at your sides, extend your arms outward and raise them even with your shoulders. Estimate the distance from your outstretched fingers on one hand to your outstretched fingers of the other hand. About how long is your fathom? Express your answer in feet. Next, work with a partner and measure each other's fathoms. Are they the same? Speculate on the value of standard units of measurement. Why are standard units of measurement important?

3–19   Linear Measurement: Obsolete Units   ★★

Ancient societies did not use the systems of measurement we use today. The ancient Egyptians, for example, used parts of their hands and arms to measure length.
Following are some units of Egyptian measurement for length:

4 digits (fingers) ≈ 1 palm (the width of a hand)

2 palms ≈ 1 span (the width of an outstretched palm from the tip of the pinkie to the tip of the thumb)

2 spans ≈ 1 cubit (the length of a forearm)

Problem: How many digits equal 1 cubit?

3–20   Linear Measurement: Obsolete Units   ★★

Some measurements found in the Bible are in cubits and spans. A cubit was the length of a forearm, which is approximately 18 inches. A span was the diagonal measure of an outstretched hand from the tip of the pinkie to the tip of the thumb, which is about 8 inches. Using body parts for measurement was troublesome, because people are different and one person's "span" frequently did not equal another's.

Problem: In the Bible, Goliath was described as being 6 cubits and 1 span in height. Approximately how tall was he? Round your answer to the nearest foot.

3–21   Linear Measurement: Quotation   ★★

The following is taken from the Special Olympics: "How far is far? How high is high? You'll never know until you try."

Problem: Explain this slogan and apply it to measurement.

3–22   Weight: English System   ★

Prepackaging is common in supermarkets. A prepackaged steak, for example, has been cut, weighed, and priced before the customer orders it. Prepackaging helps to make shopping more convenient for customers.

Problem: According to the label on the package of a turkey, the turkey weighs 14.56 pounds. It is priced $0.79 per pound. Find the cost of the turkey. Round your answer up to the penny.

| 3-23 | **Weight: English System** ★★ |

The surface gravity of a planet determines a person's weight. On planets where the surface gravity is different from Earth's, your weight would be different.

The surface gravity of the other planets in our solar system is calculated in terms of the surface gravity of Earth, which is designated as 1.00. The surface gravities of the planets are listed below:

Mercury, 0.37	Mars, 0.38	Uranus, 0.93
Venus, 0.88	Jupiter, 2.51	Neptune, 1.23
Earth, 1.00	Saturn, 1.07	Pluto, 0.04

Based on the values above, you would weigh less than half your Earth-weight on Mars, but more than two-and-a-half times your Earth-weight on Jupiter.

Problem: What would a 127-pound Earthling weigh on Jupiter? On Pluto? On which planets would you weigh about as much as you do on Earth? Explain your answer.

| 3-24 | **Weight: English System** ★★ |

Environmentalists estimate that during a lifetime, an average person will throw away garbage that is equivalent to 600 times his or her adult weight.

Problem: Using the information above, about how much would an adult who threw away 54 tons of trash weigh?

| 3-25 | **Weight: English System** ★★ |

In the English system of measurement, ounces, pounds, and tons are three common units of measurement for weight.

16 ounces (oz.) = 1 pound (lb.)

2000 pounds = 1 ton (T.)

Problem: Arrange the nine weights below in order from least to greatest.

1 lb.	2000 lb.	30,000 oz.
32 oz.	1 lb. 5 oz.	0.75 T.
1.5 lb.	200 lb.	1.25 lb.

3-26 | Weight: English System—Operations and Conversions ★★

Adding, subtracting, multiplying, and dividing units of measure involve regrouping or expressing one unit as another. In all cases, answers should always be in simplest form.

Problem: Three of the four problems below have the same answer. Find these three problems and their common answer. Then find the answer to the remaining problem.

(a) 3 lb. 15 oz.
    + 4 lb. 12 oz.

(b) 13 lb. 13 oz.
    − 5 lb. 2 oz.

(c) 3 lb. 15 oz.
                    × 2

(d) 4)‾3‾4‾ ‾l‾b‾.‾ ‾1‾2‾ ‾o‾z‾.‾

3-27 | Weight: Metric System ★

The metric system is based on ten. Following are metric units for weight:

10 milligrams (mg) = 1 centigram (cg)
10 centigrams = 1 decigram (dg)
10 decigrams = 1 gram (g)
10 grams = 1 decagram (dag) or dekagram (dkg)
10 decagrams = 1 hectogram (hg)
10 hectograms = 1 kilogram (kg)

Problem: Use >, <, or = to make each statement below true.

(a) 350 mg _____ 0.35 g

(b) 20 cg _____ 2 mg

(c) 0.1 g _____ 1 cg

(d) 15 mg _____ 150 cg

(e) 3.50 g _____ 35 kg

(f) 0.54 g _____ 54 cg

3-28 | Weight: Metric System ★★

Most dinosaurs were big, but their brains were small. The weight of a stegosaurus's brain was about 80 grams, which was about 0.004% of the stegosaurus's weight.

Problem: Find the weight of the stegosaurus in kilograms.

3–29 | Weight: English System and Metric System ☆

The heaviest domestic dog is the St. Bernard. It weighs up to 100 kilograms and stands 70 centimeters high at the shoulder.

Problem: Express this weight in pounds and the height in inches. (*Hint:* 1 kilogram ≈ 2.2 pounds and 1 centimeter ≈ 0.39 inches.)

3–30 | Weight: Using Balances ☆

The ancient Egyptians used balances much like the one to the right as early as 3000 B.C. Objects of known weight were placed on one side and objects of unknown weight could be placed on the other. Weights could then be added to or taken away from either side until the two sides balanced.

Problem: Suppose only three weights are available. One of the weights equals 1 gram, another equals 2 grams, and the third equals 5 grams. What amounts could be weighed? (*Hint:* You may wish to make a table or chart to help you organize your information.)

3–31 | Weight: Using Balances ☆☆

Balances similar to those used by Egyptians as early as 3000 B.C. are still used today. Picture a scale used in your science lab that has two pans for balancing. This scale is remarkably similar in basic design to those used about 5,000 years ago.

Problem: Suppose that you have only three weights. The first is a 1-gram weight, the second is a 3-gram weight, and the third is a 7-gram weight. Without making any adjustments on the scale, what amounts could be weighed? Explain your answer.

3-32 Capacity: English System ★

The relationships between units of liquid measure are summarized below:

8 fluid ounces (fl. oz.) = 1 cup (c.)

2 cups = 1 pint (pt.)

2 pints = 1 quart (qt.)

4 quarts = 1 gallon (gal.)

Problem: Each blank below can be filled with one of the following numbers: 1, 4, 8, or 24. Some numbers will be used more than once. Fill in the blanks so that the relationships are correct.

(a) 2 gal. = _____ qt.

(b) 4 qt. = _____ gal. = _____ pt.

(c) 3 c. = _____ c. _____ pt. = _____ fl. oz.

(d) 12 fl. oz. = _____ c. _____ fl. oz.

3-33 Capacity: English System ★★

The relationships among ounces, cups, pints, quarts, and gallons are summarized below:

8 fluid ounces (fl. oz.) = 1 cup (c.)

2 cups = 1 pint (pt.)

2 pints = 1 quart (qt.)

4 quarts = 1 gallon (gal.)

Problem: Fill in the blanks with the correct unit.

(a) 4 c. = 2 _____

(b) 5 pt. 3 c. = 6 _____ 1 c. = 3 _____ 1 c.

(c) 2 qt. = 0.5 _____

(d) 4 gal. = 16 _____ = 512 _____

3-34 | Capacity: English System ★★

Cans of frozen juice concentrate include directions for mixing the contents of the can with water. A 12-fluid ounce can of orange juice concentrate provides these mixing directions:

Mix the contents with 3 cans of cold water. Stir or shake briskly.

Problem: How many fluid ounces of orange juice will this make? Will a 1-quart pitcher be large enough to hold the contents? Explain your answer.

3-35 | Capacity: English System ★★

Some units of measure are not always listed in textbooks, but they are frequently used in measuring liquids in medicine. Some of these units are noted below:

3 teaspoons (t.) = 1 tablespoon (T.)

2 tablespoons = 1 fluid ounce (fl. oz.)

8 fluid ounces = 1 cup (c.)

Problem: A bottle of medicine contains 4 fluid ounces. One dose of medicine is 3 teaspoons. How many doses of medicine are in the bottle?

3-36 | Capacity: English System ★★

A 10-gallon hat is the name for the large hat that many cowboys of the old west wore. Although this hat was big, it only held about $\frac{3}{4}$ of a gallon.

Problem: How many quarts did the 10-gallon hat actually hold? What percent of a 10-gallon container would that fill?

3–37   Capacity: English System   ★★

The following recipe for rye cakes has been handed down for generations.

> Start with an equal amount of rye meal and flour, a pinch of salt, and four eggs. Mix with milk, making a thick batter. Bake for 15 minutes in a slow oven, and increase the fire a little at a time. This makes about 15 rye cakes.

Problem: Would you have enough information from this recipe to bake rye cakes? Write an explanation.

3–38   Capacity: English System—Operations and Conversions   ★★

Cooking involves careful measurements and knowledge of basic operations with fluid ounces, cups, pints, and quarts.

8 fluid ounces (fl. oz.) = 1 cup (c.)

2 cups = 1 pint (pt.)

2 pints = 1 quart (qt.)

4 quarts = 1 gallon (gal.)

Problem: In each statement below the units of measure have been omitted. Fill in the blanks with the correct unit of measurement.

(a) 6 _____ + 10 _____ = 16 _____ = 2 c.

(b) 6 _____ – 2 qt. = 5 _____ 2 qt.

(c) 8 _____ × 4 = 32 _____ = 4 gal.

(d) 8 _____ ÷ 2 = 4 _____ = 1 qt.

3-39 Capacity: Metric System ★

The metric system has three basic units of capacity: the kiloliter, liter, and milliliter.

1 kiloliter (kL) = 1,000 liters (L)

1 liter = 1,000 milliliters (mL)

Problem: Match each item below with the most likely unit of measurement.

(a) Bottle of soda	1. 1 mL
(b) Gas tank (underground)	2. 10 mL
(c) Watering can (for flowers)	3. 2 or 3 L
(d) Liquid in an eyedropper	4. 4 L
(e) Dose of medicine (for adults)	5. 2 kL

3-40 Capacity: Metric System ★

Kiloliters, liters, and milliliters are three common units used to measure capacity in the metric system. They are related as follows:

1,000 milliliters (mL) = 1 liter (L)

1,000 liters = 1 kiloliter (kL)

Problem: The numbers on the left of the equal signs are correct, but some decimal points and/or zeroes are incorrect in the numbers to the right of the equal signs. Correct the decimal points and/or zeroes to make each statement true.

(a) 3.6 L = 0.00036 kL	(b) .13 mL = 0.0013 L
(c) 400 L = 4 kL	(d) 23 L = 0.00023 mL
(e) 6 mL = 600 L	(f) 7.3 kL = 73000000 mL

3–41 | Capacity: Metric System ⭐⭐

The three basic units of capacity in the metric system are related as follows:

1 kiloliter (kL) = 1,000 liters (L)

1 liter = 1,000 milliliters (mL)

Problem: Fill in the blanks below with kiloliters, liters, milliliters, or the correct number to make each statement true.

(a) 27 _____ = 27000000 _____ = 27000 _____

(b) 5 _____ = 5000 _____ = 0.005 _____

(c) _____ mL = 0.0000094 _____ = 0.0094 _____

(d) _____ L = 0.0673 _____ = 67300 _____

3–42 | Time: Calculation ⭐

The symbol π (pi) is a special one in mathematics. In most texts pi is written as a decimal and rounded to 3.14. Actually, pi goes on forever without repeating or terminating. The most accurate measurement of pi passed the 1-billionth mark.

In 1987 a Japanese man recited from memory the value of pi to 40,000 places. According to the *Guinness Book of World Records,* it took him 17 hours and 21 minutes, including four 15-minute breaks!

Problem: How many hours and minutes was he actually reciting?

3–43 | Time: Calculation ⭐

Bamboo, a tall, treelike grass found in tropical or semitropical regions, may grow as much as 1.5 feet per day. It may reach a maximum height of 120 feet.

Problem: If bamboo grows at its fastest rate (1.5 feet per day), how long would it take to reach its maximum height?

3–44 Time: Calculation ☆

Good cooks know that a tasty meal requires careful preparation and timing.

Problem: Kathy plans to cook a turkey dinner for her family. The turkey, which weighs about 16 pounds, takes 6 hours to cook. Before serving, however, it must set for 30 minutes. What time should Kathy start to cook the turkey if she wants dinner to begin at 7 P.M.?

3–45 Time: Units ☆☆

The relationships among the units of time are summarized below:

60 seconds (sec.) = 1 minute (min.)   52 weeks = 1 year (yr.)

60 minutes = 1 hour (hr.)   10 years = 1 decade

24 hours = 1 day (d.)   10 decades = 1 century

7 days = 1 week (wk.)

Problem: Fill in the missing numbers to make the statements below true.

(a) one-quarter hr. = _____ min.

(b) 90 sec. = _____ min. _____ sec.

(c) $3\frac{1}{2}$ hr. = _____ hr. _____ min.

(d) $3\frac{1}{2}$ hr. = _____ min.

(e) $3\frac{1}{2}$ hr. = _____ sec.

(f) 48 hr. = _____ d.

(g) 63 d. = _____ wk.

(h) 45 yr. = _____ decades

(i) _____ yr. = 1 century

3–46 Time: Dates ☆☆

When people from different countries write the date in numbers, they may write it differently.

For example, in the U.S., September 10, 1998 would be written 9/10/98. 9 refers to September, the 9th month of the year, and it is followed by the day and year. In England, however, the same date would be written as 10/9/98. The day is written before the month.

Problem: When would both methods record the same date the same way? Give an example. When would a date written with the U.S. method make no sense in England? Give an example.

3–47 Time: Interpretation ★★

Some problems found in math texts are not always entirely accurate in the real world. Following is an example of a problem that might appear in a math text:

Suppose Sam runs a lap around the high school track in 2.5 minutes. How long will it take him to run 6.5 laps? The answer would be 16.25 minutes.

Problem: In real life this answer is possible, but unlikely. Why would Sam's time probably not be 16.25 minutes? Write an explanation.

3–48 Time: Interpretation ★★

Sometimes numbers can be confusing, especially in measurement when we try to compare different things. For example, consider the following statement:

Since 3 dollars and 15 cents can be written as $3.15, 3 hours and 15 minutes should be written as 3.15 hours.

Problem: Do you agree or disagree with the above statement? Write an explanation of your answer.

3–49 Time: A Tricky Problem ★★

Can you figure out the following tricky time problem?

Problem: It occurs once in a minute, twice in a moment, not at all in a thousand years but begins and ends a millennium. What is it?

3–50   Time: The 24-hour Clock   ★★

The 24-hour clock counts time by the hours from 1 through 24. Following are the hours in a 24-hour clock:

12 midnight—0000 (2400)	12 noon—1200
1 A.M.—0100	1 P.M.—1300
2 A.M.—0200	2 P.M.—1400
3 A.M.—0300	3 P.M.—1500
4 A.M.—0400	4 P.M.—1600
5 A.M.—0500	5 P.M.—1700
6 A.M.—0600	6 P.M.—1800
7 A.M.—0700	7 P.M.—1900
8 A.M.—0800	8 P.M.—2000
9 A.M.—0900	9 P.M.—2100
10 A.M.—1000	10 P.M.—2200
11 A.M.—1100	11 P.M.—2300

Time on the 24-hour clock can be expressed in various ways. For example, 1400 can be "fourteen hundred," "fourteen hundred hours," or "fourteen double-0."

Problem: What are some advantages of a 24-hour clock? What are some disadvantages? Would you prefer to use the 24-hour clock instead of our current system? Explain your answer.

3–51   Time: Milestones   ★★

Certain numerical milestones are important and are looked upon with anticipation (or remorse). The age when you first begin school, the year you become old enough to drive, and the year you will graduate high school are examples of some numerical milestones.

Problem: What are some numerical milestones that you have either passed or are anticipating? Write a paragraph explaining these events and why they are important to you.

3–52   Time: Leap Year   ★★

People have always had trouble designing calendars. Most calendars are based on the solar year, which is the time it takes the Earth to make a complete orbit around the sun.

In 45 B.C., upon the advice of a Greek astronomer named Sosigenes, Julius Caesar decided that Rome should use a solar calendar. Known as the Julian calendar, this calendar had a year of 365 days and a leap year every fourth year of 366 days. It was based on the belief that the solar year was $365\frac{1}{4}$ days long, but the solar year is actually 365 days, 5 hours, 48 minutes, and 45.5 seconds long. The difference of about 11 minutes adds up over the years.

By 1582, the calendar was off by 10 days. This was becoming a serious problem for the Church because Christian holidays weren't falling on the days they were supposed to. Pope Gregory XIII issued a decree dropping 10 days from the calendar and ordered a new calendar. This calendar provided that century years divisible evenly by 400 should be leap years and that all other century years should be common years. 1600 was a leap year, but 1700, 1800, and 1900 were not, even though they are divisible by four. This, he believed, would solve the problem. Although it doesn't solve the problem entirely, the Gregorian calendar is more accurate than any other calendar before it.

Problem: Is 2000 a leap year? Explain your answer.

3–53 Time: Time Zones ✭✭✭ G

Time zones are necessary to ensure that time around the world is standard. A day officially begins at the International Dateline at midnight and progresses westward, because the Earth spins in an easterly direction. The world is divided into 24 time zones, which correspond to the 24-hour day. The contiguous United States is divided into four times zones, with Alaska and Hawaii having time zones of their own. Although this system allows anyone, anywhere to know what time it is, it can be confusing, especially if you are moving across time zones.

Problem: George's company is negotiating new contracts with a company that has offices in New York, Chicago, Denver, and Los Angeles. George must meet with the managers of all three offices. He leaves his New York office at 10 A.M. on Monday morning and flies to Chicago. The flight and stayover in Chicago lasts 8 hours. Next, George flies to Los Angeles, the flight and stayover totaling 12 hours. He then flies to Denver, the flight and stayover totaling 28 hours. He is now ready to fly home. What time is it in Denver when he is leaving?

3–54 Time: Time Words ✭✭ G

Many words in English denote time. Some, like *minutes, hour,* and *day,* are obvious. Others, like *biannual* and *biennial,* aren't.

Problem: Brainstorm a list of time words. Include their meanings and numerical significance. A day, for example, is 24 hours long. When you are done, compare your list with the lists of others. Which words appear most often?

| 3–55 | **Time: Comparison of Heartbeats**   ✭✭ |

An average adult's heart beats 80 times per minute. An average canary's heart beats 130 times in 12 seconds.

Problem: Of the two heartbeats above, which is the faster, and about how many times as fast is it? What factors might increase a person's heartbeat? Write an explanation.

| 3–56 | **Time: Measuring Your Pulse**   ✭✭ G |

To check your pulse rate, you can count the number of times your heart beats in a minute.

First, you must find your pulse on the side of your neck or your wrist. (On the side of your neck, it is just below your jaw. Press gently and feel carefully and you should find it. On the underside of your wrist, your pulse should be between a half-inch and inch from the palm of your hand.) After you have found your pulse, count the beats as a partner keeps track of a minute passing on a clock or watch. The total number of beats you count in a minute is your pulse rate.

A shortcut is to count the number of beats for 10 seconds and multiply by 6. Another shortcut is to count the number of beats for 6 seconds and multiply by 10.

Problem: Explain why each of the shortcuts will work. Which shortcut is more accurate? (You may have to take your pulse a few times.) Is either shortcut likely to be as accurate as counting the beats for a whole minute? Explain your answer.

| 3–57 | **Time: Tides**   ✭✭✭ G |

As the moon orbits the Earth, the pull of its gravity affects the tides of the Earth's oceans.

If you visit the shore often, you probably know that high tide occurs twice each day. Most people assume that since each day has 24 hours, high tides occur every 12 hours. This isn't true, though. High tides occur about 12 hours, 25 minutes. This is because a lunar day lasts about 24 hours, 50 minutes.

Problem: Using this information, explain why high tides are about 12 hours, 25 minutes apart. What other factors might affect the timing and height of high tides. Where might you find information listing the times of the tides?

3–58   Time: Operations and Conversions   ✯✯✯

Adding, subtracting, multiplying, and dividing units of time require regrouping and expressing your answer in the simplest form.

Problem: In each problem below, at least one number is missing. Find the missing numbers to make the problems correct.

(a)   6 hr. 50 min.
       + 4 hr. 30 min.
       ‾‾‾‾‾‾‾‾‾‾‾‾‾‾‾
       10 hr. ___ min. = 11 hr. ___ min.

(b)   7 d. ___ hr.
       – 2 d. 12 hr.
       ‾‾‾‾‾‾‾‾‾‾‾‾
        4 d. 18 hr.

(c) (2 yr. 4 mo.) × ____ = 8 yr. 16 mo. = ____ yr. 4 mo.

(d) (13 wk. 5 d.) ÷ 6 = ___ w. ___ d.

3–59   Time: Using Formulas   ✯✯✯

Have you ever wondered about the function of a pendulum on some grandfather clocks? The pendulum helps the clock to keep accurate time, because the time it takes the pendulum to swing back and forth (or oscillate) is always the same. This is called the period.
You can use the following formula to compute the period of a pendulum:

$$T = 0.35\sqrt{L}$$

T equals the time of a period in seconds, and L is the length of the pendulum in feet.

Problem: Find the period if the length of a pendulum is 9 feet. What would the period be if the length of the pendulum is 4 feet? What do you think happens to the period if the pendulum is shorter?

3-60   Temperature   ☆

Even without knowing the specific temperature of things, most people can describe them as being hot, cold, or lukewarm.

Problem: Without using any math, arrange the items below hottest to coolest, based on their temperatures.

(a) a normal human body temperature

(b) a hot oven

(c) normal room temperature

(d) a "cool" fall day

(e) a pot of boiling water

(f) ice water

(g) frozen yogurt

3-61   Temperature: Fahrenheit and Celsius   ☆

Two common scales for measuring temperature are the Fahrenheit scale (named after its inventor, Gabriel Fahrenheit) and the Celsius scale (named after Anders Celsius). Temperatures are measured in degrees, which are written as the number, degree symbol, and a capital F or C to designate Fahrenheit or Celsius; for example, $35°F$.

Following are some important temperatures on each of the scales:

boiling point of water $= 100°C = 212°F$

normal human body temperature $= 37°C = 98.6°F$

freezing point of water $= 0°C = 32°F$

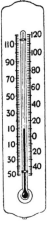

Problem: Study the thermometer shown here. Based on the temperatures above, do you think the thermometer would be best suited to measure temperatures on the Celsius or Fahrenheit scale? Explain your answer.

3-62 | Temperature: Freezing Points ⋆⋆

Most people associate freezing with water, which freezes at 0°C or 32°F. Other materials freeze, too, but at different temperatures—some at temperatures much colder than water and some much, much hotter.

Problem: Find the freezing points of vinegar, gasoline, salt, and sugar on the Fahrenheit scale by using the clues below.

The freezing point of salt is 26° less than 5 times the freezing point of sugar.

The freezing point of gasoline is 102° less than the freezing point of water.

Vinegar freezes at 30° less than water.

The freezing point of sugar is 150 times the freezing point of vinegar.

3-63 | Temperature: Conversion, Celsius to Fahrenheit ⋆⋆

–273.15°C is the temperature at which heat is no longer present. It is as cold as anything can get. (On the Kelvin thermometer, this temperature is known as 0 or absolute zero.)

Although many people use the Celsius thermometer for temperature, many others better understand temperatures on the Fahrenheit thermometer. The following formulas may be used to convert temperatures from Celsius to Fahrenheit.

$$F = \frac{9}{5}\,C + 32$$

$$F = (C \times 1.8) + 32$$

Problem: Use one of the formulas above to express –273.15°C as a Fahrenheit temperature. (Although you may use either formula to solve this problem, one of them is easier to use to find the answer than the other.) Which formula did you choose? Explain why you chose this one.

3-64 Temperature: Conversion, Celsius to Fahrenheit ★★

Because the degrees on Celsius and Fahrenheit thermometers are not equivalent, you must use a formula to convert the temperature of one to the other. Below are the formulas you may use to convert degrees Celsius to degrees Fahrenheit.

$$F = \frac{9}{5} C + 32$$

$$F = (C \times 1.8) + 32$$

Problem: Use either of the two formulas above to convert the following temperatures from Celsius to Fahrenheit.

(a) Melting point of lead, $327°C$

(b) Broiled steak, $60°C$

(c) A high fever, $40°C$

(d) A snowy day, $-11°C$

3-65 Temperature: Conversion, Fahrenheit to Celsius ★★

It is easy to convert temperatures from Fahrenheit to Celsius if you use the following formulas:

$$C = \frac{5}{9} (F - 32)$$

$$C = (F - 32) \div 1.8$$

Problem: Use either of the formulas above to convert the following temperatures from Fahrenheit to Celsius.

(a) Hot soup, $176°F$

(b) Hot bath water, $113°F$

(c) Ice water, $33°F$

(d) Frozen yogurt, $12°F$

3–66 Temperature: Using a Formula ☆

A cricket can help you to estimate the temperature of the air. To find the Fahrenheit temperature, count the number of times a cricket chirps in a minute, divide by 4 and add 37. This is summarized in the formula below:

$$F = \frac{n}{4} + 37$$

In this formula, F is the temperature in degrees Fahrenheit, and n is the number of times a cricket chirps per minute.

Problem: Estimate the Fahrenheit temperature if a cricket chirps 140 times a minute, 130 times a minute, and 115 times a minute. What can you say about the cricket chirps as the temperature decreases?

3–67 Measurement: Cords of Wood ☆

A *cord* is a stack of wood that measures $8 \times 4 \times 4$ feet, or $8 \times 8 \times 2$ feet. Firewood is frequently sold in cords.

Problem: Although the dimensions of a cord of wood indicate that a cord contains 128 cubic feet, the actual wood in a cord may measure anywhere between 65 to 100 cubic feet. Write an explanation of how this could be.

3–68 Measurement: Nails ☆☆

Most nails today range in size from 2d to 60d. "d" is the British symbol for pence, which is why we often refer to a 2d nail as a 2-penny nail, a 3d nail as a 3-penny nail, and so on.

In England in the 1400s a certain-sized nail cost 2 pence per hundred. (This became the 2d nail.) The prices of other nails were set in the same way. 100 16-penny nails, for example, sold for 16d. Although nails these days are usually sold by the pound, many people still refer to them as penny nails. The chart below provides a guideline for the length of common nails today.

Size	Length
2d	$1''$
3d	$1\frac{1}{4}''$
4d	$1\frac{1}{2}''$
5d	$1\frac{3}{4}''$

Problem: Use the chart to predict the length of 10d nails.

3-69 Measurement: Points in Printing ✮✮

Despite advances in technology and increasingly accurate forms of measurement, some "old" measures are still used today. A good example is printer's type, which is measured in points. In printer's type, 1 point = $\frac{1}{72}$ inch or 0.35 millimeters.

Problem: Determine the size of 10-point type. What is the size of 18-point type?

3-70 Measurement: Computer Memory ✮✮✮

The prefix *kilo* in the metric system means 1,000, but in computer memory a *kilobyte* is 1,024 bytes. (A *byte* is a unit of memory that can store a character such as a letter, number, punctuation mark, or blank.) A *megabyte* is equal to 1,048,576 bytes.

Problem: Answer the following questions about computer memory.

(a) How many bytes are in 640 kilobytes?

(b) How many kilobytes are in a megabyte?

(c) How many kilobytes are in 26 megabytes?

(d) A gigabyte is equal to one billion bytes. How many kilobytes is this?

3-71 Measurement: Astronomical Units and Parsecs ✮✮

An *astronomical unit* is 93 million miles, based on the Earth's average distance from the sun. Astronomical units are often used to measure distances in the solar system.

A *parsec* is equal to 200,000 astronomical units. After our sun, the closest star to the Earth is Proxima Centauri at a distance of about 1.3 parsecs.

Problem: About how many astronomical units is 1.3 parsecs? Express 1.3 parsecs in miles.

3–72   Measurement: Escape Velocity   ★★★

The *escape velocity* is the minimum velocity (speed) that an object needs to overcome the pull of gravity from another object. For a spacecraft to leave Earth, it would need to achieve an escape velocity of about 7 miles per second. This is faster than the speed of sound, which travels at about 760 miles per hour (at $32°F$ or $0°C$).

Problem: Express the Earth's escape velocity in miles per hour. About how many times the speed of sound is this?

3–73   Measurement: Light Years   ★★★ G

A *light year* is the distance light travels in one Earth year. The speed of light is about 186,000 miles per second. In one year light travels about 5,878,000,000,000 miles.

Problem: After our sun, the nearest star to the Earth is Proxima Centauri, which is about 25,000,000,000,000 miles away. About how many light years is this? Assuming a spaceship could travel at 50,000 miles per hour (which is fast for our current technology), about how many years would it take to reach Proxima Centauri? (Remember, the speed of light is calculated in miles per second.)

3–74   Measurement: Parsecs and Light Years   ★★★

A *light year* is the distance a ray of light travels in one year (about 186,000 miles per second). After the sun, the next nearest star to the Earth is Proxima Centauri at about 4.3 light years away.

A *parsec* is another way to measure great distances in space. Proxima Centauri is about 1.3 parsecs from the Earth.

Problem: About how many parsecs equal a light year? About how many light years equal a parsec?

3–75 Measurement: Star Brightness ★★★

The *magnitude* of a star refers to its brightness. Astronomers rank stars according to their magnitude. Most of the brightest stars seen by the naked eye are magnitude 1 and the faintest are magnitude 6.

A magnitude 1 star is 2.512 times brighter than a magnitude 2 star. A magnitude 2 star is 2.512 times brighter than a magnitude 3 star, and so on.

Problem: How many times brighter is a magnitude 1 star than a magnitude 6 star?

3–76 Quotation ★★

Proverbs, or words of wisdom, may mean many things to many people. Consider the following: "May you never be so rich as to feel poor, nor so poor as to envy the rich."

Problem: Write a paragraph explaining what these words mean to you. How might you apply them to measurement?

Section 4

GEOMETRY

4–1 **Naming Lines, Rays, and Segments** ☆

Lines, rays, and segments are named by points.
A *line* has no endpoints. It continues in both directions.

A *ray* has one endpoint and continues forever. A good example of a ray is a beam of light.

A *segment* (or *line segment*) has two endpoints.

Problem: Write the name, symbol, and number of endpoints for each figure below.

(a) C ————————— D

(b) ←— X —————— Y —→

(c) E ————— F —→

(d) ←— M —————— N —→

4–2 **Naming Lines, Rays, and Segments** ☆☆

Lines, rays, and segments are found in many geometric figures.

Problem: Name all the lines, rays, and segments in the figure below. (There are 21.)

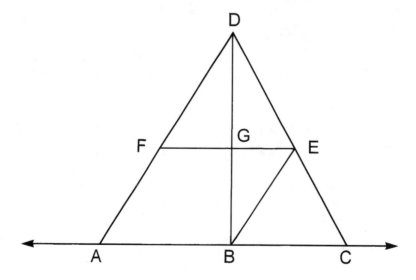

4–3   Naming Lines and Segments   ★★

The word *line* is taken from the Latin term *linum,* which means "flaxen chord." Cords made of flax were used to produce linen cloths and ropes. A sturdy flaxen chord was used to measure lengths because it was so durable.

Problem: Name the line below in three ways. Name the segment below in two ways. Explain the relationship between the segment and line.

4–4   Naming Segments and Lengths   ★★

It is important to know and use precise language when you study geometry. For example: $\overline{AB}$ denotes line segment AB, which is pictured below.

AB refers to the length of the segment. "AB = 3 inches" means that the line segment is 3 inches long.

Problem: Each statement below applies to the diagram. Identify the statements that are incorrect and correct them.

```
        5     10        15
◄───•─────•─────────•───────•───►
    A     B         C       D
```

(a) AB + BC + CD = AD

(b) $\overline{AB}$ + $\overline{BC}$ = AC

(c) 2AB = $\overline{BC}$

(d) $\overline{AB}$ + $\overline{BC}$ + $\overline{CD}$ = 30

4–5 | Lines, Line Segments, and Infinity ★★★

The concept of infinity has perplexed mathematicians (as well as many other people) throughout the ages. It wasn't until the 17th century that John Wallis, an Englishman, created the symbol ∞ for infinity. Lines and line segments may be used as examples in attempts to explain infinity.

Problem: Explain the following statement: An infinite amount does not necessarily take up an infinite amount of space. Give an example to show that this is true.

4–6 | Collinear Points ★★

Collinear points are any points that lie on the same line. Also, if A, B, and C represent three collinear points, and AB + BC = AC, then B is between A and C.

Problem: A, B, C, D, E, and F are collinear. Locate the points on a number line using the information below.

E and F are between no other points labeled on the number line.

CA + AB = CB

DB + BF = DF

CA + AD = CD

4-7   Intersection of Lines, Segments, and Rays ✮✮✮

The *intersection* of two figures, designated by the symbol ∩, is the set of points that lie in both figures. Lines, segments, and rays intersect to form geometric figures.

For example, in the diagram below $\overleftrightarrow{XY}$ intersects $\overline{AB}$ at point Z.

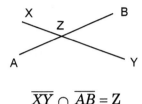

$$\overleftrightarrow{XY} \cap \overline{AB} = Z$$

Problem: Label the collinear points A, B, C, and D on the number line so that C is between A and B, and B is between C and D. Then use the number line to describe the geometric figure in each part below.

(a) $\overline{AB} \cap \overline{CD}$

(b) $\overline{AC} \cap \overline{CB}$

(c) $\overline{AC} \cap \overline{BD}$

(d) $\overleftrightarrow{AC} \cap \overleftrightarrow{BD}$

(e) $\overrightarrow{AC} \cap \overrightarrow{BD}$

(f) $\overrightarrow{AC} \cap \overrightarrow{DB}$

4-8   Unions of Lines, Segments, and Rays ✮✮✮

The *union* of two geometric figures is the set of points that are in at least one of the figures. The union is designated by the symbol ∪.

For example, in the figure below, $\overline{AB} \cup \overrightarrow{CD} = \overrightarrow{AD}$.

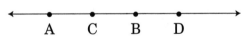

Problem: Use the diagram below to name the geometric figures.

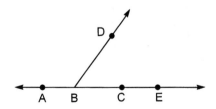

(a) $\overrightarrow{BD} \cup \overrightarrow{BC}$

(b) $\overline{AC} \cup \overline{CE}$

(c) $\overline{AC} \cup \overrightarrow{BE}$

(d) $\overleftrightarrow{AC} \cup \overline{BE}$

(e) $\overrightarrow{BD} \cup \overrightarrow{BA}$

(f) $\overrightarrow{CE} \cup \overrightarrow{CA}$

4–9   Naming Angles   ☆

An *angle* is formed by two rays with a common endpoint. The *vertex* is another name for the endpoint. The *rays* are the sides of the angle.

There are several ways to name an angle. Angles may be named by using a point on one side, the vertex, and a point on the other side. They may also be named by a number or letter inside the angle, or by the letter that identifies the point of the vertex.

Problem: Match each angle below with its name. (Some of the names may be used more than once and some may not be used at all.)

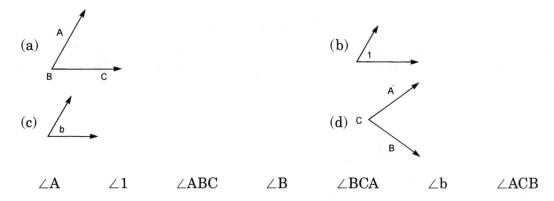

∠A   ∠1   ∠ABC   ∠B   ∠BCA   ∠b   ∠ACB

4–10   Naming Angles   ☆☆

An angle may be named with a capital letter at its vertex if only one angle is formed. For example:

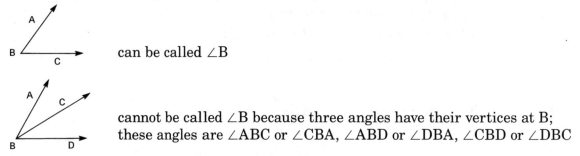

can be called ∠B

cannot be called ∠B because three angles have their vertices at B; these angles are ∠ABC or ∠CBA, ∠ABD or ∠DBA, ∠CBD or ∠DBC

Problem: Name the 10 angles in the diagram below.

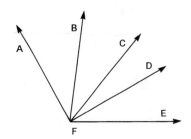

4–11 Types of Angles ☆

Angles are grouped according to their degrees.

An *acute angle* is an angle whose measure is greater than 0° and less than 90°.

A *right angle* is an angle whose measure is 90°.

An *obtuse angle* is an angle whose measure is greater than 90° and less than 180°.

A *straight angle* is an angle whose measure is 180°.

Problem: Name all the types of angles that are described below.

(a) A 30° angle

(b) The sum of two acute angles

(c)

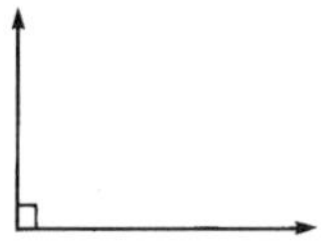

(d) The sum of two right angles

(e)

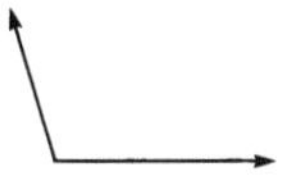

(f)

(g) A 91° angle

(h) A 90° angle

4–12 The Measurement of Angles ☆☆

A magnifying glass is a lens that makes objects appear larger than they really are. Sherlock Holmes, the great fictional detective, was often described as looking at evidence through a magnifying glass.

Problem: Suppose a 35° angle is observed through a magnifying glass that enlarges objects to twice their actual size. How big is the angle when viewed through this magnifying glass? Write an explanation of your answer.

4–13 The Measurement of Angles ★★ G

Digital clocks don't have an "angle" on time like clocks with minute and hour hands. (Three o'clock, for example, makes an angle of 90°, also called a right angle.)

Problem: Imagine the hands of a clock and identify the types of angles—acute, obtuse, or right—the hands would form if the times were the following. (*Hint:* You may wish to sketch a clock to help you visualize times and angles.)

(a) 9:00   (b) 11:20   (c) 10:00   (d) 7:00

(e) 6:45   (f) 3:40   (g) 11:50   (h) 1:30

4–14 The Measurement of Angles: Degrees and Minutes ★★

To measure angles more precisely than a degree, each degree is divided into 60 equal parts called *minutes*. The symbol ′ represents minutes. Each minute in turn is divided into 60 equal parts called *seconds,* represented by the symbol ″.

$1° = 60′$
$1′ = 60″$

For example, $41\frac{3}{5}°$ can be written as 41° 36′. ($60′ = 1°$ and $\frac{3}{5}° = \frac{3}{5} \times \frac{60}{1} = 36′$.)

Problem: Fill in the blanks below to make true statements.

(a) $54\frac{2}{3}° = 54°$ _____ ′   (b) $54.7° = 54°$ _____ ′

(c) 54 _____ ° $= 54° 30′$ (d) 54 _____ ° $= 54° 54′$

4–15   Complementary and Supplementary Angles   ✭

Complementary angles are two angles whose sum equals 90°. One angle is the *complement* of the other.

Supplementary angles are two angles whose sum equals 180°. One angle is the *supplement* of the other.

Problem: Each row below contains five angles. Two are complementary, two are supplementary, and one is neither. Identify the complementary angles and supplementary angles in each row.

(a) 15°	115°	125°	65°	75°
(b) 40°	50°	60°	150°	120°
(c) 90°	70°	100°	80°	20°
(d) 1°	90°	90°	89°	178°

4–16   Pairs of Angles: Adjacent, Vertical, Complementary, and Supplementary Angles   ✭

Special pairs of angles have their own names and distinguishing features.

Adjacent angles are two angles that have a common vertex, a common side, and no common interior points.

Vertical angles are two nonadjacent angles formed by two intersecting lines. Vertical angles always have the same measure.

Complementary angles are two angles whose sum is 90°.

Supplementary angles are two angles whose sum is 180°.

Problem: Consider the angles below. Identify the angles as being adjacent, vertical, complementary, and/or supplementary.

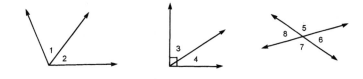

(a) ∠1 and ∠2	(b) ∠3 and ∠4	(c) ∠5 and ∠6
(d) ∠5 and ∠8	(e) ∠6 and ∠7	(f) ∠6 and ∠8

4-17 | Linear Pairs ⋆⋆

A *linear pair* are two adjacent angles whose noncommon sides are opposite rays.

For example, in the diagram below, ∠1 and ∠2 are a linear pair. Two angles that form a linear pair are supplementary.

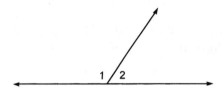

Problem: Study the diagrams of the angles below. Identify which of the following pairs of angles are linear pairs. If the angles are not linear pairs, explain why they are not.

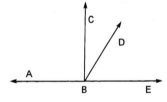 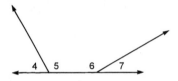

(a) ∠ABD and ∠DBE

(b) ∠CBD and ∠DBE

(c) ∠6 and ∠7

(d) ∠5 and ∠6

4-18 Angles Formed by a Transversal ★★

A *transversal* is a line that intersects two or more lines in the same plane. As it does, it forms several special types of angles.

Interior angles are angles inside the region bounded by the two lines.

Exterior angles are angles outside the region bounded by the two lines.

Same side interior angles are two nonadjacent interior angles that are on the same side of the transversal.

Alternate interior angles are two nonadjacent interior angles that are on opposite sides of the transversal.

Alternate exterior angles are two nonadjacent exterior angles that are on opposite sides of the transversal.

Corresponding angles are two nonadjacent angles (one is an interior angle and the other is an exterior angle), on the same side of the transversal.

Problem: Label the eight angles with a number from 1 to 8 on the diagram below using the following clues:

The odd-numbered angles are exterior angles.

$\angle 5$ and $\angle 4$ are vertical angles.

$\angle 2$ and $\angle 4$ are same side interior angles.

$\angle 7$ and $\angle 2$ are corresponding angles.

$\angle 4$ and $\angle 6$ are alternate interior angles.

$\angle 8$ and $\angle 7$ are vertical angles.

$\angle 2$ and $\angle 3$ are vertical angles.

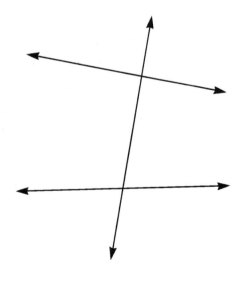

4–19 Parallel Lines and Transversals ✮✮✮

Parallel lines are lines that lie in the same plane and never intersect. The word *parallel* is taken from the Greek word *parallelos,* which means beside one another. The symbol for parallel lines is ‖.

When two parallel lines are cut by a transversal, the following special pairs of angles are formed:

Corresponding angles
Alternate interior angles
Alternate exterior angles
Vertical angles
Supplementary angles
Same side interior angles
Linear pairs

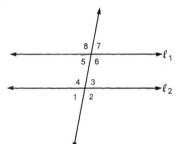

Problem: In the diagram above, $\ell_1 \parallel \ell_2$. Angles are numbered by their vertices. Find the measures of all the angles if the measure of $\angle 5 = 95°$. Then find the measure of all the angles if the measure of $\angle 2 = x°$.

4–20 Perpendicular Lines ✮

The word *perpendicular* is taken from two Latin words: *per,* which means thoroughly, and *pendre,* which means to hang. A weight hanging from a horizontal bar attached to a base would be perpendicular to the base. The symbol for perpendicular is ⊥.

Two perpendicular lines form four right angles. A right angle is an angle with a measure of 90° and is identified with the symbol ⌐ at its vertex.

Problem: In the diagram, $\ell_1 \perp \ell_2$. $m\angle 1 = 45°$. (This means that the measurement of $\angle 1 = 45°$.) Find the measure of each angle that follows.

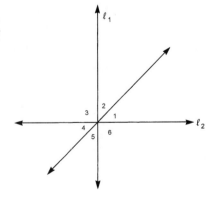

(a) $m\angle 3 =$ _____

(b) $m\angle 4 =$ _____

(c) $m\angle 1 + m\angle 2 =$ _____

(d) $m\angle 6 =$ _____

(e) $m\angle 1 + m\angle 2 + m\angle 6 =$ _____

(f) $m\angle 1 + m\angle 2 + m\angle 3 + m\angle 4 + m\angle 5 + m\angle 6 =$ _____

4–21   Polygons   ☆

A *polygon* is a closed plane figure bounded by straight line segments as sides. The term *polygon* comes from the Greek term *polygonos,* which means many angles. Unlike mathematicians today, who refer to polygons by their sides, the Greeks referred to them according to their angles and not their sides.

Problem: Do you think the number of sides and the number of angles in a given polygon is always the same? Write an explanation and provide a diagram to support your answer.

4–22   Types of Polygons   ☆

Polygons are closed plane figures bounded by straight line segments. They are named by the number of sides.

Problem: Use your knowledge of prefixes to match the name of the polygon with the number of its sides.

Decagon	4
Hexagon	8
Pentagon	12
Quadrilateral	3
Dodecagon	5
N-gon	9
Nonagon	11
Triangle	6
Undecagon	n
Heptagon	10
Octagon	7

4-23   Concave Polygons   ☆

The word *concave* comes from the Latin word *concavus,* which means hollow. Following is a test to see if a polygon is concave.

If you can choose any two points in the interior of a polygon, connect them with a straight line, and a part of the line lies outside of the polygon, then the polygon is concave.

Problem: Several polygons are pictured below. Which are concave? State which points would be connected to support your answer(s).

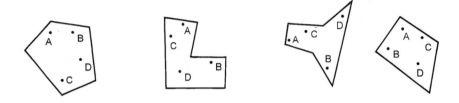

4-24   Convex Polygons   ☆

A polygon is *convex* if every two points in the interior can be connected by a line that lies entirely in the interior of the polygon.

Problem: Draw five convex polygons.

4–25 | **Diagonals of Polygons** ★★

A *diagonal* is a line segment joining two nonconsecutive vertices. The word diagonal comes from two Greek terms: *dia*, which means across, and *gonia*, which means angle.

Problem: Draw the diagonals in each figure below. Then complete the table.

  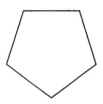 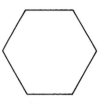

Number of Sides	Number of Diagonals
3	
4	
5	
6	
n	

4–26 | **Sum of the Angles of a Polygon** ★

The sum of the measures of the angles of a convex polygon can be found if the number of sides is known. The following formula can be used:

$$S = (n - 2)(180°)$$

S represents the sum of the measures of the angles and *n* stands for the number of sides.

Problem: Complete the chart below.

Type of Polygon	Number of Sides	Sum of the Measures of Angles
Triangle		
	4	
Pentagon		
	6	
Heptagon	7	
Octagon	8	

4–27 | Polygons and Right Angles ✭✭

Right angles, which are formed by perpendicular lines, are found just about everywhere. A glance around your classroom will reveal several right angles—windows, floor and ceiling tiles, file cabinets, desks, book shelves, books, papers, doors, and projector screens.

Problem: Some statements below are true; some are false. If the statement is true, draw the geometric figure. If it is false, explain why the statement is false.

(a) It is possible for a triangle to have two right angles.

(b) It is possible for a quadrilateral to have four right angles.

(c) It is possible for a quadrilateral to have only three right angles.

(d) It is possible for a pentagon to have three right angles.

4–28 | The Measure of Each Interior Angle of a Regular Polygon ✭✭

A *regular polygon* has congruent sides and congruent angles.

An *interior angle* of a regular polygon is an angle formed by two adjacent sides. The measure of each interior angle is $\frac{(n-2)(180°)}{n}$ where n is the number of sides.

Problem: The measure of each interior angle of a regular polygon is listed below. Find the number of sides.

(a) 60°   (b) 120°   (c) 90°   (d) $128\frac{4}{7}$°   (e) 135°   (f) 108°

4–29 | The Average Size of an Angle in a Polygon ✭✭

The average size of an angle in a polygon is the sum of the measures of the angles divided by the number of angles. You can use this formula:

$$\frac{(n-2)(180°)}{n}$$

n stands for the number of sides.

You will note that this is the same formula for finding the measure of each interior angle of a regular polygon.

Problem: Explain why the same formula can be used to find the average size of an angle in a polygon and the measure of each interior angle of a regular polygon.

4–30 The Measure of Each Exterior Angle of a Regular Polygon ✭✭

An *exterior angle* of a polygon is formed by using an auxiliary ray.
In the figure below, an auxiliary ray $\overrightarrow{DF}$ is used to form $\angle EDF$. $\angle EDF$ is an exterior angle of the pentagon.

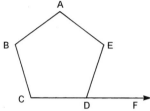

The measure of each exterior angle of a regular polygon is $\dfrac{360°}{n}$. n represents the number of sides. In the figure above, the $m\angle EDF = \dfrac{360°}{5} = 120°$.

Problem: Consider the following regular polygons: a triangle, quadrilateral, hexagon, heptagon, octagon, nonagon, and decagon. Which one of these polygons has exterior angles that are mixed numbers? Find the exterior angles of this polygon.

4–31 The Sum of the Measures of Each Exterior Angle of a Regular Polygon ✭✭

In the diagram below, $\angle BCD$ is an exterior angle of $\triangle ABC$. To find the measure of $\angle BCD$, use the formula $\dfrac{360°}{n}$ where n is the number of sides of a regular polygon.

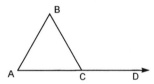

Problem: Complete the chart below. What do you notice about the sum of the measures of the exterior angles?

Regular Polygon	Number of Sides	Measure of Each Exterior Angle	Sum of the Measure of the Exterior Angles
Triangle	3	120°	360°
Quadrilateral			
Pentagon			
Hexagon			
Octagon			
Decagon			
N-gon	n		

4-32 **Classifying Triangles by the Lengths of Their Sides** ★

Triangles come in numerous shapes and sizes. They may be classified according to the lengths of their sides.

To classify triangles by the lengths of their sides, use the definitions that follow:

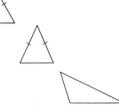

Equilateral triangle—all three sides have the same length.

Isosceles triangle—at least two sides have the same length.

Scalene triangle—all three sides have different lengths.

Problem: Classify each triangle below as equilateral, isosceles, or scalene if the sides are as follows.

(a) 3 ft., 3 ft., 1 yd.

(b) 1.5 ft., 1 ft., 12 in.

(c) 30 cm, 30 cm, 30 mm

(d) 1 yd., 4 ft., 5 ft.

4-33 **Classifying Triangles by the Measures of Their Angles** ★

To classify triangles by the measures of their angles, it may be necessary to find the measure of each angle in the triangle. (Remember that the sum of the angles of a triangle equals 180°.)

To classify triangles according to the measures of their angles, use the definitions that follow:

Equiangular triangle—all angles are equal.

Acute triangle—all angles are acute (less than 90°).

Right triangle—one angle measures 90°.

Obtuse triangle—one angle is obtuse (larger than 90°).

Problem: The measure of *at least one* angle of a triangle is listed below. Classify the triangles as equiangular, acute, right, or obtuse.

(a) 60, 20, 100

(b) 60, 60

(c) 90, 30, 60

(d) 120

(e) 45, 45, 90

(f) 80, 80, 20

4–34   Included Sides and Angles of a Triangle   ★★

A triangle has three sides and three angles.

An angle is *included* between two sides of a triangle if the endpoint of the two line segments is the vertex of the angle. In the triangle below, ∠C is included between $\overline{BC}$ and $\overline{AC}$.

A side is *included* between two angles of a triangle if each endpoint of the side is a vertex of each angle. In the example above, $\overline{BC}$ is included between ∠B and ∠C.

Problem: The triangles below are named by their vertices. Decide whether each statement is true or false. If it is false, explain why. (*Hint:* You may wish to sketch the triangle.)

(a) Consider ΔDEF. ∠D is included between $\overline{EF}$ and $\overline{ED}$.

(b) Consider ΔHIJ. ∠H is included between $\overline{HI}$ and $\overline{HJ}$.

(c) Consider ΔACD. $\overline{CD}$ is included between ∠C and ∠D.

(d) Consider ΔACH. $\overline{AH}$ is included between ∠A and ∠C.

4–35   Opposite Sides and Angles of a Triangle   ★

In a triangle, the side opposite an angle does not have the vertex of the angle as an endpoint. The angle opposite a side of a triangle has a vertex that is not an endpoint of the segment. This is illustrated below.

In ΔABC, $\overline{BC}$ is the side opposite ∠A. ∠A is the angle opposite $\overline{BC}$.

In any triangle the longest side is opposite the largest angle, and the largest angle is opposite the longest side. Conversely, the shortest side is opposite the smallest angle, and the smallest angle is opposite the shortest side.

Problem: Consider the diagrams below. Identify the longest and shortest sides. (*Hint:* The sum of the measures of the angles of any triangle equals 180°.)

(a)   (b) 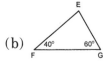   (c)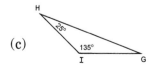

4–36   Finding the Measures of the Angles in a Triangle   ✮✮ G

There are many true statements about triangles, including:

- Vertical angles are congruent.
- Angles that form a linear pair are supplementary.
- Tick marks (or slashes) are used to show congruent sides and congruent angles.
- In an isosceles triangle, the angles opposite congruent sides are congruent.
- In an isosceles triangle, the sides opposite congruent angles are congruent.
- In an equilateral triangle, each angle has a measure of 60°.
- The sum of the measures of the angles in a triangle equals 180°.

Problem: Using the information listed above, find the measures of the numbered angles in the triangles below.

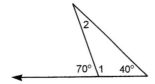

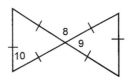

4–37   Using the Triangle Inequality Theorem   ✮✮

The *Triangle Inequality Theorem* states that the sum of the lengths of any two sides of a triangle is greater than the length of the third side. The examples below show why this is true.

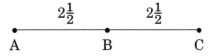
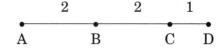

The three segments, $\overline{AB}$, $\overline{BC}$, and $\overline{AC}$, cannot be a triangle if AB = BC = $2\frac{1}{2}$ inches and AC = 5 inches.

The three segments, $\overline{AB}$, $\overline{BC}$, and $\overline{AD}$, cannot be a triangle if AB = BC = 2 inches and AD = 5 inches.

Problem: The triangles below are not drawn to scale. Some cannot be triangles if the lengths of the sides are as they are labeled. Identify the triangles that could have sides of the indicated lengths. Correct the lengths of the longest sides of the other triangles.

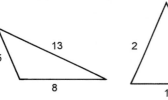
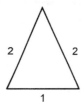
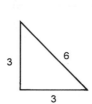
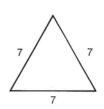

4–38   Identifying Line Segments Associated with Triangles   ✰✰

Some line segments associated with triangles are listed below.

- *Angle bisector*—a line segment that bisects an angle and extends to the opposite side.
- *Median of a triangle*—a line segment drawn from any vertex of a triangle to the midpoint of the opposite side.
- *Altitude of a triangle*—a line segment drawn from any vertex, perpendicular to the opposite side. (In an obtuse triangle, two altitudes are outside of the triangle.)
- *Perpendicular bisector of a side of a triangle*—a line segment that bisects a side and is perpendicular to the side.

Problem: Consider $\triangle ABC$ below. Match each line segment with its name. (Some names may be used more than once.)

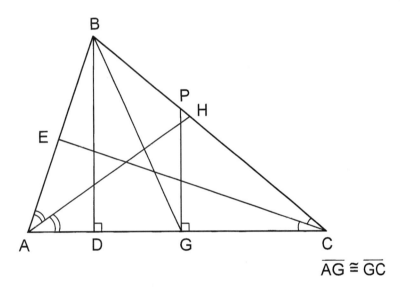

$\overline{AG} \cong \overline{GC}$

(a) $\overline{PG}$
(b) $\overline{BD}$
(c) $\overline{BG}$
(d) $\overline{EC}$
(e) $\overline{AH}$

1. angle bisector
2. median
3. altitude
4. perpendicular bisector

4-39   Using the Pythagorean Theorem to Find the Length of the Hypotenuse ☆

Pythagoras (570–500 B.C.) was one of the world's most interesting mathematicians. He believed that everything followed a strict pattern and "the essence of all things is numbers."

The Pythagorean Theorem, which states $a^2 + b^2 = c^2$ where a and b are the lengths of the legs of a right triangle and c is the length of the hypotenuse, is credited to him.

Problem: The lengths of the legs of right triangles are listed or pictured below. Find the length of the hypotenuse for each triangle.

(a) 3, 4   (b) 9, 12   (c)   12   5   (d)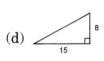

4-40   Using the Pythagorean Theorem to Find the Length of a Leg ☆☆

$a^2 + b^2 = c^2$ is the Pythagorean Theorem, named after the Greek mathematician Pythagoras who lived in the 6th century B.C. The theorem applies to right triangles where a and b stand for the lengths of the legs, and c stands for the length of the hypotenuse.

To find the length of a missing leg, substitute the length of the leg you know for a or b (it doesn't matter which one), substitute the length of the hypotenuse for c, square each number, and solve.

Problem: The length of a leg and the length of the hypotenuse are listed below. (The hypotenuse is the longest segment.) Find the length of the other leg. Express your answer in radical form.

(a) 6, 7   (b) 1, 5   (c) 5, 10   (d) $\sqrt{5}$, 7

4-41   Generating Pythagorean Triples ☆☆

A *Pythagorean triple* is a set of integers, a, b, and c, that could be sides of a right triangle if $a^2 + b^2 = c^2$. The steps below show how to generate Pythagorean triples.

1. Square an odd integer that is greater than 1.
2. Find two consecutive integers whose sum is equal to the square of the number in Step 1.

The number you squared and the other two numbers are a Pythagorean triple.

Problem: Choose a number and generate a Pythagorean triple. Substitute it into the Pythagorean Theorem to check your results.

4–42   Testing for Acute and Obtuse Triangles ★★

The Pythagorean Theorem states that $a^2 + b^2 = c^2$ for any right triangle if a and b stand for the lengths of the legs and c stands for the length of the hypotenuse.

It follows that if $c^2 \neq a^2 + b^2$, then the triangle is not a right triangle.

If $c^2 < a^2 + b^2$ where c is the longest side, then the triangle is acute. (Remember that an acute triangle has three acute angles.)

If $c^2 > a^2 + b^2$ where c is the longest side of a triangle, then the triangle is obtuse. (Remember that an obtuse triangle has one obtuse angle.)

Problem: Which of the triangles having sides with the lengths below are acute? Which are obtuse? Show the work to justify your answer.

   (a) 5, 5, 7   (b) 6, 8, 9   (c) 6, 8, 11   (d) 9, 12, 16

4–43   Finding the Length of the Hypotenuse in a 45°–45°–90° Triangle ★★

A 45°–45°–90° triangle is an isosceles right triangle. The legs of this triangle are congruent. The hypotenuse equals the length of a leg times $\sqrt{2}$.

In the diagram below, $\overline{AB}$ is the hypotenuse, and $\overline{AC}$ and $\overline{BC}$ are legs. $AB = AC\sqrt{2}$ and $AB = CB\sqrt{2}$. If $AC = 7$, then $AB = 7\sqrt{2}$.

Problem: Find the length of the hypotenuse (in simplest form) if a leg of a 45°–45°–90° triangle is:

   (a) 4   (b) $\sqrt{6}$ (c) $\sqrt{2}$ (d) $7\sqrt{2}$

4–44 **Finding the Length of a Leg in a 45°–45°–90° Triangle** ★★

The legs of a 45°–45°–90° triangle, as in any isosceles triangle, are congruent.

To find the length of a leg, divide the length of the hypotenuse by $\sqrt{2}$ and simplify (if possible).

Another way of stating this is to multiply $\frac{1}{2}$ the hypotenuse by $\sqrt{2}$ and simplify (if possible). For example, if the hypotenuse is $12\sqrt{2}$ cm, then the leg equals $\frac{1}{2} \cdot 12\sqrt{2} \cdot \sqrt{2} = 12$.

Problem: The length of a hypotenuse of a 45°–45°–90° triangle is listed in the first column. Match it with the length of its leg expressed in simplest form. Some "legs" will not be used.

(a) 8   1. $2\sqrt{2}$

(b) 4   2. $4\sqrt{2}$

(c) 38   3. 12

(d) $6\sqrt{2}$ 4. $3\sqrt{4}$

                                   5. 6

                                   6. $19\sqrt{2}$

4–45 **Finding the Length of the Hypotenuse in a 30°–60°–90° Triangle** ★★

The length of the hypotenuse of a 30°–60°–90° triangle is related to its legs in the following manner.

The hypotenuse is twice the length of the shorter leg.

The hypotenuse is $\frac{2}{3}$ of the length of the larger leg times $\sqrt{3}$.

If the shorter leg of a 30°–60°–90° triangle is 6, then the length of the hypotenuse is 12.

If the longer leg of a 30°–60°–90° triangle is $6\sqrt{3}$, then the length of the hypotenuse is $\frac{2}{3} \cdot 6\sqrt{3} \cdot \sqrt{3} = 12$.

Problem: Find the hypotenuse if the legs of a 30°–60°–90° triangle are as follows.

(a) Longer leg is $10\sqrt{3}$ (b) Shorter leg is 7

(c) Longer leg is $5\sqrt{3}$ (d) Longer leg is $9\sqrt{3}$

(e) Shorter leg is 8   (f) Shorter leg is 10

4–46 Finding the Length of the Legs in a 30°–60°–90° Triangle ★★

In a 30°–60°–90° triangle, the shorter leg is opposite the 30° angle. The longer leg is opposite the 60° angle. The relationship between the legs and the hypotenuse is stated below.

The length of the shorter leg is $\frac{1}{2}$ of the hypotenuse.

The length of the longer leg is $\frac{1}{2}$ of the hypotenuse times $\sqrt{3}$ (or the length of the short leg times $\sqrt{3}$).

The length of the hypotenuse is the longest side of the triangle.

Problem: The length of the hypotenuse is listed below on the left. The length of legs of right triangles are listed on the right. Match the hypotenuses with the legs to make 30°–60°–90° triangles. (Some legs will not be used.)

Hypotenuse		Legs		
15				
	10	$10\sqrt{3}$	3	$5\sqrt{3}$
10				
	12	5	12	30
6				
	7.5	$3\sqrt{3}$	$7.5\sqrt{3}$	14
20				

4–47 Finding the Missing Lengths of the Sides of a 45°–45°–90° and a 30°–60°–90° Triangle ★★★

The triangles below will allow you to apply your understanding of the relationships between the legs and the hypotenuse of special right triangles.

Problem: Using the information given, find the missing sides of the triangles below.

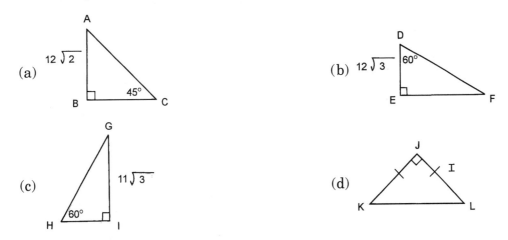

4–48   Identifying Congruent Triangles   ☆

Congruent triangles have the same shape and the same size. They may be flipped or turned, but as long as the size and shape are the same, the triangles are congruent. The symbol for congruency is ≅.

Problem: Of the six triangles pictured below, some are congruent. Identify the congruent triangles.

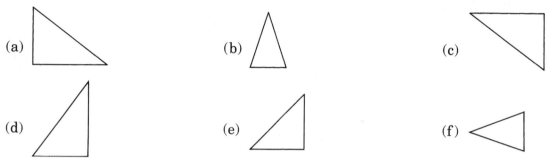

4–49   Writing a Statement of Congruence and Identifying Corresponding Parts   ☆☆

Two triangles are congruent if and only if corresponding angles are congruent and corresponding sides are congruent. ΔUVW ≅ ΔXYZ is a congruence statement for the example that follows.

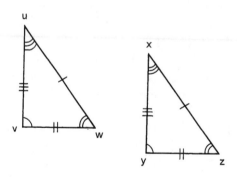

Problem: Consider the triangles below. Write a statement of congruence. List three congruent angles and three congruent sides.

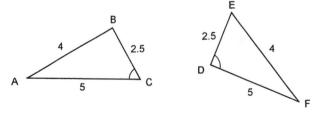

4–50 | Identifying Corresponding Parts in Overlapping Triangles ✭✭

Sometimes a geometric figure is made up of several different figures. In the diagram below, there are four triangles: ΔABF, ΔEDF, ΔACD, and ΔECB.

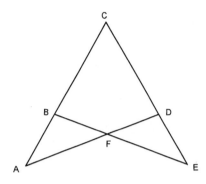

Problem: Consider the diagram above. ΔACD ≅ ΔECB. Fill in the blanks.

(a) $\overline{AB}$ ≅ _____

(b) $\overline{BC}$ ≅ _____

(c) ∠A ≅ _____

(d) ∠CBF ≅ _____

4–51 | Using SSS, SAS, and ASA to Verify Congruent Triangles ✭✭

Three of the ways to prove that two triangles are congruent are listed below.

- *SSS*—If three sides of one triangle are congruent to corresponding sides of the other triangle, then the two triangles are congruent.
- *SAS*—If two sides and the included angle of one triangle are congruent to the corresponding parts of the other triangle, then the triangles are congruent.
- *ASA*—If two angles and the included side of one triangle are congruent to the corresponding parts of the other triangle, then the two triangles are congruent.

Problem: Decide which triangles below are congruent and write a congruence statement to verify your choices. Choose from SSS, SAS, or ASA.

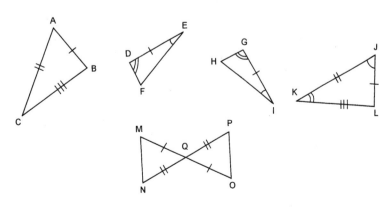

4-52 Using AAS and HL to Verify Congruent Triangles ★★

You can prove that two triangles are congruent by using the AAS method and the HL method.

- *AAS*—If two angles and the side opposite one of the angles in a triangle are congruent to corresponding parts of the other triangle, then the triangles are congruent.
- *HL*—If the hypotenuse and either leg of one right triangle is congruent to corresponding parts of another triangle, then the triangles are congruent.

Problem: Consider the diagrams below. Decide which triangles are congruent and write a congruence statement. Use AAS or HL to support your statement.

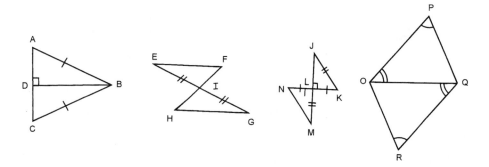

4-53 Similar Triangles ★

Similar triangles are triangles in which corresponding angles are equal and corresponding sides are in proportion.

Problem: Sketch or draw at least two examples of similar triangles.

4–54 Using AA, SSS, and SAS to Prove that Triangles Are Similar ★★

Similar triangles have the same shape, but are not necessarily the same size. Each of the methods below can be used to show that two triangles are similar.

- *AA*—If two angles of one triangle are congruent to two angles of another triangle, then the triangles are similar.
- *SSS*—If the corresponding sides of one triangle are in proportion to the corresponding sides of the other triangle, then the triangles are similar.
- *SAS*—If a pair of corresponding angles are congruent and the sides that include these angles are in proportion, the triangles are similar.

Problem: Decide which of the pairs of triangles are similar. Verify your choices using AA, SSS, or SAS.

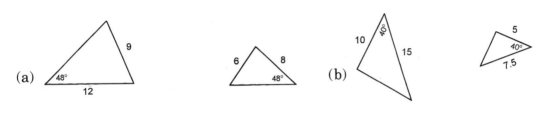

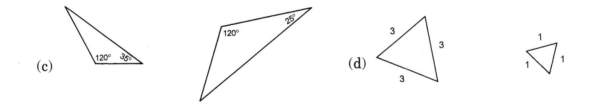

| 4–55 | **Writing a Similarity Statement and Finding the Scale Factor** ★★ |

Similar triangles have the same shape, but are not necessarily the same size. The pairs of corresponding sides are proportional. The symbol ~ means "is similar to," and was first used by Gottfried Wilhelm Leibniz in an article published in 1679.

A *similarity statement* is a correspondence between figures, and the vertices of the angles must be listed in corresponding order. In the diagram below, △ABC ~ △EDF.

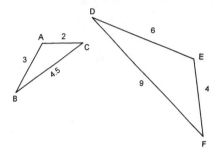

The *scale factor* is the ratio of the corresponding sides. In the diagram above, the scale factor of △ABC to △EDF is 1:2.

Problem: Write a similarity statement for each pair of triangles below. Then find the scale factor. (Use the ratio of the length of the side of the first triangle to the length of the corresponding side of the second triangle.)

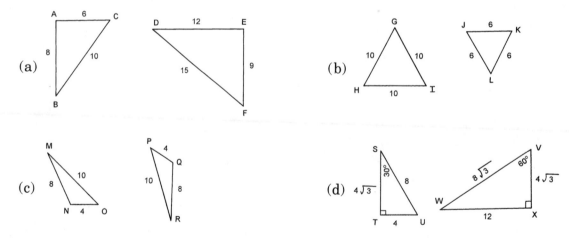

4–56 Finding the Lengths of the Sides of Similar Triangles ✯✯✯

If two triangles are similar, then their corresponding angles are congruent and corresponding sides are in a constant ratio called the scale factor.

If the lengths of two corresponding sides of a triangle are given, you can find the scale factor. This is usually the ratio of the length of a side of the first triangle to the corresponding length of a side of the second triangle. You can then write a proportion and solve to find the length of the other side.

For example, in the diagram below, △ABC ~ △EFD. The scale factor is BC:FD = 2:1.

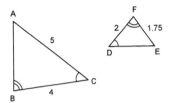

Problem: Each pair of triangles below is similar. Write a proportion and solve for x and y.

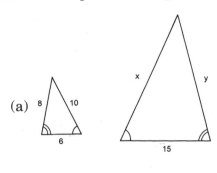

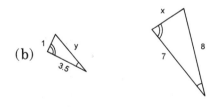

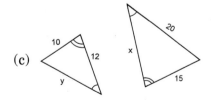

4–57 Finding the Perimeter of a Triangle ☆

The *perimeter* of a triangle is found by adding the lengths of its sides. (The units of measurement must be the same.) The formula is P = a + b + c, where *P* is the perimeter and *a, b,* and *c* are the lengths of the sides.

Problem: Find the perimeter of each triangle below.

(a)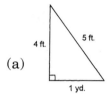

(b)

(c)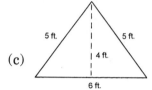

4–58 Finding the Perimeter of a Triangle ☆☆

The formula for finding the perimeter of a triangle is P = a + b + c, where *P* equals the perimeter and *a, b,* and *c* are the lengths of the sides.

Problem: Two other formulas for finding the perimeter of special triangles are written below. Identify the type of triangle to which each formula applies and write an explanation of your reasoning.

(a) P = 3a

(b) P = 2a + b

4-59   Finding the Perimeter of a Triangle   ✰✰✰

The kitchen is often considered to be the most important part of a home. Home econo-mists note that there are three main work areas in every kitchen: the sink, the stove, and the refrigerator. The most practical and efficient kitchen is designed so that these work areas are arranged at the vertices of a triangle. This is called the "work triangle." The ideal distances between the work areas are noted below.

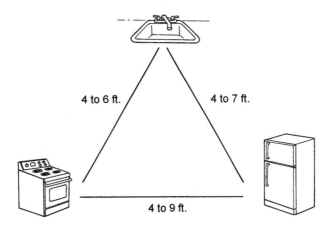

Problem: What is the largest perimeter of the ideal work triangle? What is the smallest perimeter of the ideal work triangle? What do you think your ideal kitchen work area would be? Why?

4–60   Finding the Area of a Triangle   ★

The formulas for finding the area of a triangle are $A = \frac{1}{2} bh$ or $\frac{bh}{2}$. In the formulas, A is the area, b equals the length of the base of the triangle, and h equals the height, which is also called the altitude. The height and the base form a right angle. See the examples below.

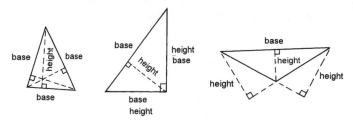

Each triangle has three altitudes. Notice that each altitude of an acute triangle is inside the triangle. Each leg of a right triangle is an altitude and the other altitude is inside the triangle. Two altitudes of an obtuse triangle are outside the triangle, and the other is inside the triangle.

When finding the area of any triangle, always be sure that the units of measurement are the same. Area is measured in square units.

Problem: Find the area of each triangle below.

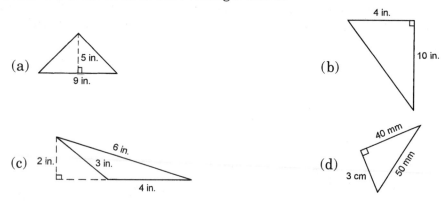

4–61   Finding the Area of a Triangle   ★★ G

Many first-class thinkers agree that you truly understand something only when you can apply your knowledge of it.

Problem: Create a short quiz for your classmates. The quiz will consist of four problems that require students to find the areas of triangles. (Remember to create an answer key.) Exchange quizzes with other students and solve each other's problems.

4–62   Finding the Area of a Triangle   ✰✰✰

Sometimes it is possible to compare areas without knowing any of the lengths. This requires careful analysis of what you already know.

Problem: In the diagram below, $\ell_1 \parallel \ell_2$. Which of the following triangles has the largest area: $\triangle ABC$, $\triangle DBC$, or $\triangle EBC$? Write an explanation of your answer.

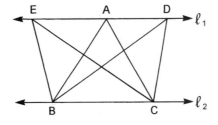

4–63   Finding the Area of a Triangle: Hero's Formula   ✰✰✰

In the 1st century A.D. Hero of Alexandria devised a formula for finding the area of a triangle. It is aptly called Hero's Formula and is stated below.

$$A = \sqrt{s(s-a)(s-b)(s-c)}$$

A stands for the area, s is half of the perimeter, and a, b, and c are the lengths of the sides.

Problem: Using Hero's Formula, find the area of a triangle whose sides have lengths of 8, 10, and 12. Round your answer to the nearest hundredth.

4–64   Identifying Types of Quadrilaterals   ☆

A *quadrilateral* is any four-sided polygon. Some types of quadrilaterals are listed below.

- A *trapezoid* is a quadrilateral that has only one pair of parallel sides.
- A *parallelogram* is a quadrilateral whose opposite sides are parallel.
- A *rectangle* is a parallelogram that has four right angles.
- A *rhombus* is a parallelogram that has four congruent sides.
- A *square* is a rectangle that has four congruent sides; also a *square* is a rhombus that has four right angles.

Problem: Six quadrilaterals are pictured below. Choose all the names that apply to each.

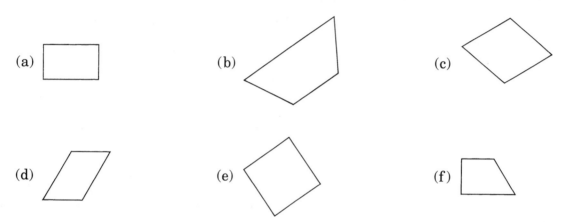

4–65   Identifying Trapezoids and Parallelograms   ☆

A *trapezoid* is a quadrilateral that has only one pair of parallel sides. It is *not* a *parallelogram,* because parallelograms have two pairs of parallel sides.

Problem: Choose the *best* name for each figure below. (Your selection could include a parallelogram, trapezoid, rectangle, square, and rhombus.)

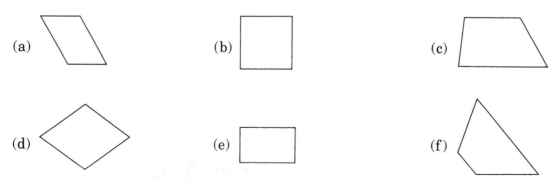

4-66   Trapeziums, Trapezoids, and Parallelograms   ✭✭

A *quadrilateral* is a four-sided polygon. Following are descriptions of some special quadrilaterals.

- A *parallelogram* is a quadrilateral that has two pairs of parallel sides.
- A *trapezoid* is a quadrilateral that has one pair of parallel sides.
- A *trapezium* is a quadrilateral that is neither a parallelogram nor a trapezoid.

Problem: How many parallel sides does a trapezium have? How many interior angles are congruent? Sketch a trapezium and explain your answer.

4-67   Classifying Quadrilaterals   ✭✭

Because quadrilaterals can be named in many ways, they are often confused. A working knowledge of the names that apply to quadrilaterals will help to eliminate confusion.

Problem: Decide whether each statement is true or false. If the statement is false, correct it.

- (a) All squares are rectangles.
- (b) Some rhombi are squares.
- (c) All parallelograms are rectangles.
- (d) Some trapezoids are parallelograms.
- (e) All squares are rhombi.
- (f) All rectangles are squares.

4–68   Drawing Quadrilaterals   ★★

Following are some facts about quadrilaterals:

- A *trapezoid* has one pair of parallel sides.
- A *parallelogram* has two pairs of parallel sides.
- A *rectangle* has four right angles.
- A *rhombus* has four congruent sides.
- A *square* has four right angles and four congruent sides.

Problem: Draw each quadrilateral described below. If it cannot be drawn, write "impossible" and explain why it cannot be drawn.

(a) A rectangle that is not a square.

(b) A rhombus that is not a square.

(c) A parallelogram that is not a rectangle.

(d) A trapezoid with four congruent sides.

(e) A square that is not a rectangle.

4–69   Squares   ★★ G

A checkerboard contains eight squares along the sides of the board and eight squares along the top and bottom. Each of these squares is 1 by 1. The total number of 1 by 1 squares is 64.

Problem: Find the total number of squares on a checkerboard. (Include 2 by 2 squares, 3 by 3 squares, and so on.)

4–70   Rectangles   ★★ G

A checkerboard has 64 small squares.

Problem: How many different-sized rectangles are there on a checkerboard? (Remember, a square is a rectangle.) List the dimensions of the different-sized rectangles. Keep in mind that a 1×2 rectangle is the same as a 2×1 rectangle.

4-71 Parallelograms ✫✫

The parallelogram below is drawn to scale. $\overline{AB}$ and $\overline{AC}$ are line segments drawn from two vertices of the parallelogram.

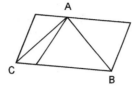

Problem: How does $\overline{AB}$ compare with $\overline{AC}$? What type of triangle is ∆ABC?

4-72 Kites and Parallelograms ✫✫

A *kite* is a quadrilateral that has two pairs of congruent adjacent sides. In the example of the kite below, $\overline{CD} \cong \overline{AD}$ and $\overline{CB} \cong \overline{AB}$.

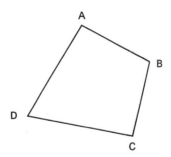

A *parallelogram* is a quadrilateral in which both pairs of opposite sides are parallel and congruent.

Problem: Are some parallelograms kites? Are all kites parallelograms? Write an explanation of your answers.

4–73   Properties of Quadrilaterals   ★★

Parallelograms, rectangles, squares, and rhombi (the plural of rhombus) share some but not all properties.

Problem: A list of properties of quadrilaterals is below. Write the names of the quadrilaterals that have the property. Choose from the following: parallelogram, rectangle, square, and rhombus. (Be careful, because some quadrilaterals possess more than one of the properties.)

(a) Opposite sides are parallel.

(b) Opposite angles are congruent.

(c) Opposite sides are congruent.

(d) All angles are right angles.

(e) All sides are congruent.

4–74   Properties of Diagonals of Quadrilaterals   ★★

A *diagonal* of a quadrilateral is a line segment drawn from a vertex to the opposite nonadjacent vertex. Quadrilaterals may be classified by the properties of the diagonals.

Problem: Identify the quadrilaterals whose diagonals have the properties listed below. Choose from among the following: parallelogram, rectangle, square, and rhombus. (Some quadrilaterals possess more than one of the properties.)

(a) The diagonals bisect each other.

(b) The diagonals are congruent.

(c) The diagonals are perpendicular to each other.

(d) Each diagonal bisects two angles.

4–75   Finding the Area of a Square   ★

Each side of a checkerboard measures 40 centimeters. The board contains eight rows of eight squares per row.

Problem: Find the area of each small square on the board.

4-76 Finding the Area of a Square ⋆⋆

The area of a square is found by multiplying the length of a side by the length of the side.

If the side of a square is 1 unit, the area is 1 square unit. If the side is 2 units, the area is 4 square units. If the side is 3 units, the area is 9 square units. If the side is 4 units, the area is 16 square units.

1, 4, 9, 16, and so on are called perfect squares. They are obtained by squaring an integer.

Problem: Is the area of a square always a perfect square? Include an example in your explanation.

4-77 Finding the Area of a Square ⋆⋆⋆

You may use the formula $A = \dfrac{d^2}{2}$ to find the area of a square. In this formula, A is the area and d equals the length of a diagonal.

Problem: Write an explanation of why this formula may be used to find the area of a square. (*Hint:* Use a $45°–45°–90°$ triangle and show the relationship of the diagonal to a leg of the triangle.)

4-78 Area and Perimeter of Squares ⋆⋆⋆

The *perimeter* is the distance around a square. The *area* is the space inside the square, represented by square units.

Problem: Statements about squares are listed below. Identify and correct the false statement(s).

(a) All squares that have the same area have the same perimeter.

(b) If the side of a square is doubled, the perimeter is doubled.

(c) If the side of a square is tripled, the area is 9 times the original area.

(d) The ratio of the area of a square to its perimeter is always greater than or equal to 1.

4–79 | Finding the Area of a Rectangle ☆

The size of a dollar bill today is smaller than the dollar bills printed before 1929. The dimensions of those bills were 7.42 by 3.13 inches. The bills in circulation today are 6.14 by 2.61 inches.

Problem: Find the area of each. How does the area of the larger bill compare with the area of the bills of today?

4–80 | Finding the Area of a Rectangle ☆

The 1897 *Farmer's Almanac* included some good advice for chicken farmers regarding the specifications for building a chicken house.
"Ten feet is wide enough and every ten feet in length will afford space for fifteen hens."

Problem: According to the specifications in the *Farmer's Almanac,* find the area of a coop that could accommodate 60 hens.

4–81 | Finding the Area of a Rectangle ☆☆

Roofing shingles are packaged in groups called "squares." One square covers 100 square feet of a roof.

Problem: The roof of a house is made of two rectangles, each 13 feet by 36 feet. The rectangles meet to form the peak of the home. How many squares of shingles are needed?

4–82   Finding the Area of a Rectangle   ★★

The word *acre* comes from the word *aecer,* which means "field" in old English. A field referred to a plot of land that was suitable for farming.

An acre is a unit of measurement for area.

$$1 \text{ acre} = 4{,}840 \text{ square yards}$$

Problem: Make a sketch of a plot of land that has an area of 1 acre. Label the dimensions.

4–83   Area of a Rectangle   ★★

Before the reign of England's Edward I, an acre was the amount of land a yoke of oxen could plow in a day. Because the performance of oxen varied greatly, Edward fixed an acre at an area of 40 rods long and 4 rods wide. That measurement has not changed.

Problem: If a rod is 16.5 feet long, express an acre in terms of square yards.

4–84   Area of a Rectangle   ★★ G

Rectangles may sometimes be arranged to form a square. One such arrangement, using tiles, is pictured below.

Problem: What is the smallest square that can be made by using 2-inch by 3-inch tiles? How many tiles would be required? How many tiles would be required to make the next larger square? What is its area?

| 4–85 | **Finding the Area and Perimeter of a Rectangle**   ✯✯ G |

The formula for finding the area of a rectangle is A = l × w. *A* is the area, *l* is the length of a side of the rectangle, and *w* is the width.

The formula for finding the perimeter of a rectangle is P = 2l + 2w. *P* is the perimeter, *l* is the length of a side of the the rectangle, and *w* is the width.

Problem: A rectangle has an area of 12 square inches. Find the smallest perimeter possible if the length and width are whole numbers. Then find the largest perimeter if the length and width are whole numbers.

| 4–86 | **Finding the Area of an Irregular Figure**   ✯✯ |

A 1-inch by 12-inch rectangle has an area of 12 square inches. A standard sheet of typing paper is $8\frac{1}{2}$ inches by 11 inches and has an area of 93.5 square inches.

Problem: Pedro claims he can cut a 1-inch by 12-inch rectangle from a standard sheet of typing paper. Explain how he can do this. After Pedro cuts the 1-inch by 12-inch rectangle from the paper, what is the remaining area?

| 4–87 | **Finding the Area of an Irregular Figure**   ✯✯ G |

Remodeling a house may involve making a room larger or adding a room or rooms.

The Joneses wish to add on a family room and a deck to their living room and kitchen. The "before" and "after" plans in a simplified form are shown below.

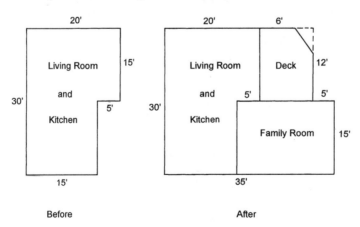

Problem: Find the area of the living room and kitchen, area of the family room, area of the deck, and the total area of the rooms and deck in the "after" plan.

4-88   Finding the Area of a Cyclic Quadrilateral   ☆☆

A *cyclic quadrilateral* is a quadrilateral that can be inscribed in a circle, as in the following figure.

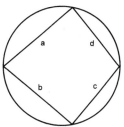

The formula for finding the area of a cyclic quadrilateral is noted below.

$$A = \sqrt{(s-a)(s-b)(s-c)(s-d)}$$

In this equation A is the area, and s is the sum of the four sides divided by 2. a, b, c, and d are the lengths of the sides.

Problem: Find the area of a cyclic quadrilateral if a = 4, b = 4, c = 3, and d = 3.

4-89   Area of a Parallelogram   ☆

A *parallelogram* is a quadrilateral that has two pairs of parallel sides. The area of a parallelogram is found by multiplying the length of the base times the height.

$$A = b \times h$$

Problem: Write an explanation of how the area of a parallelogram is similar to the area of a rectangle.

4-90 | Area of a Trapezoid ☆

A *trapezoid* is a quadrilateral that has only one pair of parallel sides. To find the area of a trapezoid, you can use the formula below.

$$A = \tfrac{1}{2}(b_1 + b_2)h$$

In this formula A is the area, b_1 is the length of one parallel side, b_2 is the length of the other parallel side, and h is the height.

Problem: Which trapezoids below have the same area? What are the areas?

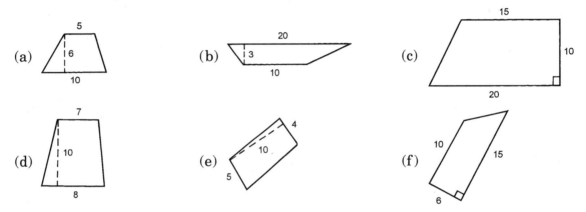

(a)   5, 6, 10

(b)   20, 3, 10

(c)   15, 10, 20

(d)   7, 10, 8

(e)   4, 10, 5

(f)   10, 15, 6

4-91 | Finding the Area of a Regular Polygon ☆☆

An *apothem* of a regular polygon is the distance from the center to a side of the polygon. See the figure below.

An apothem may be used to find the area of a regular polygon by using the formula $A = \dfrac{nsa}{2}$. In this formula, A is the area, n is the number of sides, s is the length of a side, and a stands for the apothem.

Problem: Find the area of a regular hexagon if each side is 4 inches and the apothem is 5 inches.

4–92   Circles   ☆

A symbol is something that has meaning beyond itself. Throughout history circles have always been powerful symbols. Even today, many businesses and organizations use circles in their logos.

Problem: List at least three places a circle is used as a symbol. Why do you think circles are used as symbols?

4–93   Radius   ☆

Radius is a Latin word that means "the spoke of a wheel."

Problem: Write an explanation of how the radius of a circle resembles the spoke of a wheel.

4–94   Diameter   ☆

The word *diameter* comes from the Greek word *diametros,* which means "a line that measures through."

Problem: Explain what a diameter measures through and draw an illustration to support your answer.

4–95   Finding the Diameter   ★★

Sometimes a different "slant" on a problem can make it easier to solve.

Consider rectangle OABC inside the circle pictured below. The center of the circle is O and AC = 5.

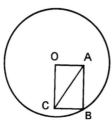

Problem: How long is the diameter of the circle? Explain your answer.

4–96   Radius and Diameter   ★★

The *radius* is a line segment from the center of a circle to a point on the circle. The *diameter* is a chord that passes through the center of a circle. A *chord* is a line segment that has its two endpoints on the circle.

The length of the radius equals half of the length of the diameter. Conversely, the length of the diameter is twice the length of the radius.

Problem: Create a math problem in which the radius and diameter of a circle are key facts. Exchange your problem for the problem of another student. Solve each other's problem.

4-97 **Finding the Circumference** ✫

The *circumference* of a circle is the distance around a circle. To find the circumference you may use either of two formulas.

$$C = \pi d \text{ or } C = 2\pi r$$

In the formulas, C is the circumference, d is the length of the diameter, and r is the length of the radius. π is approximately equal to 3.14 or $\frac{22}{7}$.

Problem: Find the circumferences for the circles below given the following information. (Use 3.14 for π.)

(a) r = 10 in.

(b) d = 15 in.

(c)

(d)

4-98 **Circumference** ✫✫

The diameter of a standard basketball rim is 18 inches, and the circumference of a basketball is 30 inches.

Problem: Explain why these dimensions are appropriate to make scoring challenging but not impossible.

4-99 **Finding the Area of a Circle** ✫

Area is the space inside a region. The *area* of a circle is the space inside the circle. You may use the following formula to find the area of a circle.

$$A = \pi r^2$$

Problem: A beam of light from a lighthouse may be seen for 30 miles in all directions. What is the area in square miles in which the light may be seen? What factors might interfere with the light being seen in this area?

4–100 | Finding the Area of a Circle ★★

A compact disc that is 120 millimeters in diameter can hold up to 74 minutes of music. The unrecorded portion of this disc has a diameter of 50 millimeters.

Problem: Find the area of the recorded portion of this disc.

4–101 | Finding the Area of a Circle ★★

The diameter of an archery target is 48 inches. The diameter of the innermost circle is 9.6 inches.

Problem: How does the area of the smallest circle compare with the area of the target?

4–102 | Finding the Area of a Circle ★★★

An ancient Palestinian formula for finding the area of a circle is $A = \dfrac{11d^2}{14}$, where A is the area and d is the diameter of the circle.

Problem: Using the formula above, find the area of a circle whose diameter is 10 inches. Then find the area of the same circle using the formula $A = \pi r^2$. Compare the answers. Explain why they might be different.

4-103 Comparing the Area of a Square and a Circle ★★

The circumference of a circle is equal to the length of the diameter times π. The perimeter of a square is equal to 4 times the length of a side.

Problem: Suppose the circumference of a circle is 31.4 inches, and the perimeter of a square is 31.4 inches. Which figure has the larger area?

4-104 Concentric Circles ★

Concentric circles are two or more circles in the same plane that have the same center. *Concentric* is taken from the Greek words *con,* which means same, and *centrom,* which means center.

Problem: List at least three examples of concentric circles you see in your daily routines.

4-105 Area of an Annulus ★★

An *annulus* is the area between two concentric circles. A good illustration of an annulus is a target used for archery.

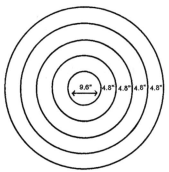

The target consists of five concentric circles. The bull's-eye is the circle in the center of the target and is 9.6 inches in diameter. Surrounding the bull's-eye are four concentric circles.

Problem: Using the archery target above as an example, find the area of the annulus of the outermost circle and the circle closest to it. Round your answer to the nearest whole number.

4-106 Tangent Circles ★★

Circles are *tangent* if they "touch" at only one point. They may be internally tangent or externally tangent as noted below.

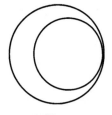

internally tangent

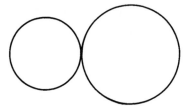

externally tangent

Problem: Three circles are pictured below. Draw the circles that are tangent to all three. (*Hint:* There are eight possible answers.)

4-107 Great and Small Circles ★★

A *small circle* is the intersection of a sphere and plane that does not pass through the center of the sphere.

A *great circle* is the intersection of a sphere and plane that passes through the center of the sphere.

Problem: Consider the sphere below. How many small circles are there? How many different great circles are there? Which circle has the larger area? Which has the larger circumference?

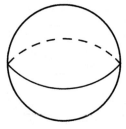

4-108 Angles in a Circle ☆

Thousands of years ago the Babylonians, a people living in a region of the Middle East known as Mesopotamia, counted things in groups of 60. We still use this number system when we measure time. There are 60 seconds in a minute and 60 minutes in an hour.

The Babylonians were fine mathematicians and enjoyed geometry. They divided the circle into 360 equal parts. We use this system today, too, and call each part a degree. A quarter of a circle contains 90° and a semicircle contains 180°.

Problem: Write an explanation of the relationship between 360° in a circle and the number of seconds in an hour. (*Hint:* Think of a circular clock.)

4-109 Types of Arcs ☆☆ G

An *arc* is part of a circle. Arcs are classified as a minor arc, major arc, or semicircle.

- A *minor arc* has a measure of less than 180°.
- A *major arc* has a measure of more than 180°.
- A *semicircle* has a measure of 180°.

The three types of arcs are shown below.

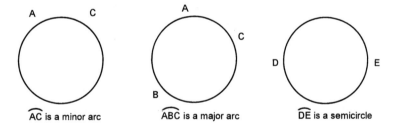

Problem: A small Ferris wheel is pictured below. The cars are labeled with the letters A through H. List all minor arcs, major arcs, and semicircles.

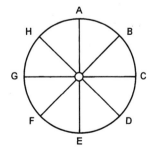

4-110 Central and Inscribed Angles ★★

A *central angle* is an angle whose vertex is at the center of a circle. Its sides are along the radii. The measure of a central angle is the same as the measure of its intercepted minor arc.

An *inscribed angle* is an angle whose vertex is on the circle and whose sides are along the two chords. The measure of an inscribed angle is half the measure of its intercepted minor arc.

Problem: Consider the circle below. O is the center and the m∠BOC = 60°. List all of the congruent angles. Then state the measure of each.

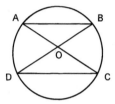

4-111 Arcs and Angles of Circles ★★

Circles can be separated into parts called arcs. In the figure below, $\overarc{AC}$ is read "arc AC." Following are some facts about arcs.

- The measure of a *minor arc* is the measure of its central angle.
- A *semicircle* has a measure of 180.
- The measure of a *major arc* is the difference between its related minor arc and 360.
- The measure of a *central angle* is equal to the measure of its intercepted minor arc.
- The measure of an *inscribed angle* is $\frac{1}{2}$ the measure of its intercepted arc.

Problem: Consider circle O. The m∠ACB = 60 and the $\overarc{AC}$ = 120. What type of triangle is △ABC? What type of triangle is △AOB?

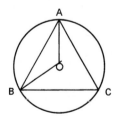

4-112 Secants and Tangents ✮

Although a circle is round, many special line segments may be associated with it. Diameters, radii, and chords are the most common. Secants and tangents are two others.

A *secant* is a line that contains a chord.

A *tangent* is a line that meets the circle at one point.

Problem: Consider circle O. List all the lines or segments that may be a diameter, radius, chord, secant, or tangent. (There are nine.)

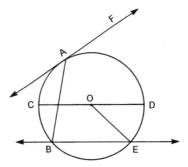

4-113 Measures of Angles: Chord–Tangent Angle Theorem and Chord–Chord Angle Theorem ✮✮✮

The *Chord–Tangent Angle Theorem* states that the measure of an angle formed by a tangent and a chord drawn from the point of tangency is equal to $\frac{1}{2}$ the measure of the intercepted arc.

The *Chord–Chord Angle Theorem* states that the measure of an angle formed by two chords intersecting in the interior of a circle is equal to $\frac{1}{2}$ the sum of the intercepted arcs.

Problem: Consider circle O. Use the theorems above and facts about semicircles and inscribed angles to find the measure of each arc below.

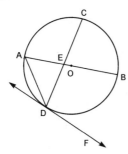

$\overleftrightarrow{DF}$ is tangent to the circle at D

$m\angle AEC = 110$

$m\angle CDF = 100$

$m\angle ADC = 50$

(a) m$\overarc{AB}$ =   (b) m$\overarc{CBD}$ =   (c) m$\overarc{AC}$ =

(d) m$\overarc{BD}$ =   (e) m$\overarc{CB}$ =   (f) m$\overarc{AD}$ =

4-114   **Measures of Angles Formed by Secants and Tangents Drawn from a Point Outside the Circle** ★★★

The measure of an angle formed when two secants, two tangents, or a secant and a tangent are drawn from a point outside the circle is equal to $\frac{1}{2}$ the difference of the intercepted arcs.

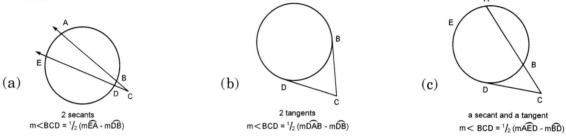

(a)

2 secants
m<BCD = ¹/₂ (m$\widehat{EA}$ - m$\widehat{DB}$)

(b)

2 tangents
m<BCD = ¹/₂ (m$\widehat{DAB}$ - m$\widehat{DB}$)

(c)

a secant and a tangent
m< BCD = ¹/₂ (m$\widehat{AED}$ - m$\widehat{BD}$)

Problem: Suppose m∠BCD = 80 and m$\widehat{BD}$ = 50 in each diagram above. Find the measure of the intercepted arc in a and c. Write an explanation of why it is impossible for two tangents, as pictured in *b*, to form an 80° angle and intercept an arc whose measure is 50. (Note: The illustrations are not drawn to scale.)

4-115   **Length of Segments: Chords Intersecting in the Interior of a Circle** ★★

A *chord* is a line segment whose endpoints are on the circle. When two chords intersect in the interior of a circle, the product of the lengths of the segments of one chord equals the product of the lengths of the segments of the other chord.

In the diagram below, ab = cd.

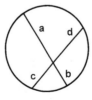

Problem: Consider the diagram above where ab = cd. Can you conclude that a = d? Write an explanation of your answer and provide an example to support your reasoning.

4-116 | Length of Segments: Secant and Tangent Segments ★★★

The two diagrams below show the relationship of two segments drawn from an exterior point to the circle.

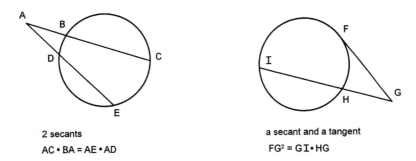

2 secants

AC • BA = AE • AD

a secant and a tangent

FG² = GI • HG

Problem: Compare and contrast these two relationships.

4-117 | Arc Lengths ★★★

The measure of a minor arc of a circle is the same as the measure of its central angle. The length of an arc is a portion of the circumference of the circle.

If $m\overarc{AB} = x$, then the length of $AB = \dfrac{x}{360} \cdot 2\pi r$, where r is the radius of the circle.

Problem: Using the relationship above, explain how all three arcs below are part of the same circle. (They are, even if they don't look like they are.)

4-118 Area of a Sector ★★

A *sector* of a circle is the part of a circle bound by two radii and the intercepted arc. A slice of pizza is a sector of the circular pie.

$A = \dfrac{x}{360} \cdot \pi r^2$ is the formula for finding the area of a sector of a circle. In this formula, A is the area, x is the measure of the central angle, and r is the length of the radius.

Problem: Two pizzas have a 12-inch diameter. One pie is cut into eight equal slices, and the other is cut into six equal slices. How does the area of a slice of the 8-piece pie compare with the area of a slice of pizza from the 6-slice pie?

4-119 Area of a Minor Segment ★★★

A *minor segment* is the part of a circle between a chord and its arc. A minor segment is shaded in the diagram.

To find the area of a minor segment, find the area of the sector, find the area of the triangle, and subtract.

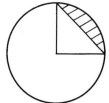

Problem: Find the area of the shaded region in the diagram above. The measure of the central angle is 90°. The measure of the radius is 4 centimeters. Express your answer in terms of π.

4-120 Figures in Space ★★

Sometimes it is easier to make a sketch than to build an actual model. A hollow crate is pictured below.

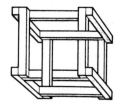

Problem: Study the crate closely. Explain why it is impossible to actually build such a figure.

4-121 Finding the Volume of a Rectangular Prism ✫

The *volume* is the space inside a container. A good example of a *rectangular prism* is a box. The volume of the box is the space inside.

To find the volume of a rectangular prism, use the formula $V = l \times w \times h$. V is the volume, l is the length, w is the width, and h is the height.

Problem: Find the volumes of the rectangular prisms with the following dimensions. (Remember that the units of measurement must be the same.)

(a) Length = 24 in.
    Width = 1.5 ft.
    Height = 18 in.

(b) Length = $2\frac{3}{4}$ ft.
    Width = $2\frac{1}{2}$ ft.
    Height = 5 ft.

(c) Length = 16 cm
    Width = 28.5 cm
    Height = 30 cm

(d) Length = 1.5 ft.
    Width = 15 in.
    Height = 2.5 ft.

4-122 Finding the Volume of a Rectangle Prism ✫✫ G

The volume of a rectangular prism is found by multiplying the length by the width by the height. You can use the formula $V = l \times w \times h$, where V is the volume, l is the length, w is the width, and h is the height.

Problem: A shoe box measures 6.5 inches by 3.5 inches by 12 inches. How many boxes of this size can be placed on a 12-inch by 25-inch shelf if the shelf is one foot from the ceiling? What is the volume of the wasted space?

4-123 Finding the Surface Area of a Rectangular Prism ✫✫✫

The *surface area* of a 3-dimensional figure is the sum of the areas of all the faces and the bases of the figure.

Dice are cubes, which are a special type of rectangular prism. Each side of a die is a face, and each die, because it is a cube, has six faces. To find the surface area of the die, you would need to find the area of each face by multiplying length times width, and then add the areas of the faces. (Because the area of each face is the same, you can simply multiply by 6 instead of adding.)

Problem: Twelve $\frac{3}{4}$ by $\frac{3}{4}$ by $\frac{3}{4}$-inch dice are boxed in two layers of two rows of three dice per row. (Six dice are in each layer.) Find the surface area of the box.

4-124 Finding the Volume and Surface Area of a Cylinder ★★★

Cylinders are found just about everywhere. Your pencil, a can of soda, paper towel rolls, and even some gym bags are cylinders.

To find the volume of a cylinder, use the formula $V = \pi r^2 h$. In this formula, V is the volume of the cylinder, r is the length of the radius, and h is the height.

To find the surface area of a cylinder, use the formula $SA = 2\pi r(h + r)$, where SA is the surface area, r is the length of the radius, and h is the height of the cylinder.

Problem: A canvas gym bag is pictured below. What is its volume in cubic feet? About how many square feet of canvas are required to make this bag?

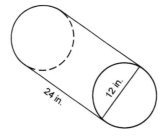

4-125 Finding the Volume of Cones ★★

Some fancy ice-cream dishes are shaped like a cone. In many restaurants you can purchase an ice-cream sundae in a tall cone-shaped dish, or in a wider cone-shaped dish that has a long pedestal.

To find the volume of a cone, use the formula $V = \frac{1}{3}\pi r^2 h$, where V is the volume, r is the length of the radius, and h is the height.

Problem: Two cone-shaped dishes are pictured below. Which has the greater volume?

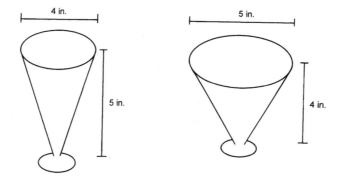

4-126 Finding the Surface Area of a Cone ★★★

Ice-cream cones vary in size and shape. Some—the cones that have a circular base and no point—are not "cones" at all but are a combination of two cylinders. Examples of real cones are waffle cones and sugar cones.

To find the surface area of a cone, use the formula $SA = \pi r(r + s)$, where *SA* is the surface area, *r* is the length of the radius, and *s* is the slant height of the cone.

Problem: A waffle cone is pictured below. The length of the diameter is 6 inches and the slant height is 8 inches. In finding the surface area of this cone, Joe used 3.14 as the value for π and found the surface area to be about 103.62 square inches. John found the answer to be about 263.76 square inches. Who is correct? What mistake was made? By whom?

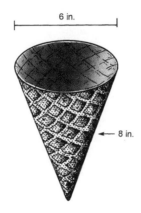

6 in.

8 in.

4-127 Finding the Volume and Surface Area of Pyramids ★★★

A *pyramid* is a 3-dimensional figure whose base is a regular polygon and whose other faces are congruent triangles.

The formula for finding the volume of a pyramid is $V = \dfrac{Bh}{3}$, where *V* is the volume, *B* is the area of the base, and *h* is the height of the pyramid.

The formula for finding the surface area is $SA = B + \frac{1}{2}ps$. In this formula *SA* is the surface area, *B* is the area of the base, *p* is the perimeter of the base, and *s* is the slant height of the triangular faces.

Problem: The Great Pyramid near Cairo, Egypt was originally 481 feet in height. (Age and erosion have since reduced its size.) The square base measured 756 feet on each side, and the slant height was 612 feet. Find the original volume and surface area of the Great Pyramid.

4–128   Finding the Volume and Surface Area of Spheres   ★★★

A *sphere* may be defined as a hollow or solid figure enclosed by a surface where every point is equidistant from the center. A baseball, basketball, and globe are examples of spheres.

To find the volume of a sphere, use the formula $V = \frac{4}{3}\pi r^3$, where V is the volume and r is the length of the radius. To find the surface area of a sphere, use the formula $SA = 4\pi r^2$, where SA is the surface area and r is the length of the radius.

Problem: The radius of a basketball is 4.75 inches. The diameter of a baseball is 3 inches. Find the volume and surface area of each. Use 3.14 for π. Round your answer to the nearest tenth.

4–129   Platonic Solids and Euler's Formula   ★★

Regular polyhedra are solid figures bounded by regular polygons in a manner such that the same number of faces meet at each vertex. There are only five regular polyhedra that are also called Platonic Solids.

Euler's Formula is V – E + F = 2, when V is the number of vertices, E is the number of edges, and F is the number of faces. The formula applies to Platonic Solids as well as other polyhedra.

Problem: Use Euler's Formula to complete the chart.

Name	Faces	Edges	Vertices
Regular Tetrahedron	4		4
Regular Hexahedron or Cube	6	12	
Regular Octahedron		12	6
Regular Dodecahedron	12		20
Regular Icosahedron	20	30	

4-130 Quotation about Geometry ★★

Plato (429–347 B.C.) was a Greek philosopher who believed that knowledge of mathematics, and particularly geometry, was essential to sound thinking.

Among the vast achievements of Plato was his founding of his Academy in Athens, which became a center of learning. Above the door of Plato's Academy was placed the following statement: "Let no one ignorant of geometry enter here."

Problem: Why might Plato have felt so strongly about the importance of the study of geometry? Do you agree with him? Why or why not?

Section 5

ALGEBRA

5–1   Simplifying Expressions: Without Exponents ☆

When simplifying expressions, you must follow a specific order of steps.

1. Simplify expressions within grouping symbols. If more than one grouping symbol is used, simplify the innermost grouping first and continue simplifying to the outermost group.
2. Perform multiplication and division from left to right.
3. Perform addition and subtraction from left to right.

Problem: Four expressions are listed below. Which will have the same value if you use the order of operations to simplify them? What are the values of each expression?

(a) $8 + 4 \cdot 3 - 1$ (b) $(8 + 4) \cdot 3 - 1$

(c) $8 + (4 \cdot 3) - 1$ (d) $8 + 4 \cdot (3 - 1)$

5–2   Simplifying Expressions: Without Exponents ☆☆ G

Numbers may always be expressed in terms of other numbers. When simplifying expressions, the order of operations must always be followed.

Problem: Using the digits 1, 2, 3, and 4, and the order of operations, write expressions that equal the numbers from 1 to 10. You must use each digit only once per expression. The first number is done for you.

$$(2 \cdot 1) - (4 - 3) = 1$$

5–3   Simplifying Expressions: Without Exponents ☆☆

A maple tree's "wings" (which contain seeds) rotate in a small circle so that they spiral downward as they fall. This slows the speed of their descent and enables the wind to disperse them. On a windy day the seeds may travel quite far from the parent tree before they reach the ground.

Problem: Use the order of operations to determine the number of feet a maple tree's wings may travel. How does this remarkable feature help the maple tree to survive?

$$5(3 + 5 \times 6 + 50 \times 2) =$$

5-4 Simplifying Expressions: With Exponents ☆

The order of operations must be followed to simplify expressions.

1. Simplify expressions within grouping symbols first. If several grouping symbols are used, simplify the innermost grouping and continue simplifying to the outermost grouping. As you do this, follow steps 2, 3, and 4.

2. Simplify powers.

3. Perform multiplication and division from left to right.

4. Perform addition and subtraction from left to right.

Problem: Place parentheses in each expression so that the result is 56.

(a) $7 \cdot 6 - 4 \cdot 4$

(b) $18 - 8 \cdot 5 + 6$

(c) $8^2 - 1 \cdot 2^3$

(d) $2^2 + 3 \cdot 9 - 1$

5-5 Simplifying Expressions: With Exponents ☆☆

The game of horseshoes is often played at picnics. For most players it is a game of skill and a bit of luck. In a standard game of horseshoes, the stakes must be set a specific number of feet apart.

Problem: Simplify the expression below to find the distance in feet between stakes in a regulation game of horseshoes.

$$2 \cdot 3^2 + 3 \cdot 2^2 + 3^2 + 1^2$$

5-6 Simplifying Expressions: With Exponents ☆☆

Of Thomas Edison's many inventions, the phonograph is one of his best known. The first words he recorded were "Mary had a little lamb." Although Edison had, without question, an "inventive" mind, he wasn't very original with his first recording.

Problem: To find the year this message was recorded, simplify the expression below.

$$9(3^2 + 2^2)^2 + 89 \cdot 2^2$$

5–7 Simplifying Expressions: With Exponents ★★

A typical symphony orchestra has a set number of instruments.

Problem: Simplify the expression below to find the number of instruments in a symphony orchestra. How does this number compare with the number of instruments in the band at your school?

$$(4^4 \div 2) - 7 \times 4 + 4$$

5–8 Simplifying Expressions: With Exponents ★★

Knowledge of numbers can increase your cultural literacy and provide you with insights in many different areas. For this problem the knowledge of algebra can even help you decipher a classic book title.

Problem: What is Fahrenheit $(7 + 8)^2 - (8 + 6)^2 + (9 + 10)^2 + 8^2 - 3$? What do you think the significance of this number is?

5–9 Simplifying Expressions: With Exponents ★★★

Imagine if you had a penny, doubled it to two pennies, then doubled the two pennies to four pennies, and continued doubling for 30 days. Do you think you'd have a lot of money at the end of the month?

Problem: Estimate how much money you would have if you started with a penny and doubled your money each day for 30 days. Then simplify the expression to find out how much money in dollars you would actually have. How does this compare with your estimate?

$$5 \times 10^6 + 3 \times 10^5 + 6 \times 10^4 + 8 \times 10^3 + 7 \times 10^2 + 9 \times 10^0 + 1 \times \frac{1}{10} + 2 \times \frac{1}{10^2}$$

5–10 Variables ☆

Not all stars shine with constant brightness. Some, called variable stars, change in brightness.

Problem: Using your experience with variables in your math classes, do you think variable stars are an appropriate name for stars that change in brightness? Explain your answer.

5–11 Words and Phrases as Mathematical Expressions ☆ G

Expressing words as mathematical symbols can be difficult but is necessary to solve equations.

Problem: Compile a list of words or phrases that may be expressed as mathematical symbols. Include the symbol for each phrase. (One example is subtraction, –. Another is pi, π.)

5–12 Writing Phrases as Algebraic Expressions ☆

An algebraic expression can be compared to a phrase. Translating a phrase into an algebraic expression is easier if you think about the meanings of the words.

Problem: Match each expression below with its algebraic expression. (Some expressions are not used.)

1. $n - 5$

(a) 5 times a number

2. $5n$

(b) 5 more than a number

3. $5 - n$

(c) A number divided by 5

4. $5 + n$

(d) 5 less than a number

5. $\dfrac{n}{5}$

6. $\dfrac{5}{n}$

5–13 Evaluating Expressions: Without Exponents ☆

In 1897 Sears, Roebuck and Company published their catalogue which listed a variety of goods, including clothing, jewelry, toys, and farm equipment.

Problem: If a = 3, b = 10, and c = 20, find the cost in cents of each item below by evaluating the expression. You may be surprised at the prices of these items back then. Why were they so inexpensive compared with prices today?

(a) One pair of steel-blade ice skates: ac + 2

(b) A baseball: $\dfrac{abc + 4ab}{b}$

(c) A catcher's mitt: 2(a + b) − 2a

(d) A deck of playing cards: a + b

5–14 Evaluating Expressions: Without Exponents ☆☆

An n × n square has *n* rows and *n* columns. There is a total of $\dfrac{n(n + 1)(2n + 1)}{6}$ squares. Some of the squares are different sizes.

For example, a 3 × 3 square has three rows and three columns, as in a tic-tac-toe drawing. If you substitute 3 in the equation, there are a total of 14 squares (nine 1 × 1 squares, four 2 × 2 squares, and one 3 × 3 square).

Problem: Use the formula above to find the total number of squares in a 12 × 12 square.

5–15 Evaluating Expressions: With Exponents ☆

Mattel produced the Barbie® doll and soon afterward introduced Ken™, Barbie's boyfriend; Midge™, her friend; and Skipper™, her sister. By 1980, Barbie was so popular that top fashion designers created clothes for her.

Problem: Evaluate the expression $a^2b + cd$, if a = 12, b = 13, c = 43, and d = 2, to find the year the Barbie® doll was first produced.

5-16   Evaluating Expressions: With Exponents   ★★

Many of the numbers in astronomy are, well, "astronomical." For example, distances are so big that they are often expressed in light years rather than miles. (A light year is the distance light travels in one year. Light travels at a speed of about 186,000 miles per second.)

Problem: Let a = 2, b = 3, and c = 5 to evaluate the expressions below.

(a) The rate at which the earth whirls around the sun (in miles per second): $ac + b^a$

(b) The rate at which the sun is moving through the Milky Way Galaxy (in miles per second): $a + ac$

(c) The number of years for the Milky Way Galaxy to complete one full turn: $a(ac)^a$

(d) The approximate distance to Polaris, the North Star (in light years): $7(ac)^a - c(c - 1)$

5-17   Evaluating Expressions: With Exponents   ★★

An n × n square has *n* rows and *n* columns. In an n × n square, there are $\dfrac{n^2(n + 1)^2}{4}$ rectangles. Some of these rectangles are different sizes. (Remember, squares are rectangles.) For example, in a 3 × 3 square, there are 36 rectangles as follows:

Nine 1 × 1 squares
Twelve 1 × 2 rectangles
Six 1 × 3 rectangles
Four 2 × 2 squares
Four 2 × 3 rectangles
One 3 × 3 square

Problem: Use the formula above to find the number of rectangles in a 12 × 12 square.

5–18   The Number Line   ☆

All numbers can be pictured as points on a number line. The origin of a number line is 0. The numbers to the right of 0 are positive numbers, and the numbers to the left of 0 are negative numbers. The *coordinate* is the number paired with a point on the number line.

Problem: Use the number line to identify the coordinates described below.

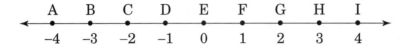

A	B	C	D	E	F	G	H	I
–4	–3	–2	–1	0	1	2	3	4

(a) The origin.

(b) The natural numbers.

(c) The point halfway between D and H.

(d) The point that is the same distance from the origin as H.

5–19   The Number Line   ☆☆

The Smith family likes to take trips in the car. To help pass the time, Mrs. Smith, who assumes the role of navigator, gives clues about the towns they will pass through.

Problem: Traveling south on an interstate highway, the Smiths will pass the cutoffs for three cities: Allenville, Browning, and Cooperton. The distance from Allenville to Browning is 16 miles. The distance from Browning to Cooperton is 8 miles, and the distance from Allenville to Cooperton is 24 miles. What town is between the other two? (*Hint:* To help you visualize the towns, you might sketch a number line.)

5–20   Opposites   ☆

Positive numbers and negative numbers are opposites. For example, gaining 3 pounds is the opposite of losing 3 pounds. In football, gaining 10 yards is the opposite of losing 10 yards.

Problem: Consider the following statement. If –10° F is really cold, then 10° F is really hot. Do you agree or disagree? Explain your answer.

5–21   Absolute Value   ☆

Absolute value is the distance of a number from 0 on the number line. Note the following examples:

$\lvert 3 \rvert = 3$	$\lvert 7 \rvert = 7$	$\lvert 15 \rvert = 15$
$\lvert -3 \rvert = 3$	$\lvert -7 \rvert = 7$	$\lvert -15 \rvert = 15$

Problem: From the examples above, Abby generalized that there are always two numbers that can be written inside the absolute value symbol so that the expression equals a positive whole number. Do you agree or disagree? Explain your answer.

5–22   Comparing Integers   ☆

Integers are the group of whole numbers, 0, and the opposites of the whole numbers. The set $\{\ldots -3, -2, -1, 0, 1, 2, 3, \ldots\}$ represents integers.

Each integer can be paired with a point on the number line. The larger integers are always to the right of the smaller integers.

Problem: Each group of integers below is arranged from the least to the greatest, or the greatest to the least, but one integer is out of order. Identify this integer and rewrite the set correctly.

(a) $\{-3, -2, 1, 0, 7\}$

(b) $\{-4, -5, -6, -7, 0\}$

(c) $\{-8, -9, -7, -6, -5\}$

(d) $\{-4, 2, 4, 8, 6\}$

5–23   Integers   ☆

Integers are used in countdowns for space flights and shuttle launchings. The negative numbers designate the seconds before blastoff, and the positive numbers represent the seconds after blastoff.

Problem: How many seconds elapse between T-10 seconds and T+10 seconds? On what number would blastoff occur?

5–24 Integers ★★

Negative numbers troubled mathematicians well into the 1800s. Most mathematicians ignored them, calling them "inadequate" or "absurd," believing that negative numbers had no practical use or meaning.

Even the best mathematics texts in the 18th century interchanged the minus sign with the symbol to denote a negative number. This all changed with Leonhard Euler. In his *Complete Introduction of Algebra,* Euler stated that subtracting the opposite of a number is the same as adding the number. In Euler's words: "To cancel a debt signifies the same as giving a gift."

Problem: Explain Euler's words above. Include an example with negative numbers to support your explanation.

5–25 Adding Integers ★

A magic square is a square in which all of the numbers in each row, column, and diagonal add up to the same number.

Problem: In the first magic square, find the sum of each row, column, and diagonal. In the second magic square, each row, column, and diagonal add up to 3. Find the missing numbers.

-4	-9	-2
-3	-5	-7
-8	-1	-6

	5	0
		-1
2		

5–26 Adding Integers ★★

Tom has trouble understanding how you can add certain integers and have an answer that is less than the number you started with. For instance: $8 + (-5) = 3$.

Problem: Write an explanation of why the equation above is correct. Provide an example from everyday life that supports your explanation.

5–27   Subtracting Integers   ✮

Companies that deliver heating oil use *degree days* to estimate when their customers will require oil deliveries. After about 1,000 degree days have accumulated, an oil delivery is scheduled.

Degree days are determined by finding the average temperature of each day, and then subtracting this temperature from 68. For example, if the average temperature on Monday is 40° F, then 68 – 40 = 28 degree days. If the average temperature for another day in the winter was –3° F, the degree day would be 68 – (–3) = 71.

Problem: Why does a lower temperature result in higher degree days? What is the degree day if the average temperature is 68?

5–28   Subtracting Integers   ✮✮

When learning how to subtract integers for the first time, many students become confused because the answer is greater than the numbers they started with. For example: 20 – (–5) = 25.

Problem: Create a word problem that requires subtraction of integers in its solution. Exchange your problem for the problem of a classmate and solve each other's problem.

5–29   Adding and Subtracting Integers   ✮✮

Sometimes mathematicians are not interested in actual numbers, but simply whether or not a number is positive. A good example is the stockholder who is concerned only with whether the value of his or her stocks go up.

Problem: Describe each situation below as positive, negative, zero, or cannot be determined.

(a) The sum of two positive integers

(b) The difference of two positive numbers

(c) The sum of a number and its opposite

(d) The sum of a negative number and zero

(e) The difference of two negative numbers

5–30 | Adding and Subtracting Integers ★★

Adding and subtracting integers requires skill, accuracy, and sometimes patience.

Problem: Follow the path from start to finish. What is the final number?

(a) $3 \rightarrow +(-6) \rightarrow +9 \rightarrow -0 \rightarrow +15 \rightarrow$ _____

(b) $-3 \rightarrow -(-5) \rightarrow +10 \rightarrow +(-4) \rightarrow +6 \rightarrow$ _____

(c) $12 \rightarrow +(-5) \rightarrow +(-7) \rightarrow -(-8) \rightarrow +8 \rightarrow$ _____

(d) $0 \rightarrow +4 \rightarrow -(-12) \rightarrow -6 \rightarrow +15 \rightarrow$ _____

5–31 | Multiplying Two Integers ★

When multiplying positive and negative integers, you must determine whether your product is positive or negative. The rules for determining the sign of the product of two integers follow:

1. If both integers have the same sign, the product is positive.

2. If the integers have different signs, the product is negative.

3. If one (or both) of the factors is 0, the product is 0.

Problem: Find the product of the integers below. Then arrange the products from least to greatest and explain the pattern.

(a) $-10 \times 0 =$ (b) $-8 \times 2 =$

(c) $-4 \times -2 =$ (d) $-8 \times -2 =$

(e) $-3 \times -8 =$ (f) $+8 \times -1 =$

5–32 Multiplying More than Two Integers ★★

When multiplying integers, the order of the factors does not affect the product. There are several ways to multiply integers. You should choose the way that is easiest for you.

- You may multiply integers from left to right.
- You may multiply all the positive integers, multiply all the negative integers, and then find the product.
- You may look at the factors. If at least one of the factors is 0, the product is 0.
- You may count the number of negative integers. If this number is even, the product is positive. If this number is odd, the product is negative. (In either of the above cases, if one of the factors is 0, then the product is 0.) After finding whether the product will be positive or negative, multiply the absolute value of each number to find the product.

Problem: Write an explanation of which method of multiplying integers is easiest for you. Perhaps you use a combination of methods. If you do, explain which ones you use and why.

5–33 Multiplying More than Two Integers ★★

Multiplying integers correctly requires concentration and accuracy. Mistakes can be made in multiplication and using the correct sign.

Problem: Of the four multiplication problems in each group below, one *does not* belong with the other three. Find which should be omitted and explain your reasoning.

(a) $-3 \times -7 \times -8$ $-8 \times 2 \times -10 \times -5$

   $-6 \times -3 \times -2 \times -7$ $-1 \times -4 \times -8$

(b) $-3 \times -4 \times 0$ $-6 \times -6 \times 4$

   $8 \times -1 \times -2$ $-3 \times -3 \times -1$

(c) $-3 \times -8 \times -4$ $-1 \times 8 \times 7$

   $-6 \times -8 \times 4$ $-5 \times -3 \times 9$

5–34 Dividing Two Integers ★

The rules for dividing integers are as follows:

1. If the signs of the divisor and the dividend are the same, the quotient is positive. (Divide as you would divide whole numbers.)

2. If either the divisor or dividend is positive and the other is negative, the quotient is negative. (Divide as you would divide whole numbers.)

3. If the dividend is 0, the quotient is 0.

4. If the divisor is 0, the quotient is undefined because it is impossible to divide by 0.

Problem: Of the problems below, at least three have errors. Identify the errors and correct them.

(a) $15 \div -5 = -3$

(b) $-21 \div -7 = -3$

(c) $105 \div -5 = -21$

(d) $-166 \div -12 = 13$

(e) $-20 \div 0 = 0$

(f) $0 \div -15 = 0$

(g) $-125 \div 5 = -25$

(h) $102 \div 17 = 6$

(i) $-35 \div 7 = -5$

5–35 Dividing Two Integers ★★

A student said that if he uses the same numbers but different signs, he can make up two problems that have the same quotient. For example: $45 \div 5 = 9$ and $-45 \div -5 = 9$.

Problem: Do you think this is true for a quotient that is a negative number? Is it true if the quotient is 0? Explain your answers and provide examples.

5–36 Multiplying and Dividing Integers ★★

Multiplying and dividing are inverse operations. This means that they are opposite operations. For example:

$$-12 \times 4 = -48 \text{ is the inverse of } -48 \div 4 = -12$$

Problem: Fill in each blank with the correct number.

(a) $-12 \times \underline{\hspace{1cm}} \div -4 = -42$

(b) $\underline{\hspace{1cm}} \times -15 \div 5 = -51$

(c) $-144 \div \underline{\hspace{1cm}} \times 6 = 36$

(d) $8 \times \underline{\hspace{1cm}} \div -4 = 20$

5-37 Four Operations with Integers ★★

Only when you truly understand a topic are you able to apply your knowledge of it. This is true for mathematics as well as any other subject.

Problem: Create four problems that use integers—one for addition, one for subtraction, one for multiplication, and one for division. When you are done, exchange your problems with the problems of a partner and solve each other's integer problems.

5-38 Four Operations with Integers ★★★ G

It's nice to have help for finding the solutions to some problems. This is one of those problems.

Problem: Use the numbers 20, 10, –4, –2, and –1, and the signs +, –, ×, and ÷ to obtain the highest and lowest numbers possible. All numbers and operations must be used once for each problem, and the answers must be integers.

5-39 Simplifying Expressions ★

An expression can be compared to a phrase. To *simplify an expression,* you must combine similar terms and numbers so that the expression has the fewest possible terms.

Problem: Simplify the expressions below. If you simplified correctly, you will find a relationship between some of the answers. Describe the relationship.

(a) $3x - 4y - (-6x) + 4y + 7y + 6x$

(b) $3 + x - 2y + 7 + 3x + 4y - 5y$

(c) $x - (-3y) + 4x - 1x - 6y + 8 + 2$

(d) $7y - 4x - 10x + 21x - 2x$

(e) $8x - 3y + 4y - 9x + 10$

5–40 Simplifying Expressions ★★

To *simplify an expression* involves combining similar terms and combining numbers.

Problem: Each expression on the left of the equal sign can be simplified to the expression on the right. Fill in the missing terms.

(a) 9a + _____ + _____ + 10 = 7a + 13

(b) 2a − 4b + _____ + _____ − 3 + _____= −2a + 16b + 3

(c) −a − (−b) + c + _____ + _____ − _____ = −2a − b + 2c

(d) 3a + 2a + 6b − 4b + 10 − _____ + _____ = 2b + 2

5–41 Simplifying and Evaluating Expressions ★

While *simplifying an expression* results in an expression with fewer terms, *evaluating an expression* results in a number.

Problem: Simplify each expression below. Then evaluate the expression if a = −2, b = 3, and c = 5. What do you notice about the values of the expressions?

(a) −15 − 6c + 3b − 6c + 9 + 2a

(b) 3a − 4a + 6a − 9b + 4c − 10

(c) b − 3c + 2a − c − 4b − 6a

(d) 3c − 5a + 9b + a − b + 10

5–42 Using the Distributive Property ★

The *Distributive Property* states that if a, b, and c are real numbers, then a(b + c) = ab + ac and ab + ac = a(b + c).

Problem: One or more terms are missing below. Fill in the blanks using the Distributive Property.

(a) 4(11 − 2x) = 44 − _____

(b) −2(3x + 1) = _____ − 2

(c) 5(8 − k) − 8k = _____ −5k − 8k = _____ −_____

(d) 9 − 3(−4 + _____) + 12x = 9 + _____ − 6x + 12x = 21 + 6x

5–43 Evaluating Expressions Containing Parentheses ★★

If the expressions within parentheses cannot be simplified, use the Distributive Property and follow the order of operations.

Problem: Each expression can be simplified and evaluated for the given values of the variable. Simplify first, then evaluate to find the value of each expression. Which values are opposites?

   (a) $8(2x - 3) - 6x$ if $x = 4$

   (b) $9 - 2(4x + 5)$ if $x = -3$

   (c) $4(5 + 6x) + 3(4 - x)$ if $x = -9$

   (d) $-(6x - 1) + 3(x - 4)$ if $x = 4$

5–44 Solving One-step Equations: Transformation by Addition ★

Solving an equation is like using a balance. If you add the same number to one side of the equation, you must add the same number to the other side. This is called *transformation by addition*.

Problem: Write a word problem that can be solved by using the equation $x - 7 = 8$. Then use transformation by addition to solve the problem. Be sure to show all the steps.

5–45 Solving One-step Equations: Transformation by Subtraction ★

Transformation by subtraction involves "taking" the same amount from both sides of an equation. Think of it like this: Suppose two of your friends have the same amount of money in their wallets. If each pays $6 for a movie admission, they will still have an equal amount of money.

Problem: Which problems below can be solved by using transformation by subtraction? Use transformation by subtraction to solve them. How could you solve the other problem(s), if any?

   (a) $x + 15 = -10$ (b) $x + 11 = 12$ (c) $x + 15 = -6$

   (d) $x + 14 = 4$ (e) $x - (-13) = 13$ (f) $x + 10 = 25$

5–46 Solving One-step Equations: Transformation by Addition and Subtraction ★★

Equivalent equations are two or more equations that have the same solution. To solve an equation, try to change or transform it into an equivalent equation. Addition or subtraction are two ways this might be done.

Problem: State which problems can be solved by adding 8 to both sides. State which can be solved by subtracting 8 from both sides. Then solve each equation.

(a) $x - 8 = 15$ (b) $x - (-8) = 27$ (c) $x + 8 = -12$

(d) $x + 8 = 12$ (e) $x - 8 = -15$ (f) $x - (-8) = -24$

5–47 Solving One-step Equations: Transformation by Multiplication ★

If each side of an equation is multiplied by the same non-zero number, the resulting equation has the same solution as the original equation. This is the principle of *transformation by multiplication*.

Problem: Imagine that you are a teacher. Explain how you would teach your math class to solve $\frac{1}{4}x = 20$ using transformation by multiplication. Then solve the problem.

5–48 Solving One-step Equations: Transformation by Division ★

Dividing both sides of an equation by the same non-zero number results in an equation that has the same solution as the original equation. This is the principle of *transformation by division*.

Problem: Solve for x.

(a) $3x = 48$ (b) $6x = 48$ (c) $12x = 48$

(d) $-4x = 48$ (e) $-2x = 48$ (f) $-x = 48$

5–49 Solving One-step Equations: Transformation by Multiplication and Division ☆☆

Multiplication and division are inverse (or opposite) operations. For example, dividing a number by 2 is the same as multiplying the number by $\frac{1}{2}$. Some equations may be solved by transformation by multiplication and transformation by division, depending upon what numbers are used.

Problem: Each equation can be solved in two ways. Fill in the blanks, then solve each equation.

(a) $3x = 15$ can be solved by dividing each side by ______ or multiplying each side by ______; $x =$ ______

(b) $\frac{1}{3}x = 15$ can be solved by dividing each side by ______ or by multiplying each side by ______; $x =$ ______

5–50 Solving Two-step Equations ☆☆

Two-step equations are equations that must be solved by using two transformations.

If each side of an equation is in simplest form, then the following steps should be followed:

1. Add the same number to each side of the equation, or subtract the same number from each side of the equation.
2. Multiply or divide each side of the equation by the same non-zero number.

Problem: Of the four problems listed below, which have the same solution?

(a) $3a + 4 = -2$

(b) $2a + 14 = 0$

(c) $11 = 7 - 2a$

(d) $-3a + 18 = 39$

5–51 Solving Two-step Equations ☆☆

Creating algebra problems is sometimes more difficult than solving them.

Problem: Write a two-step equation whose solution is $x = -6$. Then write an explanation of how you created the problem.

5-52 Identifying Similar Terms ⭐

The word *coefficient* comes from two Latin words, *co* and *efficiens*, which mean "to effect together."

A *coefficient,* or a *numerical coefficient,* is the number directly in front of a variable and means multiplication. For example:

3x means 3 times x; 3 is the coefficient

x means 1 times x; 1 is the coefficient

A coefficient is an important part of the definition of similar terms, which states that similar terms are the same except for their numerical coefficients.

Problem: Two pairs of numbers below are similar terms. Name them, then rewrite the pairs of numbers that *are not* similar so that they are similar terms.

(a) $3x, 4x$ (b) $7x^2, 4x^3$ (c) $8y, 8y^2$ (d) $-x, 1x$

5-53 Solving Equations Involving Several Steps: Variables on the Same Side ⭐

The following steps will help you solve equations in which all of the variables are on the same side.

1. Simplify each side of the equation. This may involve using the Distributive Property and/or combining similar terms and numbers.

2. Add or subtract the same number from each side of the equation.

3. Multiply or divide each side of the equation by the same non-zero number.

Problem: Fill in the blanks in each step below. Then check your answers.

$$-10 + 4(3a + 10) = 18$$

$$-10 + 12a + \underline{\hspace{1cm}} = 18$$

$$12a + \underline{\hspace{1cm}} = 18$$

$$12a = \underline{\hspace{1cm}}$$

$$a = \underline{\hspace{1cm}}$$

5–54 Solving Equations Involving Several Steps: Variables on the Same Side ★★

Solving equations is a skill that has a great potential for errors, both in solving the problem and checking the solution.

Problem: The two equations below have been solved. Are they correct? Correct any mistakes you find in the equations.

(a) $a - (1 - 2a) + (a - 3) = -4$

   $a = 0$

(b) $-9 - 3(2a - 1) = -18$

   $a = 2$

5–55 Solving Equations Involving Several Steps: Variables on Both Sides ★★

Sometimes equations have variables on both sides of the equation. If this is the case, you may add or subtract the variable expression on both sides of the equation. Remember, variables represent numbers.

Problem: Which solutions to the problems below are even numbers? What are these solutions?

(a) $9n = 7n + 16$

(c) $5(2 + n) = 3(n + 6)$

(b) $12n - 84 = 5n$

(d) $5(2n + 3) - (1 - 2n) = 2(6 + 7n)$

5–56 Solving Equations Involving Several Steps: Variables on Both Sides ★★

Sometimes the final transformation is equivalent to a false statement, such as $3 = 8$ or $-6 = 15$. These equations have no root and are denoted by the symbol $\varnothing$.

If the final transformation is equivalent to a statement that is always true, such as $x = x$ or $3 = 3$, then the equation is called an *identity* and is true for all real numbers.

Problem: Which equations below have no root? Which are true for all real numbers?

(a) $3n = 2n + n$

(d) $2n - 7 = 7 + 2n$

(b) $4c = c$

(e) $3(n + 5) - 6 = 3(n + 3)$

(c) $a + 4 = 1 + a$

(f) $6a - 2(2 - a) = 4(2a - 1)$

5-57   Using Inequality Symbols   ☆

Some inequality signs are listed below:

> means "is greater than"

< means "is less than"

≥ means "is greater than or equal to"

≤ means "is less than or equal to"

≠ means "is not equal to"

Problem: Explain what you think ⊁ means? Write an inequality using this symbol.

5-58   Solving Inequalities   ☆☆

When solving inequalities, transformations can produce equivalent number sentences. A list of the transformations that produce an equivalent inequality follows.

1. Add the same real number to or subtract the same real number from each side of the inequality.
2. Multiply or divide each side of the inequality by the same positive real number.
3. Multiply or divide each side of the inequality by the same negative real number and reverse the direction of the inequality.

Problem: Supply the missing inequality symbol in each inequality.

(a) $3(x + 5) > -18$

    $3x + 15$ _____ -18

    $3x$ _____ -33

    x _____ -11

(b) $3x + -4x + 4 < 8$

    $-x + 4$ _____ 8

    $-x$ _____ 4

    x _____ -4

(c) $-3(-x + 8) - 14x \geq -2$

    $3x - 24 - 14x$ _____ -2

    $-11x$ _____ 22

    x _____ -2

5-59° Graphing Inequalities on the Number Line ★★ G

Numbers can be represented as points on the number line. Larger numbers are to the right of smaller numbers. A number is graphed on the number line by placing a dot on the line.

A dot means a number is included in the solutions to an inequality.

An empty circle means the coordinate that corresponds to the empty circle is not included in the solution.

Problem: Solve each inequality. Then match the solutions with its graph on the number line.

(a) $3(x - 4) \leq -9$

1.

(b) $5x < 4x + 6$

2.

(c) $7(2 - x) \geq -(x - 8)$

3.

(d) $1 + 2x > 7 + x$

4.

5-60 Transforming Equations ★★ G

Equations are transformed by expressing them in terms of another variable.

Problem: Identify each formula below. Then solve for the variable after the semicolon.

(a) $C = 2\pi r; r$

(b) $V = \dfrac{Bh}{3}; h$

(c) $C = \dfrac{5}{9}(F - 32); F$

(d) $P = 2(l + w); l$

5-61 Coordinate Plane ✮

The *horizontal axis,* called the x-axis, and the *vertical axis,* called the y-axis, divide the plane into four parts called *quadrants.* The point (0,0) is called the *origin* and is where the x-axis and y-axis intersect.

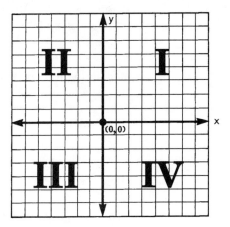

Problem: Of the four statements below, at least three are false. Identify the false statements and rewrite them to make them true.

   (a) If the x-coordinate is greater than 0, the point is always in the first quadrant.

   (b) If the y-coordinate is 0, the point is always on the y-axis.

   (c) If the signs of the x and y coordinates are the same, then the point is always in the third quadrant.

   (d) If the signs of the x and y coordinates are different, then the point could be in the fourth quadrant.

5-62 Graphing Points on the Coordinate Plane ✮

When people attend a concert, major sporting event, or theater presentation, they find their seats by checking the row and seat number on their tickets. Without having this information, they would likely have trouble finding their seats.

Problem: Explain how locating a seat in a theater or arena is similar to plotting points on a coordinate plane.

| 5-63 | **Equations and Ordered Pairs** ★★ G |

Solutions to equations that have one variable are numbers. However, the solutions to equations that have two variables are pairs of numbers. This pair is called an *ordered pair*. The first number is a value of the term that is first alphabetically, and the second number is a value of the term that is second alphabetically.

Problem: Use two variables to write three equations of which (3, −4) is a solution. Then exchange papers with the members of another group, and have them check your equations for accuracy while your group checks theirs.

| 5-64 | **Finding the Slope of a Line** ★★ |

The coordinates of pairs of points can be used to find the slope of a line. The slope of a line is always constant. If the points are on a line, the slope is always the same regardless of which points you use.

To calculate the slope of a line, use any two points (x_1, y_1) and (x_2, y_2) and substitute them into the formula: slope $= \frac{y_2 - y_1}{x_2 - x_1}$ where $(x_1 \neq x_2)$. Note, if $x_1 = x_2$, then the line has no slope because division by 0 is not defined.

Problem: Determine whether the points below are on the same line. Then find the slope. If a point is not on the line, correct it so that it is on the same line. Then find the slope.

    (a) (−1, 8), (−2, 10), (−3, 12), (−5, 16)

    (b) (0, 0), (3, 3), (4, 4), (7, 7)

    (c) (8, −3), (7, −4), (5, −5), (3, −8)

| 5-65 | **Slopes of Horizontal and Vertical Lines** ★ |

    $m = \frac{y_2 - y_1}{x_2 - x_1}$ is the formula for finding the slope of a line through two points having coordinates (x_1, y_1) and (x_2, y_2), provided that $x_1 \neq x_2$.

Problem: Write an explanation of why a horizontal line has a slope of 0. Choose two points on a horizontal line to support your reasoning. Then write an explanation of why the slope of a vertical line is undefined, and choose two points on a vertical line to support your reasoning.

5–66   Finding the Slope   ★★

Slopes are used in planning and constructing roofs of buildings. The slope of a roof is called the *pitch*. You can find the pitch of a roof with the following formula.

pitch = rise of the roof ÷ $\frac{1}{2}$ the span of the roof

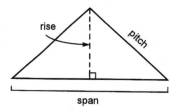

Problem: If the rise of a roof is 10 feet and the span is 24 feet, find the pitch. Compare the pitch of a roof to the slope of a line, using the formula *slope* = $\frac{rise}{run}$.

5–67   Using the Slope-intercept Method to Graph Linear Equations   ★★

One way to graph linear equations is by using the slope-intercept method described below.

1. Transform the equation into the form of y = mx + b. If there is no *y* term, then the graph is a vertical line and you should solve for *x*. This is the x-intercept.

2. Using the equation y = mx + b and assuming there is a *y* term, graph the point (0, b). This is the y-intercept.

3. Write the slope *m* as a fraction, remembering that m = rise/run.

4. From the y-intercept, count out the rise and run. Graph this point. If the rise is positive, count up. If the rise is negative, count down. If the run is positive, count to the right. If the run is negative, count to the left.

5. Draw a straight line through the y-intercept and the point plotted by using the slope. This is the graph of the line.

Problem: Four equations are graphed below. Write the equation of each in slope-intercept form. (y = mx + b)

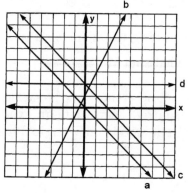

5–68   Describing Graphs of Linear Equations   ✫✫

Plumbers are sometimes paid by the hour, plus a given service charge.

Problem: EZ Plumbing charges a $40 service fee and a rate of $45 per hour. Quality Plumbing charges a $40 service fee and a rate of $50 per hour. These costs can be represented below.

EZ Plumbing: y = 45x + 40

Quality Plumbing: y = 50x + 40

x represents the number of hours worked and *y* represents the total charge.
Sketch each graph on the same coordinate plane. Then write an explanation of their similarities and differences.

5–69   Using the Graphing Method to Solve Systems of Equations   ✫

A *system of equations* is two or more equations in the same variables. To use the graphing method, graph each equation on the same graph.

If the lines intersect, the point of intersection is the solution to both equations.

If the lines are parallel, there is no solution.

If the lines coincide—meaning they are the same—there is an infinite number of solutions.

Problem: Find the point of intersection or the missing equation of the line for each graph below. Then substitute the solution into the equation to check your work.

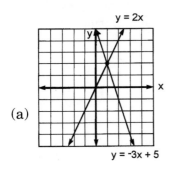

(a)

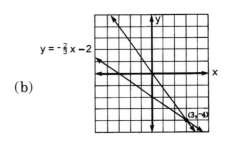

(b)

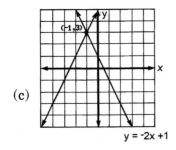

(c)

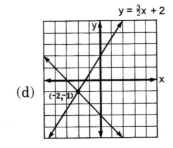

(d)

5–70 Using the Substitution Method to Solve Systems of Equations ★★

The substitution method is one of the many algebraic methods that may be used to solve a system of equations. It is most convenient to use when the coefficient of one of the variables is 1 or –1.

A list of steps used to solve equations with the substitution method follows.

1. Solve one equation for one of the variables whose coefficient is one.
2. Substitute this expression in the equation you have not used. This results in an equation in one variable. Solve this equation.
3. Substitute this expression in the equation you used in Step 1 and solve it.
4. Check your answers in both original equations.

Problem: Each system of equations can be solved by using the substitution method. Identify for which variables the substitution method could be used. Solve each system by using the substitution method.

(a) $y - 5x = 0$
$\quad\ x + y = 12$

(b) $3x + 4y = 19$
$\quad\ 4x = y + 19$

(c) $5x - y = -17$
$\quad\ 3x = 4y$

5–71 Using the Addition-or-Subtraction Method to Solve Systems of Linear Equality ★★

If the coefficients of one of the variables are the same, or if the coefficients are opposites, then the addition-or-subtraction method can be used to solve a system of equations. The method is described below.

1. Add or subtract equations to eliminate one variable. Add the equations if the coefficients of one of the variables are opposites. Subtract the equations if the coefficients of one of the variables are the same.
2. Solve the equation that results from Step 1.
3. Substitute this value in either of the original equations.
4. Check your answer in both of the original equations.

Problem: Manuel received a score of 75% on his quiz on solving systems of equations using the addition-or-subtraction method. His work is shown below. Explain how you think his teacher graded the quiz.

(a) $4x - y = 0$
$\quad\ x + y = 10$

$\quad\ 5x = 10$
$\quad\quad\ x = 2$
$\quad\quad\ y = 8$

(b) $3y - x = 0$
$\quad\ 5y - x = 18$

$\quad -2y = -18$
$\quad\quad\ y = 9$

(c) $2x - 3y = 17$
$\quad\ 2x + 3y = -1$

$\quad\ 4x = 16$
$\quad\quad\ x = 4$
$\quad\quad\ y = -3$

(d) $2x - 5y = 14$
$\quad\ 2x + 3y = 10$

$\quad -8y = 4$
$\quad\quad\ y = -\frac{1}{2}$
$\quad\quad\ x = 16\frac{1}{2}$

5–72 Using Multiplication with the Addition-or-Subtraction Method to Solve Systems of Equations ★★

To use the multiplication method to solve systems of equations, multiply one or both equations so that the coefficients of one of the variables will be the same or opposite. Then use the addition-or-subtraction method.

The multiplication method is usually used for the following conditions:

- To clear the equation(s) of fractions.
- If the coefficients of a variable are relatively prime (have a greatest common factor of 1).
- If one of the coefficients of a variable is a factor (other than 1) of the other.

Problem: There are two ways to solve $5x - 9y = 51$ and $4x + 3y = -17$.

John said to multiply the second equation by 3 and then use the addition method. Maria said to multiply the first equation by 4, the second equation by 5, and use the subtraction method. Explain which method you like better and why. Use the method you selected to solve the system of equations.

5–73 Using Positive Exponents ★★

An *exponent* is the number written in the upper right-hand corner of a number. In the expression 3^5, 5 is the exponent and 3 is the base. 3^5, which is read 3 to the fifth power, means $3 \times 3 \times 3 \times 3 \times 3 = 243$.

The word *exponent* comes from the Latin word *exponere,* which means "to expound." The base of an expression is expounded upon by the exponent.

Problem: The word "expound" means to explain by presenting in detail; in other words, to make a detailed statement about something. Explain how the base is expounded upon by the exponent in the expression 3^5.

5–74 Using Positive Exponents ★★

In the expression 2^3, 3 is the exponent and 2 is the base. The expression means that 2 is a factor three times or $2 \times 2 \times 2 = 8$.

Whenever a number or group of numbers is written in parentheses with an exponent, the number or group of numbers is the base. For example, $(8 + 2)^3$ means $10 \times 10 \times 10$ or 1,000. This is not the same as $8 + 2^3$ which means $8 + 2 \times 2 \times 2$ or 16.

Problem: Simplify each expression below.

(a) $(-5)^2$ (b) -5^2 (c) $5 + 2^4$

(d) $(5 + 2)^4$ (e) -5×3^3 (f) $(-5 \times 3)^3$

5–75 Multiplying Monomials ★★

To multiply monomials, first multiply the numerical coefficients. Then use the rule of exponents, which states $a^m \cdot a^n = a^{m+n}$ where m and n are natural numbers.

Problem: There are seven errors in the equations below. Find the mistakes and correct them.

(a) $(3a^3)(5a^5) = 8a^5$ (b) $(6x^3)(3x^3) = 18x^9$

(c) $(2c)(3c) = 5c$ (d) $(a^4)(a^3) = a^7$

(e) $(4c^2)(-2c^3) = 8c^5$ (f) $(5r^3s^2)(-3s)(2r^3s^4) = -30r^6s^6$

5–76 Multiplying Monomials ★★ G

Geometry and algebra are connected. Geometry is the study of angles and polygons, but the length of the sides of the figures may be algebraic expressions rather than simple numbers.

Problem: Show that the volume of the cylinder equals the volume of the sphere plus the volume of the cone, if the dimensions are as shown.

5–77 Powers of Monomials ★★

Rules of exponents are very specific for multiplying powers of monomials.

The rule of exponents for a power of a power is $(a^m)^n = a^{mn}$ where m and n are natural numbers.

The rule of exponents for a power of a product is $(ab)^m = a^m b^m$ where m is a natural number.

Problem: In each row, one expression does not belong because it is not equivalent to the others. Identify these expressions.

(a) $a^2 \cdot a^2 \cdot a^2$ $(a^2)^3$ a^5 a^6

(b) $16a^{12}$ $(4a^6)(4a^6)$ $(2a^3)^4$ $8a^7$

(c) $9a^2$ $-9a^2$ $-(3a)^2$ $-3a^2 \cdot 3$

(d) $2a^6b^8$ $4a^6b^8$ $2(a^3b^4)^2$ $2a^3b^4 \cdot a^3b^4$

5–78 Powers of Monomials ★★

The volume of a cube is found by raising the length of a side to the third power.

Problem: One cube has a side whose length is 2x. Another cube has a side whose length is 6x. How does the volume of the larger cube compare with the volume of the smaller cube?

5–79 Dividing Monomials ★

The rule of exponents for division states: If m and n are rational numbers and a is a real number not equal to 0, then:

$$\frac{a^m}{a^n} = a^{m-n} \qquad\qquad \frac{a^m}{a^n} = \frac{1}{a^{n-m}} \qquad\qquad \frac{a^m}{a^n} = 1$$

$$\text{if } m > n \qquad\qquad\qquad \text{if } n > m \qquad\qquad\qquad \text{if } m = n$$

Problem: Write an explanation of the rule of exponents for division. Use the examples below to help you.

$$\frac{a^5}{a^2} \qquad\qquad\qquad\qquad \frac{a^8}{a^9} \qquad\qquad\qquad\qquad \frac{a^3}{a^3}$$

5–80   Dividing Monomials   ☆

The word *billion* comes from two French words, *bi,* which means two, and *million,* which means "million." A billion may be represented as 10^9. A million may be represented as 10^6.

Problem: How many times greater is a billion than a million?

5–81   Dividing Monomials   ☆☆

Division of monomials can be checked the same way as division of whole numbers. For example, $12 \div 4 = 3$ can be checked by multiplying 4×3, which equals 12. Likewise, $\dfrac{12a^6}{3a^4} = 4a^2$ can be checked by multiplying $4a^2 \times 3a^4$, which equals $12a^6$. In each case, the quotient is multiplied by the divisor.

Problem: Check the problems below to make sure they are correct. Find the correct quotient for the incorrect problem(s). (Assume no denominator equals 0.)

(a) $\dfrac{a^9}{a^2} = a^7$ (b) $\dfrac{a^8b^3}{a^6b^4} = \dfrac{a^2}{b}$ (c) $\dfrac{24a^6b^3}{8a^2b^3} = 3a^3$ (d) $\dfrac{5a^2b^5}{25a^3b} = \dfrac{1b^4}{5a}$

5–82   Finding the GCF of Monomials   ☆

The greatest common factor of two or more monomials is the common factor that has the greatest coefficient and the greatest degree in each variable.
To find the greatest common factor (GCF) follow the steps below.

1. Find the GCF of the numerical coefficients.
2. Find the smaller power of each variable that appears in both monomials. For example, the greatest common factor of $20x^2 y$ and $15x^3$ is $5x^2$.

Problem: Match the pairs of monomials with the greatest common factor.

(a) 8x, 2xy   1. 1

(b) $14x^3y^2$, $21x^3y^3$ 2. $2x^2y^7$

(c) $2x^2$, 3y   3. xy

(d) $4x^2y^7$, $6x^5y^{10}$ 4. 2x

(e) $15x^2y^3$, $10x^2y^3$ 5. $5x^2y^3$

(f) $12x^3y^2$, 5xy   6. $7x^3y^2$

5–83   Polynomials   ✫ G

A *polynomial* is an algebraic expression that has more than one term. Polynomials have many uses. For example, they are often used to determine an individual's (or team's) score in basketball.

The following formula may be used:

$S = 3t + 2g + f$, where S is the total score, t is the number of 3-point goals, g is the number of 2-point goals, and f is the number of free throws.

Problem: Evaluate the total score for a basketball player who scored two 3-point goals, ten 2-point goals, and seven free throws. Write a polynomial to determine the score in another sport.

5–84   Adding and Subtracting Polynomials   ✫

Binomials and trinomials are special types of polynomials. Whereas a *polynomial* is an algebraic expression that has more than one term, a *binomial* has two terms, and a *trinomial* has three terms.

To add or subtract polynomials, you must first combine similar terms. A polynomial is simplified if no two of its terms are similar.

Problem: Polynomials are either added or subtracted to obtain the sum or difference. Find the missing polynomials below.

(a)
$$\begin{array}{r} 3a - 2 \\ + \underline{} \\ \hline 8a + 7 \end{array}$$

(b)
$$\begin{array}{r} 5n + 3 \\ - (\underline{}) \\ \hline 3n - 4 \end{array}$$

(c) $(7x^2 - 3xy + 4y^2) + (\underline{}) = 9x^2 - 4xy + 3y^2$

(d) $(3a - 5) - (\underline{}) = 2a - 7$

5–85 | Multiplying a Monomial by a Binomial ☆

The Distributive Property can be helpful in multiplying a monomial by a binomial. Just remember to "distribute" the monomial to each term of the polynomial.

Problem: Which problems below are correct? Correct those that are incorrect.

(a) $2(x - 5) = 2x - 10$

(b) $4x(x + 7) = 4x^2 + 28$

(c) $-3a(6a^2 - 4b) = -18a^3 - 12ab$

(d) $3x(x - 5) + 2x(4x + 3) = 11x^2 - 9x$

5–86 | Dividing a Polynomial by a Monomial ☆

To divide a polynomial by a monomial, divide each term of the polynomial by the monomial, then add the quotients.

Problem: There is at least one error in each problem below. Identify and correct each mistake.

(a) $\dfrac{18a - 24}{6} = 3a - 18$

(b) $\dfrac{27b^2 - 18b - 9}{-9} = -3b^2 - 2b - 1$

(c) $\dfrac{42s^2t^4 - 49st^2}{7st^2} = 6st^2 - 1$

(d) $\dfrac{45r^4s^2 - 75r^3s + 30r^2}{-15r^2} = 3r^2s^2 - 5s - 2$

5–87 Multiplying Binomials ★

FOIL is an acronym for:

> **F**irst
> **O**uter
> **I**nner
> **L**ast

Remembering FOIL may help you to multiply binomials.

1. Multiply the *first* terms of each binomial.
2. Multiply the *outer* terms (the first term of the first binomial by the last term of the second binomial).
3. Multiply the *inner* terms (the second term of the first binomial by the first term of the second binomial).
4. Multiply the *last* terms of each binomial.
5. Simplify.

Problem: Match each binomial with its product.

(a) $(x + 7)(x + 2)$ 1. $x^2 - 5x - 14$

(b) $(3x - 1)(3x + 1)$ 2. $9x^2 - 1$

(c) $(9x + 5)(x - 4)$ 3. $x^2 + 9x + 14$

(d) $(x - 7)(x + 2)$ 4. $9x^2 - 31x - 20$

5–88 Multiplying Binomials ★

If the length and width of a rectangle are binomials, then the area of the rectangle is the product of the binomials.

Problem: Four rectangles are drawn below. Find the area of each rectangle in terms of x.

(a)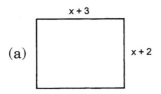

(b)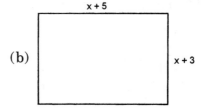

(c)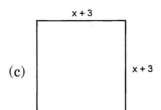

(d)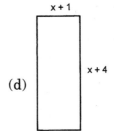

5–89   Cubes of Binomials   ★★

Cubing a binomial means to use the binomial as a factor three times. For example:

$(a + b)^3 = a^3 + 3a^2b + 3ab^2 + b^3$

$(a - b)^3 = a^3 - 3a^2b + 3ab^2 - b^3$

Problem: Substitute 4 for *a* and 6 for *b* to verify each equation above. Multiply $(a + b)(a + b)(a + b)$ to verify the first equation. Multiply $(a - b)(a - b)(a - b)$ to verify the second equation.

5–90   Perfect Powers   ★★ G

A *perfect square* is a number that is the product of a number and itself, such as $5 \times 5 = 25$. 25 is the perfect square.

A polynomial such as $a^2 + 2ab + b^2$ is a perfect trinomial square because it is the product of $(a + b)(a + b)$.

A perfect cube is the product of a number or polynomial to the third power. $2^3 = 8$ is an example of a perfect cube. Another example of a perfect cube is $(a + b)^3 = a^3 + 3a^2b + 3ab^2 + b^3$.

Problem: Make a conjecture as to the definition of a perfect power. Explain what a perfect power is and give an example.

5–91   Pascal's Triangle and the Binomial Formula   ★★★ G

Pascal's Triangle is a triangular array of numbers.

```
      1
     1 1          Note that the first and last number in each row is 1.
    1 2 1         The other numbers are obtained by adding the two
   1 3 3 1        numbers to the upper right and left of the previous row.
  1 4 6 4 1
```

Problem: How does each row of the triangle compare to the coefficients of the binomial (a + b) raised to a power? Write a general formula showing this relationship.

5–92 Factoring Differences of Squares ☆☆

"Difference" is a word that implies subtraction. A perfect square is a number (or a monomial) times itself.

Here are some examples of factoring differences of squares:

$a^2 - b^2 = (a - b)(a + b)$

$a^2 - 9 = (a - 3)(a + 3)$

$4a^2 - 25 = (2a - 5)(2a + 5)$

Problem: Explain why $(3a - 5)(3a + 5)$ is a binomial but $(3a - 5)(3a - 5)$ is a trinomial. How could you factor $9a^2 - 25$?

5–93 Factoring Squares of Binomials ☆☆

Squaring a binomial can be compared to finding the area of a square. Multiply the length of the side by itself. For example:

$(a + b)^2 = a^2 + 2ab + b^2$

$(a - b)^2 = a^2 + 2ab - b^2$

Problem: The areas of four squares are listed below. Find the length of the side. Then find the perimeter.

(a) $a^2 + 8a + 16$

(b) $a^2 - 10a + 25$

(c) $49a^2 - 56a + 16$

(d) $36a^4 - 12a^2b^3 + b^6$

5–94 Factoring Trinomials of the Form $x^2 + bx + c$ Where $c > 0$ ★★

Being able to identify patterns is an important skill in factoring binomials. For example:

$x^2 + 7x + 10 = (x + 5)(x + 2)$. Note that the 7 on the left side of the equation is equal to the sum of 5 and 2 on the right side. Also, 10 on the left side is equal to the product of 5 and 2 on the right side.

$x^2 - 11x + 10 = (x - 10)(x - 1)$. Note that the −11 on the left side of the equation is equal to the sum of −10 and −1 on the right side. Also, 10 on the left side is equal to the product of −10 and −1 on the right.

Problem: Fill in the blanks below.

(a) $x^2 + 6x + 5 = (x + \underline{\hspace{1cm}})(x + \underline{\hspace{1cm}})$

(b) $x^2 - 13x + 42 = (x - \underline{\hspace{1cm}})(x - \underline{\hspace{1cm}})$

(c) $x^2 + 9x + \underline{\hspace{1cm}} = (x + 6)(x + \underline{\hspace{1cm}})$

(d) $x^2 - \underline{\hspace{1cm}} + 45 = (x - 9)(x - \underline{\hspace{1cm}})$

5–95 Factoring Trinomials of the Form $x^2 + bx + c$ Where $c < 0$ ★★

The product of a positive number and a negative number is always negative. The sum of a positive number and a negative number may be positive, negative, or zero, depending upon the numbers. These facts are important when factoring trinomials. For example:

$x^2 - x - 12 = (x - 4)(x + 3)$. Note that the −1 (as the coefficient of x) on the left side of the equation is equal to the sum of −4 and 3 on the right side. The −12 on the left side of the equation is the product of −4 and 3 on the right side.

$x^2 + 2x - 15 = (x + 5)(x - 3)$. Note that the 2 on the left side of the equation is equal to the sum of −3 and 5 on the right side. Also, the −15 on the left side is equal to the product of 5 and −3 on the right.

Problem: Consider $x^2 + \underline{\hspace{1cm}}x - 10$. The coefficient of x is missing. List all of the coefficients of x that could be used so that the polynomial could be factored. Then factor the polynomial.

5–96 Factoring Polynomials of the Form $ax^2 + bx + c$ Where a Is an Integer > 1 ✮✮✮

Here is a method of guess-and-check for factoring polynomials.

1. List the factors of a.
2. List the factors of c.
3. Test the possibilities to see which produces the correct coefficient of x.

Problem: The area of a rectangle is $6x^2 - 7x + 2$. How does the perimeter of this rectangle compare with a rectangle whose area is $5x^2 - x - 4$? Assume $x > 0$.

5–97 Factoring by Grouping ✮✮✮

The Distributive Property, $ab + ac = a(b + c)$, is true if a is a number, monomial, or a polynomial.

For example, if a is replaced by $(x - 6)$, then $(x - 6)b + (x - 6)c = (x - 6)(b + c)$.

Remember that multiplying a polynomial by -1 results in a product that is the opposite of the polynomial.

When solving polynomials, try to group terms in ways that can be factored. Then factor out the common polynomials.

Problem: Find the missing binomial.

(a) $2(x + y) - y(x + y) = ($ _____ $)(x + y)$

(b) $x + 3y - a(3y + x) = ($ _____ $)(x + 3y)$

(c) $6a - 3ax + 7x - 14 = 3a($ _____ $) + 7($ _____ $) = (3a - 7)($ _____ $)$

(d) $4y^2 + 8xy - y - 2x = y($ _____ $) + 2x($ _____ $) = (y + 2x)($ _____ $)$

5–98 Factoring Sums and Differences of Cubes ★★★

Patterns are apparent in factoring the sums of differences of cubes. For example:

$a^3 + b^3 = (a + b)(a^2 - ab + b^2)$

$a^3 - b^3 = (a - b)(a^2 + ab + b^2)$

Problem: The formula $V = Bh$, where V is the volume, B is the area of the base, and h is the height, can be used to find the volume of a rectangular prism. Solve for V, B, or h in terms of the variable in each problem below.

(a) $B = m^2 + 3m + 9$ (b) $B =$ (c) $B =$

     $h = m - 3$ $h =$ $h =$

     $V =$ $V = z^3 + 1$ $V = 8x^3 - y^3$

5–99 Finding Square Roots ★

Finding a square root is the inverse of squaring a number. Since $4 \times 4 = 16$, then $\sqrt{16} = 4$. $\sqrt{16}$ is read, "the square root of 16."

Problem: Explain why $\sqrt{-25}$ results in an error message on your calculator. List other square roots that result in error messages.

5–100 Expressing Square Roots in Radical Form ★★

Expressions such as $\sqrt{49}$ and $\sqrt{25}$ are called *radicals*. The symbol $\sqrt{\ }$ is the radical sign. The word *radical* is taken from the Arabic word *jidr,* which means plant root, because the Arab texts explained that square numbers grow out of root numbers. For example, 49 grows out of 7. 25 grows out of 5.

The product and quotient property for square roots states that $\sqrt{ab} = \sqrt{a} \cdot \sqrt{b}$ if a and b are non-negative numbers, and $\sqrt{\dfrac{a}{b}} = \dfrac{\sqrt{a}}{\sqrt{b}}$ if a is non-negative and b is positive.

Problem: Identify which problems below are simplified incorrectly and then correct them.

(a) $\sqrt{25} = 5$ (b) $\sqrt{98} = 7\sqrt{2}$ (c) $\sqrt{.01} = \dfrac{1}{10}$ (d) $\sqrt{54} = 9\sqrt{6}$

5–101   Expressing Radical Expressions in Simplest Form   ★★

A radical is in simplest form when:

- No radicand has a square root factor other than 1. (The radicand is the expression beneath the radical sign.)
- The radicand is not a fraction.
- No radicals are in the denominator.

Problem: Mike received a grade of 80% on his quiz on simplifying radicals. The problems and his answers are shown below. Do you agree or disagree with his score? Explain your answer.

(a) $\dfrac{3}{\sqrt{7}} = \dfrac{3\sqrt{7}}{7}$

(b) $\dfrac{5\sqrt{3}}{4\sqrt{5}} = \dfrac{25\sqrt{15}}{4}$

(c) $\dfrac{9\sqrt{3}}{\sqrt{24}} = \dfrac{9}{\sqrt{8}}$

(d) $3\sqrt{\dfrac{48}{9}} = \sqrt{48}$

(e) $\sqrt{\dfrac{10}{36}} = \dfrac{\sqrt{10}}{6}$

5–102   Adding and Subtracting Radicals   ★★

To simplify sums and differences of radicals, do the following:

1. Express each radical in simplest form.
2. Add or subtract radicals with like radicands.

Problem: One expression is omitted from each problem below. Fill in the blanks with the correct expression.

(a) $6\sqrt{17} -$ _____ $+ 3\sqrt{17} = 7\sqrt{17}$

(b) $\sqrt{12} + \sqrt{3} =$ _____

(c) $\sqrt{18} +$ _____ $= 4\sqrt{2}$

(d) $-11\sqrt{27} - 7\sqrt{12} =$ _____

5–103 | Multiplying Binomials Containing Radicals ★★★

If b and d are both non-negative, then the binomials $a\sqrt{b} + c\sqrt{d}$ and $a\sqrt{b} - c\sqrt{d}$ are called *conjugates* of one another.

Conjugates differ by the sign of one term, and if a, b, c, and d are integers, the product of $(a\sqrt{b} + c\sqrt{d})(a\sqrt{b} - c\sqrt{d})$ is an integer.

Problem: Alberto claims that the product of conjugates is like multiplying binomials of the form $(a - b)$ and $(a + b)$. Explain the similarities of these two products. Use examples to support your ideas.

5–104 | Rationalizing the Denominator that Contains Radicals ★★★

Rationalizing the denominator is the process of rewriting a fraction with an irrational denominator as a fraction with a rational denominator. Conjugates are used to rationalize binomial denominators that contain radicals.

Problem: Match each fraction with its simplest form.

(a) $\dfrac{2}{\sqrt{5} - 2}$

1. $2\sqrt{5} + 4$

(b) $\dfrac{8}{3\sqrt{5} + 4}$

2. $-1 - \sqrt{5}$

(c) $\dfrac{\sqrt{5} - 4}{\sqrt{5} + 2}$

3. $\dfrac{24\sqrt{5} - 32}{29}$

(d) $\dfrac{4}{1 - \sqrt{5}}$

4. $13 - 6\sqrt{5}$

5–105 | Solving Radical Equations ★★★

A *radical equation* is an equation that has a variable in the radicand.

To solve a radical equation, isolate the radical and then square both sides. Since squaring both sides of an equation does not always result in an equation that is equivalent to the original equation, be sure to check every solution by substituting it in the original equation.

Problem: Solve for x. (*Hint:* Each radical equation has only one solution.)

(a) $\sqrt{2x + 3} = 9$ (b) $\sqrt{x^2 + 1} = 1 - x$ (c) $4\sqrt{x} = 28$

5–106 Using Polynomial Equations ★★

A *polynomial equation* is an equation whose sides are both polynomials. Polynomial equations are named by the term of the highest degree. If a ≠ 0, then:

- ax + b = 0 is a linear equation of the first degree.
- $ax^2 + bx + c = 0$ is a quadratic equation of the second degree.
- $ax^3 + bx^2 + cx + d = 0$ is a cubic equation of the third degree.

When he was only 20 years old, Carl Friedrich Gauss (1777–1855), a German-born mathematician, proved the Fundamental Theorem of Algebra, which relates the number of solutions of a polynomial equation to its degree.

Problem: Use the facts below to make a conjecture about the Fundamental Theorem of Algebra.

- A polynomial equation of degree 1 has one solution.
- A polynomial equation of degree 2 has two solutions.
- A polynomial equation of degree 3 has three solutions.
- A polynomial equation of degree *n* has *n* solutions.

Complete this sentence: Every polynomial equation has a number of solutions equal to

_____ .

5–107 Using the Zero-Product Property ★

The *Zero-Product Property* states that if the product of two or more factors is 0, at least one of the factors is 0, and if at least one of the factors is 0, then the product is 0.

Problem: Write an explanation of why this property is true. Include examples to support your explanation.

5–108 Solving Quadratic Equations by Factoring ✸✸

Many polynomial equations can be solved by factoring and applying the Zero-Product Property.

1. If the polynomial is factored, then solve it by using the Zero-Product Property.

2. If the equation is not in standard form, then transform it into standard form, factor it, and use the Zero-Product Property. In the standard form of a polynomial equation, one side equals zero and the other side is a simplified polynomial arranged in descending powers of the variable. Remember, not all polynomial equations can be factored.

Problem: Two of the problems below are correct, and two are partially correct. Identify the problems that are partially correct and correct them.

(a) $(n + 17)(n + 7) = 0$
$n = -17$
$n = -7$

(b) $x^2 - 13x + 36 = 0$
$(x - 9)(x - 4) = 0$
$x = -9$
$x = -4$

(c) $y^2 - y = 6$
$y^2 - y - 6 = 0$
$(y - 3)(y + 2) = 0$
$y = 3$
$y = -2$

(d) $m^3 - 4m = 0$
$m(m^2 - 4) = 0$
$m = 0$
$m = 4$

5–109 Solving Quadratic Equations of the Form $ax^2 = c$, $a \neq 0$ ✸✸

To solve equations of the form $ax^2 = c$ when $a \neq 0$, isolate the squared term and find the square root of $\frac{c}{a}$. If $\frac{c}{a} \geq 0$, then there are two square roots that are real numbers. If $\frac{c}{a} < 0$, then there are no real roots.

Problem: At least one problem below has no real roots. Find the real roots of the other problems. Express the answers in radical form.

(a) $x^2 = 49$ (b) $x^2 - 7 = 0$ (c) $3x^2 + 75 = 0$ (d) $2x^2 = 50$

5–110 Using Squares of Binomials and Perfect Squares ★★

Perfect squares are the result of squaring a number, such as $7^2 = 49$ or $(-3)^2 = 9$.

Squaring a binomial results in a trinomial such as $(x - 4)^2 = x^2 - 8x + 16$. The last term is a perfect square.

Problem: In all of the examples below, the square of half the coefficient of x, on the right side of the equation, and the perfect square are related. Write an explanation of this relationship.

(a) $(x + 6)^2 = x^2 + 12x + 36$

$$\left(\frac{12}{2}\right)^2 \quad 36$$

(b) $(x - 1)^2 = x^2 - 2x + 1$

$$\left(-\frac{2}{2}\right)^2 \quad 1$$

(c) $(x + a)^2 = x^2 + 2ax + a^2$

$$\left(\frac{2a}{2}\right)^2 \quad a^2$$

5–111 Using the ± Symbol ★★

William Oughtred (1574–1660), an Englishman, first used the symbol ± in his work, *Clavis Mathematicae*, which was published in 1631. The symbol is a short way of combining two mathematical sentences.

For example, $7 ± 3$ can be written as $7 + 3 = 10$ and $7 - 3 = 4$.

Problem: What two numbers are represented by the following? Express the answer in simplest form.

(a) $3 ± 15$

(b) $7 ± \sqrt{25}$

(c) $3 ± \sqrt{50}$

(d) $\dfrac{8 ± \sqrt{16}}{4}$

(e) $8 ± \sqrt{9}$

(f) $4 ± \sqrt{98}$

5–112 Solving Quadratic Equations by Completing the Square ✰✰✰

If an equation is not in the form $ax^2 = c$, $a \neq 0$, then it may be possible to transform the equation so that it is in that form. This method is called *completing the square*.

Although this method may always be used, it is easiest to use if the coefficient of the linear term is even. The procedure is detailed below.

1. Transform the equation so that the quadratic term plus the linear term equals a constant.

2. Divide each term by the coefficient of the quadratic term if it does not equal 1.

3. Complete the square.
   - Multiply the coefficient of x by $\frac{1}{2}$.
   - Square the value.
   - Add the result to both members.
   - Express one side of the equation as the square of a binomial and the other as a constant.

4. Solve the equation.

Problem: Column A contains three equations. Column B contains a number that is added to each member of the equation. Column C contains solutions to the equations. Columns B and C are mixed up. Arrange them so that they correspond to the equations in Column A.

A	B	C
$x^2 - 2x = 20$	4	$-3 + 3\sqrt{2}, -3 - 3\sqrt{2}$
$x^2 - 4x = 3$	9	$1 + \sqrt{21}, 1 - \sqrt{21}$
$x^2 + 6x - 9 = 0$	1	$2 + \sqrt{7}, 2 - \sqrt{7}$

5–113 Transforming Equations into the Form $ax^2 + bx + c = 0$, $a \neq 0$ ✰✰

All quadratic equations may be expressed in the form $ax^2 + bx + c = 0$, $a \neq 0$. This transformation is necessary so that the quadratic formula may be used.

Problem: Four quadratic equations are listed below. In which equation(s) are a, b, and c correctly identified? Correct those values that are incorrect.

(a) $x^2 + 3x = 4$

       $a = 1$
       $b = 3$
       $c = 4$

(b) $5x^2 - 6x = -10$

       $a = 5$
       $b = -6$
       $c = 10$

(c) $3x^2 + 4 = 7x$

       $a = 3$
       $b = 4$
       $c = -7$

(d) $4x^2 = 10x - 5$

       $a = 4$
       $b = -10$
       $c = 5$

5–114 Solving Quadratic Equations Using the Quadratic Formula $[(b^2 - 4ac) \geq 0]$ ★★

The Quadratic Formula is stated below:

$$\text{If } ax^2 + bx + c = 0, \, a \neq 0, \text{ then } x = \frac{-b \pm \sqrt{b^2 - 4ac}}{2a}$$

Problem: Match each equation in the first column with the correct solution in the second.

(a) $x^2 + 3x + 1 = 0$

(b) $x^2 + 4x = 6$

(c) $4x^2 + 5x + 1 = 0$

(d) $3x^2 + 4 = 7x$

1. $-1, -\frac{1}{4}$

2. $\dfrac{-3 + \sqrt{5}}{2}, \dfrac{-3 - \sqrt{5}}{2}$

3. $\frac{4}{3}, 1$

4. $-2 + \sqrt{10}, -2 - \sqrt{10}$

5–115 Using Imaginary Numbers ★★★

Sometimes problems cannot be solved if only real numbers are used. For example, $x^2 = -25$ has no solution in the set of real numbers. Equations like this fall into the realm of imaginary numbers.

Imaginary numbers use the imaginary unit i, which is defined to be the square root of -1.

$$i = \sqrt{-1} \qquad\qquad i^2 = -1$$

The solution to the equation $x^2 = -25$ is $x = \pm 5i$. Generally, if $x > 0$, then $\sqrt{-x} = i\sqrt{x}$.

Problem: Simplify each expression below.

(a) $\sqrt{-18}$ (b) $-\sqrt{-9}$ (c) $(3i)^2$ (d) $(i\sqrt{7})^2$

5–116   Using Powers of i ★★★

Some interesting patterns emerge for the powers of i as the exponent increases.

$i = \sqrt{-1}$
$i^2 = -1$
$i^3 = i^2 \cdot i = -i$
$i^4 = i^2 \cdot i^2 = 1$
$i^5 = i \cdot i^4 = i$
$i^6 = i^3 \cdot i^3 = -1$
$i^7 = i^3 \cdot i^4 = -i$

Problem: After studying the pattern above, complete the following statement. (Your choices for answers should include real and imaginary numbers.)

Any positive intergral power of i that is greater than 1 equals _____ , _____ , _____ ,

or _____ .

5–117   Using the Discriminate   ★★★ G

A quadratic equation of the form $ax^2 + bx + c = 0$, where a, b, and c are real numbers and $a \neq 0$, has a discriminate equal to $b^2 - 4ac$ which determines the number and kinds of solutions to the equation.

Study the chart below.

If $b^2 - 4ac$ is:	then the equation will have:
negative	two (conjugate) imaginary roots
zero	one real root (double real root)
positive	two different real roots

Problem: Write three quadratic equations as follows:

1. One that has a discriminate that is less than 0

2. One that has a discriminate equal to 0

3. One whose discriminate is greater than 0

Then solve each equation.

5–118 Sums and Products of Roots ✭✭✭

The sums and the products of the roots of quadratic equations in the form of $ax^2 + bx + c = 0$, $a \neq 0$, where a, b, and c are real numbers, are each related to the ratio of $\frac{-b}{a}$ or $\frac{c}{a}$.

Problem: Look at the sum of the roots of each quadratic equation below. Find the relationship and express it as a ratio involving a, $-b$, or c. Then do the same for the product of the roots.

Equation	Roots
$x^2 + 5x + 6 = 0$	$-3, -2$
$x^2 - 9x + 18 = 0$	$3, 6$
$3x^2 - 3x - 1 = 0$	$\dfrac{3 + \sqrt{21}}{6}, \dfrac{3 - \sqrt{21}}{6}$
$4x^2 - 12x + 9 = 0$	$\dfrac{3}{2}, \dfrac{3}{2}$
$3x^2 - 8x + 4 = 0$	$\dfrac{2}{3}, 2$

5–119 Graphing Quadratic Functions ✭✭✭

$y = f(x) = ax^2 + bx + c$, where a, b, and c are real numbers and $a \neq 0$, is a *quadratic function*. The graph of a quadratic function is U-shaped and is called a parabola. The word *parabola* comes from the Greek word *parabole*, which means "to throw beside."

If $a > 0$, the parabola opens upward.

If $a < 0$, the parabola opens downward.

The x-coordinate of the vertex is $\dfrac{-b}{2a}$.

The axis of symmetry is $x = \dfrac{-b}{2a}$.

Problem: Consider the parabola below. The value of b in the quadratic function is 2. The value of c is –3. Write the quadratic equation.

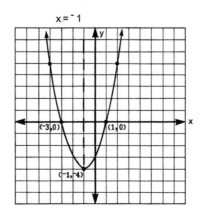

5–120 Graphing Quadratic Functions ✯✯✯ G

The function f is given by $y = f(x) = ax^2 + bx + c$ where a, b, and c are real numbers and $a \neq 0$. If x is a real number, then we know the following:

- Its graph is a parabola.
- Its vertex is the highest or lowest point on the graph, depending on the value of a.
- If $a > 0$, then the vertex is the lowest point and the parabola opens upward.
- If $a < 0$, then the vertex is the highest point and the parabola opens downward.
- The axis of symmetry is the line $x = \dfrac{-b}{2a}$.

Problem: Consider the graphs pictured below. Make a conjecture about how the y-intercept is related to c.

$y = x^2 - 4x + 3$ $y = x^2 - 4x$ $y = x^2 - 4x - 1$

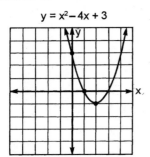 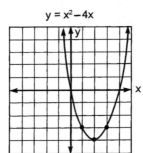 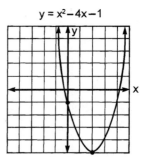

5–121 Factoring Cubic Equations of the Form $ax^3 + bx^2 = 0$ and $ax^3 + bx = 0$ Where $a \neq 0$ ✯✯✯

Some cubic, or third-degree, equations can easily be solved by factoring.

Problem: Solve each equation for x.

(a) $ax^3 + bx^2 = 0$ (b) $ax^3 + bx = 0$

5–122 Using Scientific Notation to Express Large Numbers ⋆⋆ G

A number is written in *scientific notation* when it is expressed as a product of a number greater than or equal to 1, but less than 10 with an integral power of 10. For example:

$$1,800,000 = 1.8 \times 10^6 \qquad 15,600 = 1.56 \times 10^4$$

Problem: A googol is the numeral 1 with a hundred zeroes after it. A googolplex is the numeral 1 with a googol of zeroes after it. Write a googol and a googolplex in scientific notation.

5–123 Using Scientific Notation to Express Small Numbers ⋆⋆

Extremely small numbers such as a milligram, which is 0.001 gram (a thousandth of a gram), and a picogram, which is 0.000000000001 gram (a trillionth of a gram), are difficult to picture as well as write. Recopying so many zeroes is tedious and may lead to errors. It is also easy to forget the place value names. Scientific notation eliminates these problems. For example:

1 milligram = 1×10^{-3} grams

1 picogram = 1×10^{-12} grams

23 milligrams = 0.023 grams = 2.3×10^{-2} grams

781 micrograms = 0.000781 grams = 7.81×10^{-4} grams

Problem: Pretend that you are explaining how to express 0.000081 in scientific notation. Write your explanation.

5–124 Using Scientific Notation to Express Large and Small Numbers ⋆⋆

A number is written in scientific notation when it is expressed as a product of a number greater than or equal to 1, but less than 10, and a power of 10 in exponential form.

Problem: Express each number in scientific notation.

(a) The mass of an electron: 0.0000000000000000000000000009 grams

(b) The diameter of the sun: 1,390,000,000 miles

(c) A wavelength of ultraviolet light: 0.00000136 centimeters

(d) The distance of a light year: 9,461,000,000,000 kilometers

5-125 Expressing Numbers in Standard Form ✯✯

Numbers written in scientific notation can easily be written in standard form by "moving" the decimal point.

- If the exponent is positive, move the decimal point to the right the same number of places as the exponent. For example, if the exponent is 7, move the decimal point 7 places to the right.
- If the exponent is negative, move the decimal point to the left the same number of places as the exponent.

Problem: Express each number in standard form.

(a) The number of pages of text that may be stored on a CD-ROM: 3.5×10^5

(b) The distance to the Andromeda Galaxy from Earth: 1.5×10^6 light years

(c) The length of the nucleus of a hydrogen atom: 5×10^{-7} centimeters

(d) The relationship between an attogram and a gram: 1 attogram $= 1 \times 10^{-18}$ gram

5-126 Using Negative Exponents ✯✯

A special relationship exists between the exponents of non-zero numbers: $\frac{1}{a^n} = a^{-n}$ where a ≠ 0 and n is a real number. For example:

$$\frac{1}{2^3} = 2^{-3} = \frac{1}{8} \qquad\qquad \frac{a^3}{b^4} = a^3 b^{-4}$$

Also, $a^0 = 1$ where a is a real number.

Problem: Find the missing exponent of the variable a.

(a) $\dfrac{1}{a^3} = a$ 　　　(b) $\dfrac{1}{a^3} \cdot \dfrac{1}{a^2} = a$ 　　　(c) $\dfrac{a^0}{a^{-2}} = a$ 　　　(d) $\dfrac{a^{-3}}{a^{-3}} = a$

5–127 Simplifying Expressions Using Negative Exponents ★★★

Negative exponents may be used to write expressions without using fractions. For example:

$\dfrac{a^2}{b^3}$ can be written as a^2b^{-3}

$\dfrac{15a^4}{a^7b^{-3}}$ can be written as $15a^{-3}b^3$

Problem: Rewrite the problems below without using fractions.

(a) $\dfrac{3x^{-1}}{y^5}$

(b) $\dfrac{a^{-1}b^{-2}}{b^5}$

(c) $\left(\dfrac{3}{8}\right)^{-2}$

(d) $\left(\dfrac{5a^2}{b^{-5}}\right)^2$

5–128 Quotation ★★

Jean Le Rond d'Alembert (1717–1783) discovered he had great abilities in mathematics. A specialty of his was differential equations. His later works dealt with the mathematics of music.

Problem: Write an explanation of this quote of Jean Le Rond d'Alembert: "Algebra is very generous; she often gives more than is asked of her."

Section 6

POTPOURRI

6–1 Using "Data" Correctly ☆

The word *data* is the plural form of the Latin word *datum.* Being a plural, it is important to remember to use the correct form of verbs with the word "data."

Incorrect: The data is here.

Correct: The data *are* here.

Problem: Write a math problem using the word "data" correctly. Exchange your problem for the problem of another student and solve each other's problem.

6–2 Finding the Average of a Set of Numbers ☆

The word *average* comes from the Arabic word *awariyah,* which means "damaged goods." It was originally associated with trade. If any goods of a merchant were damaged during transportation or trade, the merchant and any partners would share the losses equally. The losses were averaged among the investors.

Problem: What is the average of the first five prime numbers? Round your answer to the nearest whole number. What is the average of the first five composite numbers? Round your answer to the nearest whole number.

6–3 Finding the Mean ☆☆

Mean is another word for *average.* You can find the mean, or average, of a set of numbers by adding the numbers in a set and dividing by the amount of numbers in the set.

Problem: Each quarter, Mary's math teacher gives four tests. No test has any extra credit or bonus problems. So far, Mary's test grades are two 85s and an 89. The last test of the quarter is scheduled for next week. Can Mary obtain an "A" test average for the quarter? (In Mary's school an "A" ranges from 90 to 100.) Write an explanation of your answer.

6–4 Finding the Mean ★★

Consider the following table of western states (in the contiguous U.S.) and their record high temperatures.

State	Record High Temperature, °F
Arizona	127
California	134
Colorado	118
Idaho	118
Montana	117
Nevada	122
Oregon	119
Utah	116
Washington	118
Wyoming	114

Problem: When asked to find the mean of the record high temperatures, John took the two highest temperatures and the two lowest temperatures on the chart, added them and divided by four. He reasoned that this method should give him the mean. Do you agree or disagree? Explain your answer.

6–5 Finding Batting Averages in Baseball ★★

A *batting average* is the number of hits a batter makes, divided by the official number of at-bats he or she has had. Bases on balls and sacrifices do not count as official times at-bat. A player's batting average is expressed by a 3-digit decimal, rounded to the nearest thousandth.

Problem: What is the batting average of a player who has been to the plate 45 times, and of these times to the plate has 10 hits, 7 bases on balls, and 3 sacrifices?

6–6   Finding an On-base Average in Baseball   ⋆⋆

A player's *on-base average* is the number of times the player reaches base, divided by the number of at-bats. Unlike a batting average, the on-base average includes bases on balls, being hit by a pitch, and sacrifices as at-bats. A player's on-base average is expressed by a 3-digit decimal, rounded to the nearest thousandth.

Problem: What is the on-base average of a player who walks 5 times, singles 12 times, doubles 3 times, strikes out 5 times, grounds out 25 times, flies out 8 times, and sacrifices 2 times?

6–7   Finding a Pitcher's ERA   ⋆⋆

A pitcher's performance is measured by his or her earned run average, or ERA. An earned run is a run that is not the result of a runner reaching first base or scoring because of a fielding error. A pitcher's ERA represents the number of runs the pitcher has given up during a 9-inning game. A pitcher's ERA is rounded to the nearest hundredth.

You can find a pitcher's ERA by multiplying the number of earned runs scored by 9, then dividing by the total number of innings pitched. Note that because innings have three outs, fractions are sometimes important in determining a pitcher's ERA.

Problem: Find the ERA of a pitcher who has pitched $130\frac{1}{3}$ innings and has given up 50 earned runs. What might you conclude about a pitcher who has an ERA of 2.65 when compared with one whose ERA is 4.30?

6–8   Finding the Weighted Mean   ⋆⋆

To find the *mean,* or *average,* of a set of numbers, you add the numbers and divide by the amount of numbers you have in the set.

A *weighted mean* takes into account the importance of each quantity.

Suppose you have two test grades: 85 and 90. However, you also have a midterm exam grade of 88, which is twice as important as a single test grade. To find the weighted mean of these scores, you would add 85, 90, 88 and 88, and then divide by 4. The weighted mean is 87.75.

Problem: Using your knowledge of weighted means, find the average donation toward the purchase of a TV for Carterville's recreation center.

6 people each donated $10   4 people each donated $25
2 people each donated $50   3 people each donated $75
1 person donated $100

6–9   Average Rate   ★★★

Most average rate problems can be solved using the following formula:

Average Rate = Total Distance ÷ Total Time

Problem: A car traveled from Jackson to Smithville at an average rate of 40 miles per hour. On the return trip (along the same route), the average rate was 60 miles per hour. If the towns are 240 miles apart, what is the average rate for the round trip?

6–10   Averages in Everyday Routines   ★★ G

Averages are used often in our lives. From averages used to determine grades to average temperatures to an "average" day, the use of averages are more common than many people think.

Problem: Generate a list of situations, activities, or events in which averages are used as a form of measurement or comparison. Be ready to share your list with the members of your class.

6–11   Finding the Range   ★★

The *range* of a set of data is the difference between the greatest and least numbers in the set.
The highest point on the Earth is Mt. Everest at 29,028 feet. The lowest point is the Marianas Trench in the Northern Pacific Ocean at 38,635 feet below sea level. The distance between these points is the range of the highest and lowest points on Earth.

Problem: Find the range of the highest and lowest points on Earth. Can you conclude that the average elevation on Earth is –4803.5 feet? Explain your answer.

6–12 Finding the Range ★★

Goals are often given in ranges. A training range (or target heart rate) gives you a safety zone while exercising. It is based on your age and heartbeats per minute. Fitness experts suggest that a person should exercise at least three times per week for 20 to 30 minutes at his or her optimal heart rate.

To find your training range, do the following:

1. Start at 220 beats per minute.

2. Subtract your age.

3. Your training range is 60% to 75% of the answer in Step 2.

Problem: Find your training range. Explain why this is a range.

6–13 Finding the Range ★★

Looking only at numbers may distort your analysis of data.

Problem: The test grades of the students in Ms. Aruna's math class ranged from 100% to 20%. The student who got the 20% had been absent and had not made up the work before the test. If this student's score was eliminated, the range would be 100% to 65%. Do you think the rest of the students mastered the concepts and skills that were on the test? Explain your answer.

6–14 Finding the Mode ★★

The *mode* is the number that occurs most often in a set of data. Depending on the set of data, there can be one mode, many modes, or no mode.

Problem: Count the number of times each letter appears in the introduction to this problem. Then find the mode(s).

6–15 Median ☆

The *median* is the "middle" number when a set of data is arranged in numerical order. When there are two middle numbers, the median is their average.

Problem: When may the median of a set of data not be a member of the set of data? Explain your answer and provide an example.

6–16 Finding the Median and the Mode ☆☆

Whereas the *median* is the middle number when a set of data is arranged numerically, the *mode* is the number that appears most often.

Problem: Consider the perfect squares from 1 to 25 inclusive. List the number of factors of each perfect square, then find the median. How does the median compare with the mode?

6–17 Finding the Median and Mean ☆☆

A set of data may often be described by various statistical measures. Two of the most common of these measures are the median and mean.

Problem: The longest rivers in six of the continents are listed below. Find the median and the mean of their lengths.

Volga River, Europe: 2,290 miles

Murray River, Australia: 1,600 miles

Yangtze River, Asia: 3,400 miles

Nile River, Africa: 3,485 miles

Amazon River, South America: 4,000 miles

Mississippi River, North America: 2,330 miles

6–18 Measures of Central Tendency ✰✰

A *measure of central tendency* is a way to describe a set of numerical data. The mean, median, and mode are often referred to as measures of central tendency.

- The *mean* is the average of a set of numbers.
- The *mode* is the number that appears most often in a set of numbers.
- The *median* is the middle number of a set of numbers when the numbers are arranged in order.

Problem: Which of these three numbers—mean, median, and mode—*must* be a member of the set of data? Which of the three numbers *may* be a member of the set of data? Give an example to justify your answer.

6–19 Using the Measures of Central Tendency ✰✰

Some planets have no moons, some have one, and some have many.

Problem: The nine planets of our solar system are listed below, along with their number of moons. Find the mode, median, and mean of the set of moons.

Mercury, 0	Mars, 2	Uranus, 15
Venus, 0	Jupiter, 16	Neptune, 8
Earth, 1	Saturn, 20	Pluto, 1

6–20 Making a Frequency Table ★★

A *frequency table* consists of a category, tally marks, and frequency, which is the number of tally marks. Frequency tables are a method to organize data.

Problem: The time it takes a planet to rotate (or turn) on its axis is called a day. The Earth takes 23.9 hours to rotate, which makes our day about 24 hours long. Because the rotation rates of planets vary, the length of days on other planets are not usually as long as a day on Earth. Following are the rotation rates of the planets of our solar system, expressed in Earth time.

Mercury, 58.7 days   Saturn, 10.7 hours
Venus, 243.0 days   Uranus, 17.2 hours
Earth, 23.9 hours   Neptune, 17.0 hours
Mars, 24.6 hours   Pluto, 6.4 days
Jupiter, 9.9 hours

Complete this frequency table for the rotation of the planets.

Rotation Time	Tally	Frequency
0–24 hours		
1–10 days		
More than 10 days		

6–21 Making a Bar Graph ★

A *bar graph* uses the lengths of bars to compare data. Bars are usually separated by spaces. Bar graphs are one of the most common types of graphs.

Problem: Following are the maximum speeds of some animals for a quarter of a mile, in miles per hour. Make a bar graph to illustrate their speeds. Be sure to title your graph and label the scale. (*Hint:* Before labeling your graph, consider what the best values for the units would be.)

cat (domestic), 30 mph   giraffe, 32 mph
coyote, 43 mph   lion, 50 mph
elephant, 25 mph   rabbit, 35 mph

6–22 | Line Graphs ★★

A *line graph* displays data as points that are connected by line segments. It can be used to illustrate data that has been collected over time. As with other graphs, line graphs should have a title and vertical and horizontal axes that are clearly labeled.

Problem: Consider the line graph below. Of the following choices, which one(s) could the graph represent? Explain your answer(s).

(a) A car is traveling on a turnpike after stopping at a toll booth.

(b) A kettle of water has been placed on the stove and has been heated.

(c) Sue is walking and stops to talk to a friend.

(d) The temperature in a city for a 24-hour period.

6–23 | Line Graphs ★★

Years ago sailors used to climb up to the crow's nest of their ship so that they could see distant ships sooner. Because the Earth is a sphere, the higher the point from which a person is looking outward, the farther he or she can see.

It has been estimated that if your eye is 6 feet above the water (and your vision is normal), you can see for 3 miles. At 54 feet above the water, you can see 9 miles. At 150 feet above the water, you can see 15 miles.

Problem: Do you think a graph that shows the information above is a straight line? Explain your reasons, then sketch a graph of the data.

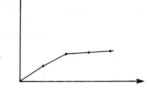

6–24   Using Stem-and-leaf Plots   ★★

A *stem-and-leaf plot* is used to condense a set of data. The greatest place value of the data forms the stem. The next greatest place value forms the leaves.

For example, a stem-and-leaf plot of the number of the New England states' electoral votes for president of the United States is pictured below.

$$\begin{array}{c|l} 0 & 34448 \\ 1 & 2 \end{array} \qquad\qquad 0\,|\,3 \text{ means 3 votes}$$

This is a shorter way of representing the number of electoral votes by state than listing each individually.

Maine, 4	New Hampshire, 4	Vermont, 3
Massachusetts, 12	Rhode Island, 4	Connecticut, 8

Problem: Construct a stem-and-leaf plot to represent the number of electoral votes of the Mid-Atlantic states.

New York, 33	New Jersey, 15	Pennsylvania, 23
Delaware, 3	Maryland, 10	

6–25   Positive, Negative, and No Relationships   ★★

Data may be graphed along the horizontal and vertical axes in a bar or broken-line graph. The data may be related in a positive manner, a negative manner, or may not be related at all.

When data is related in a positive manner, both the horizontal and vertical values increase.

When data is related in a negative manner, the horizontal values increase as the vertical values decrease.

When there is no relationship, there will be no pattern between the horizontal and vertical values.

Problem: Determine which events have a positive relationship, a negative relationship, or no relationship.

(a) Age and value of antiques

(b) Age and the value of a new car

(c) School attendance and grades

(d) Watching the news and scores on a current events quiz

(e) Practicing basketball and the ability to play well

(f) Taking a school bus and completing homework

6-26   Using Scattergrams   ★★

A *scattergram,* which is also called a *scatter plot,* suggests whether or not two sets of data are related. Whenever you graph two sets of data as ordered pairs, you make a scattergram.

To determine if the data in a scattergram are related, pretend that a line is drawn so that about half the points in the scattergram are above the line and about half are below.

If the line between the points slants up and to the right, there is a positive relationship. If the line slants downward and to the right, there is a negative relationship. If no line is apparent, there is no relationship.

Problem: Three scattergrams are shown below. Match each scattergram with the statement that describes it.

(a)   (b)   (c)

1. Field goals attempted and field goals made

2. A person's weight and the number of pets he owns

3. The outside temperature and heating costs

6-27   Step Graphs   ★★ G

A *step graph* looks like a series of steps rather than a curve or straight line. An example of a step graph is shown below.

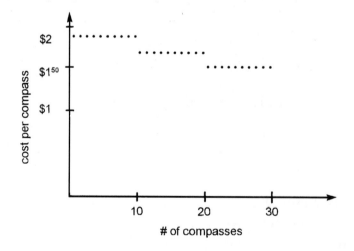

Problem: Using the step graph above, find the cost of buying 10 compasses. How does this compare with buying 11 compasses. Sketch another graph so that the horizontal axis is the same, but label the vertical axis "Total Cost."

6-28 Circle Graphs ☆

Circle graphs, also known as *pie graphs,* represent data expressed as parts of a whole. The circle equals 100%. Each part of the circle representing data is called a sector.

Problem: Ricardo is an athlete who realizes the importance of a healthy diet. He eats sensibly and follows the Food Guide Pyramid. His meals yesterday included the following servings from the different food groups:

Fats, Oils, Sweets Group: 1

Milk, Yogurt, Cheese Group: 3

Meat, Poultry, Fish, Dry Beans, Eggs, and Nuts Group: 3

Vegetable Group: 5

Fruit Group: 4

Bread, Cereal, Rice, and Pasta Group: 8

Using this data, complete the circle graph below.

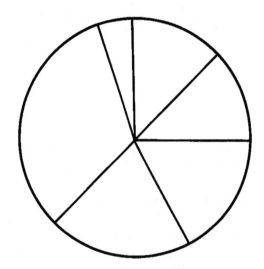

6-29 Finding Simple Probability ★★

If a day is chosen at random from the month of March, there are 31 possible outcomes. Each outcome is equally likely.

Suppose a 3 is picked. The selection of 3 is now called a favorable outcome. The likelihood, or probability, that the number 3 is picked out of 31 possible days is 3/31. This is written $P(3) = \frac{3}{31}$.

To find the probability of an event when all outcomes are equally likely, use the formula:

$$P = \text{number of favorable outcomes} \div \text{number of possible events}$$

Problem: Refer to the calendar below. State the probability of choosing each of the following.

(a) A Saturday or a Sunday

(b) St. Patrick's Day

(c) A prime number

(d) A palindrome

(e) A number that has exactly three factors

(f) A perfect square

```
        MARCH
S   M   T   W   T   F   S
        1   2   3   4   5   6
7   8   9  10  11  12  13
14  15  16  17  18  19  20
21  22  23  24  25  26  27
28  29  30  31
```

6-30 Finding Simple Probability ★★

Spinners are often used on board games. The area they spin over is usually circular and divided into equal parts called sectors. This makes each outcome equally likely. If the sectors are not equal, the probability of the events will differ.

Problem: Draw a spinner that has only the numbers 1, 2, and 3, but the following probabilities:

$P(1) = \frac{1}{4}$ $P(2) = \frac{1}{4}$ $P(3) = \frac{1}{2}$

6–31 Finding Simple Probability ⋆⋆

A standard deck of cards contains 52 cards. There are four groups of 13 cards. Each group is called a suit. Two of these suits are red and two are black. Each suit contains an ace, king, queen, jack, and the numbers 10 through 2.

Problem: Assuming a deck of cards has been shuffled, find the probability of drawing the following cards. Express your answer in simplest form.

    (a) A red card

    (b) A king

    (c) A queen or jack

    (d) An even number

    (e) The 7 of hearts

    (f) A prime number

6–32 Finding Simple Probability ⋆⋆⋆

A fast-food restaurant is trying to increase its business by sponsoring a drawing so that each customer receives a card offering a free soft drink, free sandwich, or $.25 off the next purchase. There are also cards that say, "Sorry, try again." A total of 2,000 cards will be printed.

Problem: If P ($.25 off the next purchase) = $\frac{1}{2}$, P (free soft drink) = $\frac{1}{10}$, and P (free sandwich) = $\frac{1}{20}$, find the number of cards that must be printed for each prize. How many cards that say "Sorry, try again" should be printed?

6–33 Probability of Impossible and Certain Events ⋆⋆

When it is *impossible* for an event to occur, the probability of this event is 0. When it is *certain* that an event will occur, the probability of this event is 1.

Problem: Is it possible for the probability of an event occurring to be greater than 1 or less than 0? Explain your reasoning. List three events that have a probability of 0. List three events that have a probability of 1.

6–34 Finding the Odds of an Event ★★★

Odds and probability are closely related.

To determine the odds of an event, calculate the probability of the event and then divide that by the probability of the event not occurring. The probability of an event not occurring equals 1 minus the probability of the event. You can find the odds of an event occurring by using the formula $P(A) \div [1 - P(A)]$ where A is the event.

For example, suppose you roll a die that has the numbers 1 through 6, and you want to determine the odds of rolling a 4. The odds of rolling a $4 = P(4) \div [1 - P(4)] = \frac{1}{5}$.

Problem: Consider the spinner shown here and find the odds of spinning the following.

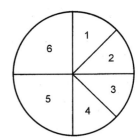

(a) A 6

(b) A number divisible by 3

(c) A prime number

(d) A number that has exactly three factors

6–35 Probability of Independent Events ★

Independent events are two or more events in which the outcome of one event does not affect the outcome of the other event(s).

To find the probability of two independent events, multiply the probability of the first event by the probability of the second event. Use the following formula:

$$P(A \text{ and } B) = P(A) \times P(B)$$

Problem: Tony's mother purchases two bags of bagels from the bagel shop. One bag contains eight plain bagels and four cinnamon–raisin bagels. The other contains two blueberry, four banana–nut, and six apple–nut bagels. What is the probability of Tony randomly selecting the following?

(a) One plain and one banana–nut bagel

(b) One plain and one apple–nut bagel

(c) One cinnamon–raisin and one blueberry bagel

(d) One onion and one apple–nut bagel

6-36 Probability of Independent Events ☆☆ G

In most games of chance that have spinners, the spinner lands on numbers. In some, however, spinners may land on names or symbols such as hearts, diamonds, clubs, or spades.

Problem: Fill in the spinners below with the correct geometric shapes so that all of the statements are correct. (The probabilities indicate the result of spinning both spinners at the same time.)

(a) Spinner A contains only triangles.
No two are congruent or similar.

(b) Spinner B contains only quadrilaterals.
No two are congruent or similar.

(c) P (each figure has no congruent sides) = $\frac{1}{12}$.

(d) P (equilateral figures) = $\frac{1}{12}$.

(e) P (two figures that have at least one right angle) = $\frac{1}{6}$.

(f) P (two figures, each of which has at least one pair of congruent sides) = $\frac{1}{2}$.

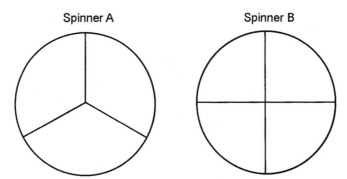

Spinner A   Spinner B

6-37 Probability of Independent Events ☆☆

Independent events are events that do not influence each other. Each toss of a coin, for example, is independent of the previous toss.

Problem: If a coin is tossed three times and comes up heads each time, what is the probability of it coming up heads on the fourth toss? Contrast this with the probability of tossing H, H, H, H. Write an explanation of why these probabilities differ.

6–38 Probability of Dependent Events ✯✯

Dependent events are two or more events in which the outcome of one event affects the outcome of the other event(s).

The probability of two dependent events is the product of the probability of the first event and the probability of the second event. You can use this formula:

$$P (A \text{ and } B) = P (A) \times P (B)$$

Problem: Suppose a jack, an ace, a 10 of hearts, and a 3 of spades are dealt to you from a standard deck of playing cards. They are not returned to the deck. Find the probability that the next two cards will be the following.

(a) 2 jacks

(b) A 5 of clubs and a 3 of diamonds

(c) An ace and a jack

(d) A 10 of clubs and a 4

6–39 Probability of Dependent Events ✯✯✯

As with independent events, the probability of two dependent events is the product of the probabilities.

Problem: Ms. Kiota collects math bonus problems. Currently there are four geometry, eight algebra, ten number theory, and three graphing questions. Each question is on a sheet of paper, folded, and placed in a jar. Every day a student from each of her five classes selects a problem and answers it. The problem is not replaced, because she does not want the problem to be redone in the same class.

What is the probability of each student selecting a number theory problem that day? Suppose each problem was returned to the jar. What is the probability that the same problem would be selected the next day in each of the classes?

6–40 Number Coincidences ★★

A fascinating thing about numbers is coincidences—events that have no seeming relationship but are linked numerically in some way. Here are some examples.

- Christopher Columbus discovered the New World in 1492, which opened the Age of Discovery. In 1942 Enrico Fermi led a team that achieved a nuclear chain reaction, which marked the beginning of the Atomic Age. By switching the middle digits of 1942, you get 1492, the year Columbus discovered the New World.
- Three American presidents—John Adams, Thomas Jefferson, and James Monroe—died on the Fourth of July.
- Harry Houdini, the master magician and escape artist, died on October 31—Halloween.

Problem: Write an explanation of your feelings about these and other mathematical coincidences of which you might be aware.

6–41 Quote about Statistics ★★

Statistics are used in providing, comparing, and analyzing information. Statistics are often the foundation of decision-making.

Problem: Explain this anonymous quote: "Some men use statistics as a tired man uses a lamppost for support rather than illumination."

6-42 | Using the Fundamental Principle of Counting ⋆⋆

The *Fundamental Principle of Counting* states that if successive choices are made, then the total number of choices is the product of the number of choices at each stage.

For example, if you have three sweaters and two pairs of jeans, then you have a total of six different outfits. Each sweater may be worn with either pair of jeans. Three sweaters times two pair of jeans equals six outfits.

Problem: A fast-food restaurant has a large menu that offers the following:

3 different sizes of fries

6 different sandwiches

3 different soft drinks, each in a small, medium, or large container

tea or coffee, each in a medium or large container

milk, regular or low-fat

3 types of salads

3 types of dressings

How many choices are there if a customer wants the following?

(a) A soft drink, sandwich, and fries

(b) A sandwich, fries, and milk

(c) A salad with dressing and tea

(d) A sandwich, salad with dressing, and coffee

6-43 | Using the Fundamental Principle of Counting ⋆⋆

The total number of possible credit card numbers greatly exceeds the total number of cardholders. (There are about 65 million cardholders.) The purpose for this is security. The larger the number of possible numbers, the smaller the chance of a sales clerk mistakenly "punching in" someone else's number when a customer is making a purchase.

Problem: A credit card has 13 digits. How many possible credit card numbers are there? Write and simplify the ratio of credit cardholders to the number of possible numbers.

6–44 Using the Fundamental Principle of Counting ★★ G

States require cars and other vehicles to be registered. Once a vehicle is registered, it receives a license plate, which is usually a combination of numbers and letters. Each vehicle receives its own license plate.

Problem: Suppose a state license plate consists of a 3-digit number followed by three letters. (Both numbers and letters may repeat.) How many license plates may be issued?

If the state needs 10 times that number, how could the license plates be changed so that enough numbers would be available? Write an explanation of your plan.

6–45 Using the Factorial Counting Rule ★

n! is the product of all counting numbers beginning with n and counting "down" to 1. You may use the formula $n! = n \times (n-1) \times (n-2) \times \ldots \times 1$. For example:

$$6! = 6 \times 5 \times 4 \times 3 \times 2 \times 1 = 720$$

The *Factorial Counting Rule* states that different items may be arranged in order n! different ways.

By definition: $0! = 1$ and $1! = 1$.

Problem: A gubernatorial candidate wants to visit the county seat of each of the 21 counties in her state. Assuming she travels from one county seat to another, how many different routes may she take to visit each county seat?

6-46 Using the Permutations Rule ✮✮

Permutations are arrangements of things in a particular order. The Factorial Counting Rule is used to determine the way a number of items can be arranged in some type of ordered sequence. If only some items (not all items) are to be included, the *Permutations Rule* can be used.

The number of permutations (or arrangements) of *n* items taken *r* at a time can be shown by the following formula:

$$_nP_r = \frac{n!}{(n-r)!}$$

Problem: Find the number of possible permutations if:

(a) A teacher must display five papers on the bulletin board. He has eight papers from which to choose.

(b) A security system with nine digits can be disarmed when three different digits are pressed. (No digit is used twice.)

(c) A building inspector only has time to visit seven out of ten buildings or offices on her list of inspection sites.

6-47 Using Circular Permutations ✮✮

P_c is the total number of *circular permutations* of *n* things arranged in a circle.

$$P_c = (n-1)!$$

In a circle, one position is fixed. The other positions are arranged around it.

Problem: The Da Silvas are planning a surprise party for their daughter. They have rented a hall and guests will sit at circular tables. Eight people will be seated at the Da Silva table, but Mr. Da Silva must be seated at a certain seat so that he has a direct view of the entrance to the parking lot. This will enable him to see his daughter arrive and alert the others. How many circular arrangements are possible?

6-48 Using the Combination Rule ⋆⋆

Combinations are a grouping of items without regard to order. The number of combinations of *n* items taken *r* at a time is $_nC_r = \dfrac{n!}{(n-r)!r!}$.

Problem: Find the number of possible combinations for the following.

(a) Three students are chosen from a group of six to form a committee.

(b) Four numbers are chosen from a group of 36 numbers.

(c) A roving reporter selects five people from 12 people who are available for an interview.

6-49 Lotteries ⋆⋆

Many states have lotteries in which people buy tickets that they hope will match the lottery's winning numbers. Prizes can sometimes be in the millions of dollars.

In a typical lottery, to win first prize the ticket holder must have the correct combination of six different numbers from 1 to 54, which are drawn randomly. The probability of winning this lottery is 1 out of 25,827,165.

Problem: Given such great odds against winning, why do you think so many people play the lottery? Explain your answer.

6-50 Palindromes ⋆

Palindromes are numbers, words, phrases, or sentences that are read the same from left to right as from right to left. Some examples of palindromes include:

Words: MOM; DAD; RADAR; WOW

Phrase: A MAN, A PLAN, A CANAL, PANAMA

Sentence: MADAM, I'M ADAM

Numbers: 22; 303; 1991

Problem: Find two palindromes whose sum is a palindrome. Find two palindromes whose difference is a palindrome. Do you think it is always true that if the sum of two palindromes is a palindrome, their difference is also a palindrome? Explain.

6–51   Palindromes   ☆

The year 2002 is a palindrome because it is the same written left to right or right to left. The year 2112 is also a palindrome.

Problem: Are there any years between 2002 and 2112 that are palindromes? What is the next year after 2112 that is a palindrome?

6–52   Palindromes   ☆☆ G

Mathematical palindromes can be both interesting and fun.
Sometimes, the product of two 2-digit palindromes is also a palindrome. For example: $11 \times 11 = 121$. Here's another: $11 \times 33 = 363$.
A product of a 2-digit palindrome and a 3-digit palindrome may also be a palindrome. For example: $22 \times 313 = 6,886$, and $11 \times 121 = 1,331$.

Problem: Find the product of two 2-digit palindromes that is also a palindrome (not using the examples above). Find the product of a 2- and 3-digit palindrome that is also a palindrome (not using the examples above).

6–53   Using Cryptarithms   ☆☆

A *cryptarithm* is a sum in which letters have been substituted for numbers. The digits 0 to 9 with different letters for different digits are used. For example:

$$
\begin{array}{r} \text{TWO} \\ + \text{TWO} \\ \hline \text{FOUR} \end{array}
\qquad
\begin{array}{r} 928 \\ + 928 \\ \hline 1856 \end{array}
$$

In the above cryptarithm T = 9, W = 2, O = 8, F = 1, U = 5, R = 6.

Problem: Solve the following cryptarithm to find the value of each letter below.

$$
\begin{array}{r} \text{ONE} \\ + \text{ONE} \\ \hline \text{TWO} \end{array}
$$

6-54 Cryptarithms ★★★ G

You can think of cryptarithms as a type of code in which letters replace numbers. Of course, all mathematical operations must be valid in cryptarithms.

Problem: Create a cryptarithm of your own and exchange it with others. Solve each other's cryptarithms.

6-55 Number Ciphers ★★

A *cipher* is a secret system of writing in which every letter is replaced with a symbol. For example, a cipher might use the code A = 1, B = 2, etc. Another example of a cipher is A = 26, B = 25, etc. (Note that not all ciphers use numbers in order to stand for letters. Of course, such ciphers can be difficult to figure out.)

Problem: Decipher the cipher below.

20-23-15   9-19   20-8-5   15-14-12-25   5-22-5-14   16-18-9-13-5

6-56 Number Ciphers ★★★

Number ciphers enable a person to write a message in code. In a number cipher, a number takes the place of a letter. For example, A = 1, B = 2, etc., or A = 5, B = 6, etc. You can select any number to replace a letter, but the numbers and letters must remain consistent in the message.

Problem: Write a short message using a number cipher. Exchange your message with the message of a partner and try to decipher each other's messages.

6-57 Using Number-box Ciphers ☆

A *number-box cipher* consists of five rows and five columns that make 25 boxes. See the example below.

	1	2	3	4	5
1	A	B	C	D	E
2	F	G	H	I	J
3	K	L	M	N	O
4	P	Q	R	S	T
5	U	V	W	xy	Z

Because there are 26 letters of the alphabet, one box must contain two letters. Since *x* is not used very often in English words, *x* and *y* may be placed in the same box. The boxes are numbered from 1 to 5 across and down.

The numbers obtained from the rows and columns represent the letters. For example, 11 (row 1, column 1) stands for A. 32 (row 3, column 2) stands for L, and 43 (row 4, column 3) stands for R.

Problem: Using the number-box cipher above, decipher the following message.

35-34-15   24-44   11   41-15-43-21-15-13-45   44-42-51-11-43-15

6-58 Using Box-and-dot Codes ☆

A *box-and-dot code* is made up of designs that look like ⌴ and/or ⌐ rotated in different positions.

The code is created on three tic-tac-toe boards. The letters A through I, J through R, and S through Z are placed in the spaces on each board. A dot is placed in each space of the second board and two dots are placed in each space of the third board. The code should look like the following:

A	B	C
D	E	F
G	H	I

J̇	K̇	L̇
Ṁ	Ṅ	Ȯ
Ṗ	Q̇	Ṙ

S̈	T̈	Ü
V̈	Ẅ	Ẍ
Ÿ	Z̈	¨

A few examples of the letters included are A = ⌴, H = ⌐, N = •, P = •⌐, T = ••, and X = ••.

Problem: Use a box-and-dot code to encode the following message.

Addition is *sum* fun.

6-59 Writing a Rebus ★★ G

A *rebus* is a word, phrase, or sentence that is written with words, numbers, and illustrations.

The rebus below states: A diameter equals 2 radii.

A 🎲 a ▭ = 2 ↗D 👁

Problem: Write a rebus to convey a math term, phrase, or principle.

6-60 Roman Numerals ★★ G

The Romans, conquerors of the ancient Mediterranean world, much of Britain, Germany, and Asia Minor, were well known for their engineering skills. Some Roman roads are still in use today. However, they never developed a practical number system. It's likely that Roman numerals were as confusing to Roman students as they are to students today.

Roman numerals are read from left to right. When a symbol of lesser value comes *before* a symbol of greater value, subtract the lesser from the greater. For example, IV = 4, which is 1 taken from 5. When a symbol of lesser value *follows* a symbol of greater value, the two values are added, such as, VI = 6, or 5 + 1. There was no symbol for 0 in Roman numerals.

Following are some examples of Roman numerals:

I = 1	X = 10
II = 2	L = 50
III = 3	C = 100
IV = 4	D = 500
V = 5	M = 1,000

Although many of the lands that had once been part of the Roman Empire continued to use the Roman number system after Rome fell, eventually the Western world came to adopt the number system developed by Arabs in the Middle East. We continue to use the Arabic system today.

Problem: Make up at least four math problems using Roman numerals. Exchange your problems with the problems created by another group and solve each other's problems. (Be sure to make a key for your answers.)

6-61 Magic Squares ✭

A *magic square* is a square array of numbers. The magic square below is of order three because it has three rows and three columns. In any magic square the sum of the numbers in each row, column, and diagonal equals the same number. In the magic square below, the sum of the numbers in each row, column, and diagonal equals 15.

6	1	8
7	5	3
2	9	4

Problem: In the magic square below, the sum of the numbers in each row, column, and diagonal equals 21. Find the missing numbers.

10		
5		
		4

6-62 Magic Squares ✭✭

Magic squares are squares whose sum of the numbers in any row, column, and diagonal equals a given number, which is called the *magic number*. Although for centuries people in many parts of the world found magic squares fascinating, it was not until the Renaissance that magic squares became popular in Europe.

Problem: Find the missing numbers in the magic square below. The magic number is 34.

		3	16
	11		5
		6	
		15	4

6-63 Magic Squares ★★

A *magic square* is a square array of numbers arranged in such a way that the sum of the numbers in each row, column, and diagonal is the same. The first record of a magic square dates to 2200 B.C. in China.

Problem: In the magic square below, the sum of the numbers in each row, column, and diagonal equals 65. Find the missing numbers.

17	24	1		15
23			14	16
		13	20	
10	12		21	3
				9

6-64 Numbers and Symbolism ★★ G

Since ancient times, many people believed that some numbers are symbolic and have meanings far greater than just the number itself. Following are the numbers 1 through 5 and some of their ancient symbolism.

1 is unique. It is the beginning of the counting numbers and is considered to be the balance point.

2 represents contradictions. A line passes through two points and extends forever in opposite directions.

3 is symbolic of the triangle. Ancient mythologies tell of three fates, three graces, and three Furies.

4 represents the four directions: north, south, east, and west.

5 represents a pentagram. The ancient Greeks considered a five-pointed star to be a secret symbol.

Problem: Make a list of expressions that include the numbers described above. Do not limit the list to math. Think of everyday terms, TV shows, and songs.

6-65 | Symbols and Letters in Math ★★

Mathematicians often use symbols and letters as a type of shorthand when writing mathematical expressions. Although using symbols and letters makes it easier to write expressions, they can sometimes be confusing.

Problem: Following are some symbols and letters used commonly in math. Identify what each means.

(a) L in the metric system

(b) l in geometric figures

(c) P in geometric figures

(d) P in number theory

(e) P as in P(A) in probability

(f) C in a temperature formula

(g) c in right triangles

(h) C in a geometry formula

6-66 | Symbols (Infinity) ★★

Sometimes symbols and numbers are confusing. A teacher explained that division by 0 is impossible. It is not defined. To show this, she used $\frac{8}{0} = \infty$ as an example.

Later she gave the class some problems to work out. One of the problems was $\frac{5}{0} = $ _____. Some students responded that $\frac{5}{0} = $ ∽.

Problem: Explain how these students misunderstood what the teacher had tried to explain. What concept was misunderstood?

6-67   Numerical Patterns   ☆

A *pattern* is a plan, diagram, or model to be followed. By finding a relationship between the items that make up the pattern, you can determine upcoming items in the pattern. Understanding patterns can be helpful in making predictions.

Problem: Find the next three numbers in the patterns below. Explain how the numbers in each pattern are related.

    (a) 1, 2, 4, 8, 16, _____, _____, _____

    (b) 1, 4, 9, 16, 25, _____, _____, _____

    (c) 100, 50, 25, 12.5, _____, _____, _____

    (d) 2, 1, 4, 3, 6, 5, _____, _____, _____

6-68   Numerical Patterns   ☆☆ G

If you understand the sequence of a mathematical pattern, it is relatively easy to predict what numbers come next.

For example, the even numbers make a simple pattern. Recognizing that the first four numbers are even, the next three can be predicted.

$$2, 4, 6, 8, \underline{\hspace{1cm}}, \underline{\hspace{1cm}}, \underline{\hspace{1cm}}$$

Problem: Create at least four numerical patterns in the manner of the example above. (You may use fractions and decimals, or even negative numbers.) When you are done, exchange your patterns with the patterns of another group and complete each other's patterns. (Be sure to make a key of your answers.)

6-69   Fibonacci Numbers   ☆☆

Leonardo of Pisa (1170–1250), known as Fibonacci, was one of the first Italian mathematicians to write about algebra. He is best known for the sequence {1, 1, 2, 3, 5, 8, 13, 21, . . . }, which is called the Fibonacci Sequence.

Fibonacci numbers are the numbers of a sequence in which successive numbers are formed by adding the two previous numbers.

Problem: Start with any two numbers and create a Fibonacci sequence. Then find the sum of the first ten numbers. How does this sum compare with the seventh term?

6–70   Figural Analogies   ★★

Figural analogies are relationships between figures. Sometimes, the figures may appear quite different, but they are related in some way. Following is an example of a figural analogy.

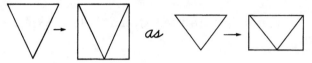

Problem: Complete the figural analogies below.

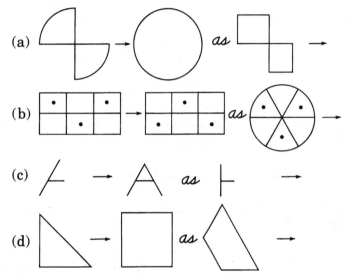

(a)

(b)

(c)

(d)

6–71   Finding the Terms of an Arithmetic Sequence   ★★

An *arithmetic sequence,* also called an *arithmetic progression,* is a special sequence in which the difference between each term and the one after it is constant.

An example of an arithmetic sequence is {7, 9, 11, 13, . . . }. The difference between each successive term is called the common difference.

The nth term of an arithmetic sequence equals a + $(n - 1)$d, where a is the first term and d is the common difference.

Problem: Consider the arithmetic sequences below. Find the designated term.

(a) {8, 12, 16, 20, . . . } 10th term

(b) {4, 3, 2, 1, . . . } 12th term

(c) {1, 3, 5, 7, . . . } 15th term

(d) {4, 4.5, 5, . . . } 8th term

6-72   Finding the Sum of an Arithmetic Series   ★★★

An *arithmetic series* is a series in which the difference between each term and the one after it is constant.

For example, $\{3 + 7 + 11 + 15 + \ldots\}$ is an arithmetic series.

The general formula for an arithmetic series is $S_n = a + (a + d) + (a + 2d) + \ldots + [a + (n - 1)d]$ where a is the first term and d is the common difference.

The sum of the n terms of an arithmetic series is $\frac{n}{2}(a + \ell)$ where ℓ is the last term.

Problem: Find the sum of the 10 terms of each arithmetic series below.

(a) $\{8 + 10 + 12 + \ldots\}$

(b) $\{7 + 10 + 13 + 16 + \ldots\}$

(c) $\{-1 + 4 + 9 + \ldots\}$

(d) $\{-5 + -4 + -3 + -2 + \ldots\}$

6-73   Finding the Terms of a Geometric Sequence   ★★

A *geometric sequence,* also called a *geometric progression,* is a special sequence in which the ratio of each term to the one after it is constant.

$\{1, 4, 16, 64, \ldots\}$ is an example of a geometric sequence. The general formula for the nth term is $u_n = ar^n$, where a stands for the first term and r stands for the common ratio. In the example at the beginning of this paragraph, the 10th term $= 1 \times 4^{10} = 1{,}048{,}576$.

Problem: Match each geometric sequence with its 10th term.

(a) $\{1, 2, 4, 8, 16, \ldots\}$ 1.   48,828,125

(b) $\{5, 25, 125, \ldots\}$ 2.   19,683

(c) $\{\frac{1}{3}, 1, 3, 9, \ldots\}$ 3.   256

(d) $\{.25, .5, 1, 2, \ldots\}$ 4.   1,024

6-74 Finding the Sum of a Geometric Series ★★★

A *geometric series* is a series in which the ratio of each term to the one after it is constant.

$\{1 + 2 + 4 + 8 + 16 + \ldots\}$ is a geometric series whose first term is 1 and the constant ratio is 2. The nth term is ar^n where a is the first term and r is the constant ratio.

If the ratio is greater than 1, then the series becomes larger and larger; it has no limit.

If the ratio is between −1 and 1, then there is a finite sum that equals $\frac{a}{1-r}$.

Problem: Find the sum (if it exists) of each geometric series.

(a) $\{1 + 2 + 4 + \ldots\}$

(b) $\{\frac{1}{3} + 1 + 3 + 9 + \ldots\}$

(c) $\{1 + .5 + .25 + .125 + \ldots\}$

(d) $\{\frac{1}{3} + \frac{1}{12} + \frac{1}{48} + \ldots\}$

6-75 Fractals ★

A *fractal* is a figure that results from iterations (repetitions) in which each new part of the figure is similar to the previous figure.

Problem: Suppose a plant has two branches. Every year each branch produces two new branches. Sketch how the plant would likely look for the first five years. (The first two years are sketched for you below.) Assuming no branch has broken or died, how many branches would be on the plant after 10 years?

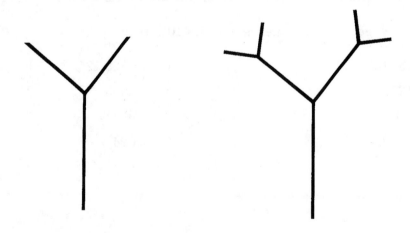

6-76 Fractals: Using the Sierpinski Triangle ★★

A *fractal* is a geometric shape that can be repeated by following the same process over and over.

Waclaw Sierpinski (1882–1969), a Polish mathematician, introduced the Sierpinski Triangle, also called the Sierpinski Gasket, which illustrates the concept of fractals. To use the Sierpinski Triangle, follow the steps below.

- *Stage 0*—Start with an equilateral triangle.

- *Stage 1*—Find the midpoint of each side and connect the midpoints, forming a "new" triangle. Shade this triangle.

- *Stage 2*—Find the midpoint of each side of each unshaded triangle and connect these midpoints, forming "new" triangles. Shade these new triangles.

The process repeats with each new figure being similar to the original.

Problem: How many unshaded triangles are in Stage 4 of Sierpinski's Triangle?

6-77 Fractals: Using the Koch Snowflake ★★★

Helge von Koch (1870–1924), a Swedish mathematician, introduced a fractal that came to be known as the Koch Snowflake. To create a Koch Snowflake, follow the steps below.

- *Stage 0*—Start with a line segment. Divide the line segment into three congruent parts.
- *Stage 1*—Remove the middle segment and replace it with an equilateral triangle. Remove the base of the triangle.
- *Stage 2*—Repeat Stage 1 with each of the four new segments.

If you start with an equilateral triangle, continue this process on each side of the triangle. The result is the Koch Snowflake.

Problem: Start with a line segment three inches long. Follow Stages 1 and 2. What is the length of the line segment?

6–78 Figurate Numbers: Triangular Numbers ☆

Figurate numbers are numbers associated with geometric figures. The ancient Greeks found figurate numbers unusual and interesting.

Triangular numbers are an example of figurate numbers that can form an arrangement that has three sides and three angles. The first three triangular numbers are shown below.

Note that the third triangular number is three more than the second.

Problem: What is the fifth triangular number? How does the fifth triangular number compare with the fourth triangular number?

6–79 Figurate Numbers: Square Numbers ☆

Figurate numbers are numbers that can be represented by geometric figures.

One type of figurate number is a *square number,* which is a number that can be represented by dots in such a way that the number of dots on each side of the square is the same. The first three square numbers are shown below.

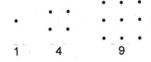

Problem: What is the tenth square number? What is another name for square numbers?

6-80 Figurate Numbers: Square Numbers ★★

A *figurate number* is a number that can be represented by a geometric figure. A *square number* is a figurate number that can be represented by the same number of dots on each side of the square. The first three square numbers are shown below.

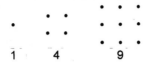

When square numbers are added, some interesting patterns emerge. One pattern relates square numbers to the sum of odd numbers.

Problem: Fill in the blanks and answer the question.

The 1st square = 1 = 1st _____ number.

The 2nd square number = 4 = sum of the 1st and 2nd _____ numbers.

The 3rd square number = 9 = sum of the _____, _____, and 3rd _____ numbers.

How could you express the seventh square number as the sum of odd numbers?

6-81 Figurate Numbers: Rectangular Numbers ★

Rectangular numbers are figurate numbers that can be represented by a rectangle that has at least two rows and two columns. Some examples are shown below.

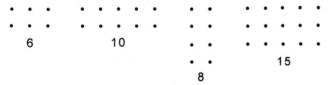

Problem: Draw a rectangular grouping of dots. Then count the dots and write the rectangular number.

6–82 | Figurate Numbers: Rectangular Numbers ☆☆

A *rectangular number* can be represented as dots in a rectangular grouping of numbers. The rectangle must have at least two rows and two columns.

Sometimes the same rectangular number may be pictured by several rectangles. Each of the rectangular groups of dots below represents the number 12.

Problem: How many ways can 18 dots be arranged? Are there any numbers, other than 1, that are not rectangular? If so, what types of numbers are they?

6–83 | Pascal's Triangle ☆

The triangular array of numbers below is called *Pascal's Triangle,* named for Blaise Pascal, a French mathematician who lived in the 17th century. After the first number (which is 1) and the numbers in the first row (which are 1, 1), each number is the sum of the numbers to its immediate upper left and immediate upper right in the previous row.

				1				Row 0
			1		1			Row 1
		1		2		1		Row 2
	1		3		3		1	Row 3
1		4		6		4		1 Row 4

. . . . . .

Problem: Continue following the described pattern to complete the triangle up to and including row 10. What are the numbers in this row?

6–84 Pascal's Triangle ★★

Pascal's Triangle is a triangular array of numbers. The first number is 1, and the numbers in the first row are 1, 1. Subsequent inner numbers of the triangle are found by adding the two numbers to the immediate left and right above them. See the example below.

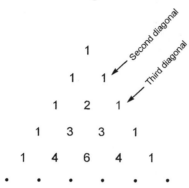

Problem: What type of numbers are listed along the second diagonal? What numbers are listed along the third diagonal? Is each row a palindrome? Explain your answer.

6–85 Pythagorean Triples ★★

The mathematicians of ancient Greece enjoyed exploring numbers and geometric figures. They were interested in finding patterns and formulas to explain the universe.

Pythagoras, one of the most famous of the ancient mathematicians, found a relationship between three numbers, *a*, *b*, and *c* in the equation $a^2 + b^2 = c^2$. The numbers that satisfy this equation are called a *Pythagorean Triple*.

To find a Pythagorean Triple, use the formula $\left(\dfrac{m^2 + 1}{2}\right)^2 = \left(\dfrac{m^2 - 1}{2}\right)^2 + m^2$ where *m* is an odd natural number.

Problem: Use the formula above to find a Pythagorean Triple. Use the Pythagorean Theorem to check your answer.

6–86 Pythagorean Triples ★★★ G

A *Pythagorean Triple* is a set of three numbers that satisfies the equation $a^2 + b^2 = c^2$.

Plato, a Greek philosopher who was also interested in mathematics, derived a formula to generate Pythagorean Triples. This formula is $(m^2 + 1)^2 = (m^2 - 1)^2 + (2m)^2$, where *m* is a natural number.

Problem: Plato's formula can be used to generate some (but not all) Pythagorean Triples. What triples satisfy the Pythagorean Theorem but cannot be obtained by using Plato's formula? Explain your answer.

6-87   The Golden Ratio ☆

The *golden ratio,* or *golden section,* is approximately 8 to 5 or 1.6. This ratio is called *phi,* the symbol for which is ϕ. The length-to-width ratio of 8 to 5 is considered esthetically pleasing and appears in nature, sculptures, paintings, and architecture, as well as every-day objects.

Problem: Find the length-to-width ratio of the following items. Which ratios are close to the golden ratio?

(a) A 3″ x 5″ note card

(b) A sheet of typing paper 8.5″ by 11″

(c) A postage stamp, $\frac{7}{8}$ ″ by 1″

(d) A CD case, $5\frac{1}{2}$ ″ by $4\frac{7}{8}$″

6-88   Line Symmetry ☆

Line symmetry is a type of symmetry where one half of a given shape covers the other half exactly. This is also called *reflexive symmetry,* because if a mirror was placed on the line of symmetry the total shape would result.

Problem: Five letters of the words LINE SYMMETRY have line symmetry. Which are they? What word(s) or what 2-digit number(s) have line symmetry?

6-89   Lines of Symmetry ☆☆

A *line of symmetry* divides a figure into two congruent parts that are mirror images of each other.

Problem: Consider the regular polygons below. Draw the lines of symmetry in each. Then make a conjecture about the number of lines of symmetry of a regular *n*-gon.

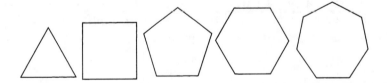

6-90 Rotational Symmetry ★★

A shape has *rotational symmetry* if, after a rotation, every point coincides with the original shape. The number of possible rotations that result in the original position of the shape is called the order of rotational symmetry.

Consider the examples below.

order of rotational symmetry is 3   order of rotational symmetry is 4

Problem: State the order of rotational symmetry of the following.

(a) A square

(b) A rectangle that is not a square

(c)

(d) A regular hexagon

6-91 Coordinate Geometry: Figures Formed by Intersecting Lines ★

Lines may intersect to form geometric figures. Some of the most common of these figures include triangles, squares, rectangles, and parallelograms.

Problem: What geometric figure is formed by the four lines whose equations are the following?

$$y = 2 \qquad x = 3 \qquad y = -2 \qquad x = -3$$

What is its area and perimeter?

6-92 Coordinate Geometry and the Distance Formula ★★

The *Distance Formula* is used to find the distance between two points in the coordinate plane. The distance is given by the Distance Formula, $d = \sqrt{(x_1 - x_2)^2 + (y_1 - y_2)^2}$ where d stands for the distance.

Problem: Three vertices of a triangle are points (0, 4), (−10, 0), and (−7, 0). What type of triangle is this? Find its perimeter and area. Round your answers to the nearest whole number.

6-93 | Coordinate Geometry and the Distance Formula ★★ G

The distance between two points on the coordinate plane may be found by using the formula $d = \sqrt{(x_1 - x_2)^2 + (y_1 - y_2)^2}$ where d is the distance.

By knowing the distance between two or more points, you may be able to determine the type of figure (if any) that is formed.

Problem: (2, 0), (5, 3), (8, 0), and (5, –3) are four points on a plane figure. What type of figure could this be? (There is more than one answer.)

6-94 | Coordinate Geometry and the Midpoint Formula ★★

The *Midpoint Formula* can be used to find the midpoint of a line segment drawn on the coordinate plane.

If (x_1, y_1) and (x_2, y_2) are two points on the coordinate plane, then the midpoint of the line segment joining these points could be found by averaging the x and y coordinates. You may use the Midpoint Formula for this.

$$\text{the midpoint} = \left(\frac{x_1 + x_2}{2}, \frac{y_1 + y_2}{2} \right)$$

Problem: Draw a rectangle with the following vertices: (–3, 2), (6, 2), (6, –4), (–3, –4). Then find the midpoint of each diagonal. Make a conjecture about the diagonals of a rectangle and write an explanation of your reasoning.

6-95 | Coordinate Geometry: Finding Congruent Figures ★★

Algebra and geometry are closely related. Apply your knowledge of congruent triangles and graphing points to solve the problem below.

Problem: Study the diagram that follows. Graph a new point F and state its coordinate so that the two triangles are congruent. (There are four answers.)

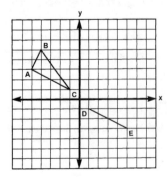

6-96 Coordinate Geometry and Lines of Symmetry ✰✰✰ G

A *line of symmetry* is a line that produces a mirror image of the original figure.

Problem: Complete the drawing below so that the dotted line is the line of symmetry. What is the equation of the dotted line?

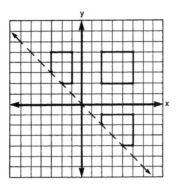

6-97 Coordinate Geometry: Using an Argand Diagram ✰✰✰

An *Argand Diagram* represents complex numbers. The diagram is similar to a graph in the coordinate plane, but the y-axis represents the imaginary part. The x-axis represents the real part. Note the diagram below.

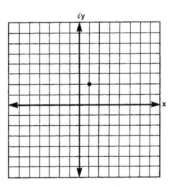

The point (1, 2) represents the complex number $(1 + 2i)$.

Problem: Graph the points that represent the following complex numbers. Then connect the points in the order you have graphed them, a to b, b to c, etc. The first point is graphed for you. What symbol have you drawn?

(a) $1 + 2i$ (b) $2 + 3i$ (c) $3 + 0i$

(d) $4 + 4i$ (e) $6 + 4i$

6–98 | Translations, Rotations, and Reflections ☆

Three rigid forms of motion are *translations, rotations,* and *reflections.*

A translation is made when a figure is moved along a straight line. Sometimes this motion is referred to as a "slide" or "glide."

A rotation is made when a figure is moved around a point. This is also called a "turn."

A reflection is made when a figure is flipped over a line. This motion is often simply called a "flip."

Problem: In the figure below, the letter M is printed in bold. It has been translated, rotated 90°, and reflected. Three lighter figures are the result of each and are labeled *a, b,* and *c.* Identify which is the result of a translation, rotation, or reflection. More than one answer is possible.

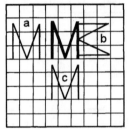

6–99 | Translations, Rotations, and Reflections ☆☆

The three rigid forms of motion are *translations* (slides or glides), *rotations* (turns), and *reflections* (flips). When a figure is moved in any of these ways, its size and shape remain the same. Only its position changes.

Problem: Consider the right triangle whose vertices are (2, 4), (2, 1), and (6, 1). Identify which triangle results from the following.

(a) A reflection over the y-axis

(b) A rotation around point (6, 1), 90° clockwise

(c) A reflection over the x-axis

(d) A rotation of 180° around the origin

(e) A reflection over the y-axis and a reflection over the x-axis

(f) A translation 5 units up

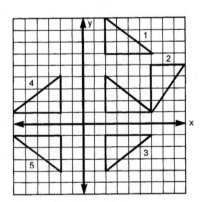

6-100 Adding Matrices ★★

A *matrix* is an array of numbers or letters in the shape of a rectangle. The order of a matrix is the size of the matrix. If a matrix has m rows and n columns, then it is of the order m by n.

Matrices (the plural of matrix) can be added, only if they have the same order, by adding corresponding elements (the numbers or letters of the matrix).

Each matrix below is 2×3.

$$\begin{pmatrix} 3 & 1 & 4 \\ 8 & 7 & 9 \end{pmatrix} + \begin{pmatrix} 2 & 1 & 5 \\ 1 & 1 & 0 \end{pmatrix} = \begin{pmatrix} 5 & 2 & 9 \\ 9 & 8 & 9 \end{pmatrix}$$

Problem: Solve for x, y, and z.

(a) $\begin{pmatrix} 1 \\ 3 \\ 8 \end{pmatrix} + \begin{pmatrix} 2 \\ 4 \\ 1 \end{pmatrix} = \begin{pmatrix} x \\ y \\ z \end{pmatrix}$

(b) $\begin{pmatrix} 1 & 0 \\ 3 & x \end{pmatrix} + \begin{pmatrix} y & 1 \\ 4 & 5 \end{pmatrix} = \begin{pmatrix} 5 & 1 \\ z & 6 \end{pmatrix}$

(c) $\begin{pmatrix} 2 & 3 & x \\ 1 & 8 & 4 \end{pmatrix} + \begin{pmatrix} y & 1 & 3 \\ 2 & 0 & 4 \end{pmatrix} = \begin{pmatrix} 8 & 4 & 5 \\ 3 & z & 8 \end{pmatrix}$

6-101 Multiplying Matrices ★★

Two matrices can be multiplied if the number of elements in the columns of the first matrix is the same as the number of elements in the rows of the second matrix. The product of two matrices is found by combining each row of the first matrix with each column of the second matrix. See the example below.

$$\begin{pmatrix} 1 & 2 & 3 \\ 4 & 5 & 6 \end{pmatrix} \times \begin{pmatrix} 8 & 2 \\ 9 & 4 \\ 1 & 6 \end{pmatrix} = \begin{pmatrix} 29 & 28 \\ 83 & 64 \end{pmatrix}$$

$1 \times 8 + 2 \times 9 + 3 \times 1 = 29$
$1 \times 2 + 2 \times 4 + 3 \times 6 = 28$
$4 \times 8 + 5 \times 9 + 6 \times 1 = 83$
$4 \times 2 + 5 \times 4 + 6 \times 6 = 64$

Problem: Multiply $\begin{pmatrix} 8 & 2 \\ 9 & 4 \\ 1 & 6 \end{pmatrix} \times \begin{pmatrix} 1 & 2 & 3 \\ 4 & 5 & 6 \end{pmatrix}$

Is multiplication of matrices commutative? Explain your answer.

6–102 Multiplying Matrices ★★★

Matrices can be multiplied, but you must follow a special procedure. The product of two matrices is found by combining each row of the first matrix with each column of the second matrix. The number of elements in the columns of the first matrix must be the same as the number of elements in the rows of the second matrix.

Problem: Create a problem using matrix multiplication. Exchange your problem with that of another student. Solve each other's problems.

6–103 Translations and Vectors ★★

A *translation* is a transformation in which a shape "slides" or "glides" without turning. Every point moves in the same direction.

Suppose a triangle has vertices at $(1, 2)$, $(3, 2)$, and $(4, 5)$, and it should be moved 5 units to the left and 4 units up. This movement can be expressed by the vector $\begin{pmatrix} -5 \\ 4 \end{pmatrix}$. To find the vertices of the resulting triangle, add $\begin{pmatrix} -5 \\ 4 \end{pmatrix}$ to each vertex. The first vertex is found for you.

$$\begin{pmatrix} 1 \\ 2 \end{pmatrix} + \begin{pmatrix} -5 \\ 4 \end{pmatrix} = \begin{pmatrix} -4 \\ 6 \end{pmatrix}$$

Problem: Find the other two vertices of the triangle. Then sketch the original triangle and its translation to verify your results.

6-104 Using Transformation Matrices: Reflection ✭✭

A transformation can be represented by a 2×2 matrix. A point (x, y) is transformed to a point (x^1, y^1) by multiplying $\begin{pmatrix} x \\ y \end{pmatrix}$ by the appropriate matrix.

The transformation matrix that produces a reflection in the x-axis is $\begin{pmatrix} 1 & 0 \\ 0 & -1 \end{pmatrix}$.

Suppose you wished to reflect the quadrilateral whose vertices are $(0, 4)$, $(3, 5)$, $(2, 8)$, and $(0, 5)$ in the x-axis. Multiply $\begin{pmatrix} 1 & 0 \\ 0 & -1 \end{pmatrix}$ by each ordered pair expressed as $\begin{pmatrix} x \\ y \end{pmatrix}$.

The first point is found for you.

$$\begin{pmatrix} 1 & 0 \\ 0 & -1 \end{pmatrix} \times \begin{pmatrix} 0 \\ 4 \end{pmatrix} = \begin{pmatrix} 0 \\ -4 \end{pmatrix}$$

Problem: Find the other three vertices of the quadrilateral. Then sketch the original quadrilateral and its reflection to verify your results.

6-105 Using Transformation Matrices: Enlargement ✭✭

An *enlargement matrix* is $\begin{pmatrix} k & 0 \\ 0 & k \end{pmatrix}$ where k is the linear scale factor and k^2 is the area scale factor.

Problem: Suppose each side of a square is to be three times as large as the original. What matrix would be used? How does the area of the new square compare with the original?

6-106 Networks ☆

A *network* is any diagram of connected lines. The three main features of a network include:

- The lines of the diagram (called *arcs*)
- The points at which the lines meet (called *nodes*)
- The areas for which the lines form a boundary (called *regions*)

A node is odd if the number of paths leaving the node is odd. A node is even if the number of paths leaving the node is even.

Problem: Classify each node in the diagrams below as even or odd.

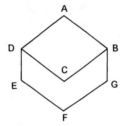 

6-107 Traceable Networks ☆☆ G

A network is *traceable* if it can be drawn without taking the pen (or pencil) off the paper or going over the same line twice.

Problem: Which networks below *cannot* be traced?

(a) 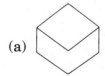   (b)   (c)   (d)

Count the number of odd and even nodes in each network. Then make a conjecture. A network is traceable if either:

(a) there are only _____ _____ nodes, or

(b) there are all _____ nodes.

6-108 Using Digraphs ✮

A *digraph* is a graph with arrows that represent a certain relationship.

Problem: The towns below are joined by a bus line. In the diagram, the → between Spotswood and South River means that a bus travels from Spotswood to South River. (The bus travels in the direction of the arrow.) Use the graph to list all of the bus routes between the towns.

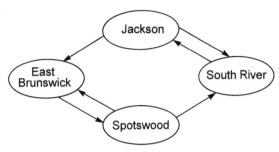

6-109 Using Digraphs ✮

A *digraph* is a graph with arrows that indicate how certain things are related.

Below are six softball teams, labeled A, B, C, D, E, and F. The symbol A → B means that team A defeated team B.

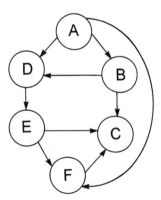

Problem: Use the digraph to answer the following. How many games were played? List the outcome of each game. Which team won the most games? Which team didn't win any games?

6-110 Using Digraphs ★★ G

Although digraphs can show relationships between quantities, like other graphs, they have limitations.

Consider the case of four girls—Elle, Lauren, Hallie, and Carla—who were making calls to plan a time to leave for a movie. In the digraph below, E → H means that Elle called Hallie.

Problem: Was each girl aware of the plans? (Several answers are possible.) Explain your answer.

6-111 Quotation about Mathematics ★★

Galileo Galilei (1564–1642), an Italian mathematician, physicist, and astronomer, was one of the foremost thinkers of his time. Although he was not a pure mathematician, his inquiries of the natural world paved the way for applied mathematics.

Problem: Write an explanation of this quote by Galileo: "Mathematics is the pen with which God has written the universe."

6-112 A Personal Quote about Mathematics ★

Although you are still in school, you have, over the years, learned much about mathematics.

Problem: Consider your knowledge of math, and especially why mathematics is important. Write a statement—a personal quote—that you would like to pass down to younger students about mathematics.

Answer Keys

SECTION 1   Whole Numbers: Theory and Operations

1-1. Answers may vary; a few include "on cloud nine," "40 winks," and "dressed to the nines"

1-2. *Biathlon,* two events—cross-country skiing and rifle shooting; *pentathlon,* five events—horseback riding, fencing, swimming, target shooting, cross-country running; *heptathlon,* seven events (for women)—hurdles, high jump, shot-put, sprint, long jump, javelin, 800-meter race; *decathlon,* 10 events—100-meter race, long jump, shot-put, hurdles, 400-meter race, 110-meter high hurdles, discus, pole vault, javelin, 1,500-meter race

1-3. 7x

1-4. 3, 6, 10, 15, 21; answers may vary. One pattern is that the sum of the first five numbers is five more than the sum of the first four numbers, or the sum of the first n numbers is n more than the sum of the n − 1 numbers.

1-5. Answers may vary; a few include single, 1; pair, 2; duo, 2; triplet, 3; quartet, 4

1-6. S, S, E. The letters are the first letter of the whole numbers written as words.

1-7. Answers may vary.

1-8. 1, 3, 6, 10, 15. Answers may vary. One pattern is that the sum of the first five numbers is four more than the sum of the first four numbers, or the sum of the first n numbers is $n − 1$ more than the sum of the n − 1 numbers.

1-9. Explanations may vary.

1-10. Answers may vary; a few possible answers include: all together, sum; product, multiplication; twice, two times; quotient, division

1-11. b and d

1-12. Smallest sum is 20 = 10 + 10; largest sum is 198 = 99 + 99

1-13. Smallest sum is 33 = 10 + 23 or 13 + 20; largest sum is 183 = 97 + 86 or 96 + 87

1-14. Answers may vary; a few include:

$$\begin{array}{r} 658 \\ +\,314 \\ \hline 972 \end{array} \qquad \begin{array}{r} 738 \\ +\,216 \\ \hline 954 \end{array}$$

1-15. Smallest sum is 39 = 15 + 24 or 14 + 25; largest sum is 176 = 94 + 82 or 92 + 84

1-16. (a) 2,858   (b) 4,122   (c) 2,280   (d) 1,069

1-17. Explanations may vary.

1-18. (a) correct   (b) 1,612   (c) 1,919   (d) 75,406

1-19.
$$\begin{array}{r} \text{(a)} \quad 6,763 \\ -\,3,929 \\ \hline 2,834 \end{array} \qquad \begin{array}{r} \text{(b)} \quad 71,146 \\ -\,4,876 \\ \hline 66,270 \end{array}$$

1-20. Nine students

1-21. 9,222. Explanations may vary.

1-22.
$$\begin{array}{r} \text{(a)} \quad 296 \\ \times\,48 \\ \hline 2368 \\ 1184 \\ \hline 14,208 \end{array} \quad \begin{array}{r} \text{(b)} \quad 183 \\ \times\,79 \\ \hline 1647 \\ 1281 \\ \hline 14,457 \end{array} \quad \begin{array}{r} \text{(c)} \quad 1,586 \\ \times\,34 \\ \hline 6344 \\ 4758 \\ \hline 53,924 \end{array} \quad \begin{array}{r} \text{(d)} \quad 2,087 \\ \times\,63 \\ \hline 6261 \\ 12522 \\ \hline 131,481 \end{array}$$

1-23.
$$\begin{array}{r} \text{(a)} \quad 438 \\ \times\,93 \\ \hline 1314 \\ 3942 \\ \hline 40,734 \end{array} \qquad \begin{array}{r} \text{(b)} \quad 5,603 \\ \times\,507 \\ \hline 39221 \\ 280150 \\ \hline 2,840,721 \end{array}$$

1-24. Problems may vary.

1-25. $431 \times 52 = 22,412$

1-26. Answers may vary; some possible answers include: $297 \times 18 = 5{,}346$; $157 \times 28 = 4{,}396$; $198 \times 27 = 5{,}346$

1-27. $832 \times 74 = 61{,}568$

1-28. a, b, and c are correct; (d) 71r40

1-29. (a) $76 \overline{\smash{)}45{,}380}$ gives 597r8

$$
\begin{array}{r}
597r8 \\
76{\overline{\smash{)}45{,}380}} \\
380 \\
\hline
738 \\
684 \\
\hline
540 \\
532 \\
\hline
8
\end{array}
$$

(b) $56 \overline{\smash{)}51{,}408}$ gives 918

$$
\begin{array}{r}
918 \\
56{\overline{\smash{)}51{,}408}} \\
504 \\
\hline
100 \\
56 \\
\hline
448 \\
448
\end{array}
$$

1-30. Explanations may vary.

1-31. (a) 46r37   (b) 80r72   (c) 1,380r5

1-32. (a) 1,235, sums of previous digits   (b) 1,369, start with 1 and multiply 1 by 3, 2 by 3, 3 by 3   (c) 4,040, subtract four, add four   (d) 9,753, subtract 2

1-33. 10 complete teams (with two players left over)

1-34. Answers may vary; one possible answer is $(5 + 6 + 9) - (1 + 2 + 3 + 7)$

1-35. 7,000 to 10,500

1-36. Two answers are possible. One person, meaning the narrator, because "met" may mean that the other group of people and animals were coming from St. Ives. If they were all going in the same direction, the answer is 2,802 which equals 1 narrator + 1 man + 7 wives + 49 sacks + 343 cats + 2,401 kits.

1-37. 1

1-38. Answers may vary.

1-39. b, c, and e

1-40. 2, 3, 5, 7, 11, 13, 17, 19, 23, 29, 31, 37, 41, 43, 47

1-41. Explanations may vary. 1 has only one factor.

1-42. $10 = 5 + 5$, also $7 + 3$; $11 = 7 + 2 + 2$, also $5 + 3 + 3$; $12 = 7 + 5$; $13 = 7 + 3 + 3$, also $5 + 5 + 3$; $14 = 7 + 7$, also $11 + 3$; $15 = 7 + 5 + 3$, also $5 + 5 + 5$

1-43. 13

1-44. 7 red stripes, 6 white stripes, 50 stars

1-45. 2099

1-46. Answers may vary. Some examples include: 2 and 3; 4 and 15; 15 and 16; 17 and 18

1-47. 3 and 17; 7 and 13. No, because 2 and 3 do not have symmetric primes. Explanations may vary.

1-48. 11 and 13; 17 and 19; 29 and 31; 41 and 43

1-49. Answers may vary. There are nine in all: 11, 13, 17, 31, 37, 71, 73, 79, and 97

1-50. 101, 107, 113, 131, 149, 151, 157, 167, 179, 181, 191, and 199

1-51. Explanations may vary.

1-52. 372

1-53. 1816

1-54. 1954

1-55. 1947

1-56. 10, 4 factors; 12, 6 factors; 14, 4 factors; 15, 4 factors; 16, 5 factors; 18, 6 factors; 20, 6 factors

1-57. Disagree. Every natural number except the number one is either prime or composite.

1-58. 1, 4, 9, 16, 25, 36, 49, 64, 81, 100

1-59. Explanations may vary.

1–60. Answers may vary. One answer is $3 \times 4 \times 5 \times 6 + 1 = 361$

1–61. 36 and 64

1–62. Four. 4 may be obtained by rolling 1 and 3 or 2 and 2. 9 may be obtained by rolling 3 and 6 or 4 and 5.

1–63. c and d

1–64. b

1–65. 48 is the number. $(1 + 2 + 3 + 4 + 6 + 8 + 12 + 16 + 24) = 76$

1–66. 6 is perfect. 12, 18, and 20 are abundant. The others are deficient.

1–67. (a) divisible by 2   (b) divisible by 2   (c) divisible by 2, 4, 8   (d) divisible by 2, 4, 8

1–68. (a) divisible by 3, 6   (b) divisible by 3, 9   (c) divisible by 3, 9   (d) divisible by 3, 6, 9, 12

1–69. 10, 5, 5, 10; examples may vary.

1–70. c and d are divisible by 7; explanations may vary

1–71. b and c

1–72. Examples may vary. One is $423 - 324 = 99$.

1–73. 1928

1–74. 144 dozen; 1,728

1–75. 12 or a multiple of 12

1–76. a is incorrect; GFC = 10

1–77.
$$\begin{array}{llll} 208\overline{)464}\;\;2r48 & 48\overline{)208}\;\;4r16 & 16\overline{)48}\;\;3 & \text{GCF} = 16 \end{array}$$

1–78. 1636

1–79. \$60

1–80. 2,484 miles

1–81. 336

1–82. c

1–83. (a) 60   (b) 50   (c) 63   (d) 493

1–84. 0, all but G; 1, B and C; 2, all except C and F; 3, all except E and F; 4, all except A, D, and E; 5, all except B and E; 6, all except B; 7, all except E, D, and G; 8, all; 9, all except E

1–85. Explanations may vary.

1–86. Explanations may vary.

SECTION 2   FRACTIONS, DECIMALS, AND PERCENTS

2–1. Explanations may vary.

2–2. Explanations may vary.

2–3. (a) 15   (b) 36   (c) 12   (d) 42

2–4. c and d

2–5. The simplified fractions are $\frac{13}{14}$, $\frac{29}{37}$, $\frac{47}{63}$, $\frac{2}{9}$. Those that must be simplified are $\frac{21}{49} = \frac{3}{7}$, $\frac{15}{21} = \frac{5}{7}$, $\frac{19}{38} = \frac{1}{2}$, $\frac{12}{18} = \frac{2}{3}$, $\frac{10}{45} = \frac{2}{9}$.

2–6. Fractions equivalent to $\frac{14}{18}$ are $\frac{21}{27}$, $\frac{63}{81}$, $\frac{77}{99}$. Fractions that can't be simplified are $\frac{20}{21}$, $\frac{9}{11}$, $\frac{3}{14}$. $\frac{7}{9}$ is in the part of the circles that overlap.

2–7. b, c, and d

2–8. (a) 37   (b) 67   (c) 47   (d) 58

2–9. The first quiz; $\frac{4}{5}$ are correct as opposed to $\frac{3}{4}$.

2–10. (a) >   (b) <   (c) correct   (d) <

2–11. $\frac{3}{5}$, $\frac{2}{5}$, $\frac{33}{75}$ are misplaced. $\frac{50}{75}$, $\frac{45}{75}$, $\frac{30}{75}$, $\frac{63}{75}$, $\frac{33}{75}$.

2-12. (a) $\dfrac{3}{7} = \dfrac{15}{35}$ (b) $\dfrac{5}{6} = \dfrac{10}{12}$

$+\dfrac{4}{5} = \dfrac{28}{35}$ $\quad\quad +\dfrac{3}{4} = \dfrac{9}{12}$

$\dfrac{43}{35} = 1\dfrac{8}{35}$ $\quad\quad \dfrac{19}{12} = 1\dfrac{7}{12}$

2-13. $1\dfrac{7}{8}$ miles

2-14. (a) $8\dfrac{7}{12} = 8\dfrac{7}{12}$ (b) $7\dfrac{5}{6} = 7\dfrac{15}{18}$

$+6\dfrac{3}{4} = 6\dfrac{9}{12}$ $\quad\quad +2\dfrac{1}{9} = 2\dfrac{2}{18}$

$14\dfrac{16}{12} = 15\dfrac{1}{3}$ $\quad\quad 9\dfrac{17}{18}$

2-15. a and c; correct answer for b is $13\dfrac{1}{20}$; correct answer for d is $9\dfrac{5}{24}$

2-16. (a) LCD = 18; answer $\dfrac{1}{18}$ (b) LCD = 15; answer $\dfrac{2}{15}$ (c) LCD = 21; answer $\dfrac{2}{21}$
(d) LCD = 40; answer $\dfrac{17}{40}$

2-17. $\dfrac{1}{12}$ cup

2-18. b and c are correct; (a) $13\dfrac{1}{4}$ (d) $4\dfrac{1}{2}$

2-19. Explanations may vary.

2-20. (a) $14\dfrac{2}{9} = 13\dfrac{11}{9}$ (b) $7\dfrac{1}{7} = 6\dfrac{8}{7}$

$-7\dfrac{2}{3} = 7\dfrac{6}{9}$ $\quad\quad -4\dfrac{3}{7} = 4\dfrac{3}{7}$

$6\dfrac{5}{9}$ $\quad\quad\quad 2\dfrac{5}{7}$

2-21. Problems may vary.

2-22. Problems may vary.

2-23. $1\dfrac{3}{4}$ feet

2-24. 5 pounds

2-25. $\dfrac{7}{2} \times \dfrac{5}{3} = 5\dfrac{5}{6}$ or $\dfrac{7}{3} \times \dfrac{5}{2} = 5\dfrac{5}{6}$

2-26. $\dfrac{1}{9}; \dfrac{1}{36}$

2-27. No. $6.25 is left. Explanations may vary.

2-28. Yes. $\dfrac{1}{3}$ of 90 = 30. Therefore, this brand of reduced-calorie dressing could have as many as 60 calories.

2-29. b is correct; (a) $\dfrac{1}{6}$ (c) $1\dfrac{5}{6}$

2-30. (a) 12 (b) $11\dfrac{1}{3}$ (c) $12\dfrac{3}{8}$

2-31. 12; explanations may vary

2-32. Problems may vary. One example is $5\dfrac{3}{4} \times 1\dfrac{1}{3} = 7\dfrac{2}{3}$. Explanations may vary.

2-33. 20

2-34. $\dfrac{7}{9} \div \dfrac{11}{2} = \dfrac{14}{99}$ or $\dfrac{7}{11} \div \dfrac{9}{2} = \dfrac{14}{99}$

2-35. b is correct; (a) $5\dfrac{1}{5}$ (c) $2\dfrac{1}{4}$

2-36. Problems may vary.

2-37. No; $2\dfrac{1}{4}$ inch nails

2-38. $12

2-39. Explanations may vary.

2-40. 513.0212 Hop should be last; 510.03 Gib should be second

2-41. Vatican City, Monaco, Gibraltar, Macao, Nauru, Tuvalu, Bermuda, San Marino, Liechtenstein, Antigua

2-42. Sullivan, 26.83; Burgess, 22.583; Webb, 21.25; Tiraboschi, 16.55

2-43. 146.5 meters

2-44. Answers may vary; some answers include $\dfrac{1}{10} = 0.1$, $\dfrac{1}{2} = 0.5$, and $\dfrac{1}{8} = 0.125$

2-45. 18.125

2-46. (a) $2\frac{3}{5}$ (b) $\frac{3}{4}$ (c) $14\frac{19}{20}$ (d) $1\frac{1}{250}$

2-47. $.1\frac{1}{9} = \frac{1}{9}$ $.6\frac{1}{3} = \frac{19}{30}$ $.7\frac{1}{7} = \frac{5}{7}$ $.33\frac{1}{3} = \frac{1}{3}$ $.83\frac{1}{3} = \frac{5}{6}$

2-48. $\frac{1}{7}, \frac{1}{9}, \frac{1}{11}$

2-49. $\frac{1}{3} = 0.\overline{3}; \frac{1}{6} = 0.1\overline{6}; \frac{1}{7} = 0.\overline{142857}; \frac{1}{9} = 0.\overline{1}; \frac{1}{11} = 0.\overline{09}; \frac{1}{12} = 0.08\overline{3}; \frac{1}{13} = 0.\overline{076923}; \frac{1}{14} = 0.0\overline{714285};$
$\frac{1}{15} = 0.0\overline{6}$

2-50. b

2-51. Yes; no. Explanations may vary.

2-52. *Whole numbers:* (a) 1 (b) 3 (c) 3 (d) 0; *tenths:* (a) 0.9 (b) 2.8 (c) 3.1 (d) 0.4; *hundredths:* (a) 0.94 (b) 2.76 (c) 3.06 (d) 0.44; *thousandths:* (a) 0.938 (b) 2.764 (c) 3.059 (d) 0.444

2-53. (a) $1.00 (b) $1.50 (c) $.67 (d) $.63

2-54. (a) 32.95 (b) 53.885 (c) 89.346 (d) 28.165

2-55. $8.75

2-56. (a) 0.92 (b) 351.4174 (c) 3.51 (d) 0.03548

2-57. *$4.11*—4 one-dollar bills, 1 dime, 1 penny; *$2.41*—2 one-dollar bills, 1 quarter, 1 dime, 1 nickel, 1 penny; *$7.00*—1 five-dollar bill, 2 one-dollar bills; *$12.40*—1 ten-dollar bill, 2 one-dollar bills, 1 quarter, 1 dime, 1 nickel

2-58. Problems may vary.

2-59. (a) 3.6×54 or 36×5.4 (b) $.78 \times .21$ (c) 324×6.5 or 32.4×65 (d) $.007 \times .03$ or $.07 \times .003$ or $7 \times .00003$. Explanations may vary.

2-60. d is correct; (a) 0.14336 (b) 1.296 (c) 6.04064

2-61. Problems may vary. One of many is $1,831.7 \times 1.4$. Explanations may vary.

2-62. Explanations may vary.

2-63. 680; explanations may vary

2-64. None are correct; (a) 7.5 (b) 0.0743 (c) 85.9 (d) 0.0085

2-65. 20 miles per gallon

2-66. Arm, 25.45 inches; leg, 36.82 inches; the average length of the human leg is longer

2-67. 35-ounce box

2-68. $289.60

2-69. Buy one get one free; explanations will vary

2-70. $10.94

2-71. $157.50

2-72. $1.05

2-73. $3.63

2-74. 10,018.8 miles

2-75. 27.12

2-76. 0.126

2-77. $13.68 \div 3.8 + 5.2 \times (2.4 - 1.7) = 7.24$

2-78. Problems may vary.

2-79. Answers may vary.

2-80. $151:42; 21:8; 2:1$

2-81. $\frac{3}{37}$; explanations may vary

2-82. *O* scale is larger; explanations may vary

2-83. a and c are proportions; (b) $\frac{5}{7} = \frac{25}{35}$ or $\frac{5}{7} = \frac{35}{49}$ (d) $\frac{10}{9} = \frac{30}{27}$ or $\frac{10}{1} = \frac{30}{3}$

2-84. Missing denominators: (a) 21 (b) 14 (c) 7 (d) 3.5. Explanations may vary. One is as the numerator of the fractions whose denominator is 7 increases, the denominator of the fractions whose numerator is 6 decreases.

2-85. 275 calories

2–86. Explanations may vary.

2–87. About 5 trees

2–88. 20 inches

2–89. Yes; a 5-inch tree on this scale = a 20-foot tree

2–90. $10,240,000

2–91. $1\frac{2}{3}$ inches; one needs to know where Washington is in relation to Jackson. Explanations may vary.

2–92. Another class that had 100% attendance joined the class

2–93. 25% of the Earth's surface is land. Asia is the largest continent, covering 7.5% of the Earth's surface. Australia is the smallest, covering 1% of the Earth's surface.

2–94. Explanations may vary. It is impossible to offer 110% off the price of auto services, because that would be more than the cost of the service. According to the sign, Fred would pay people so that he (Fred) could fix their cars.

2–95. Explanations may vary.

2–96. One-tenth, $\frac{1}{10}$, 0.1, 10%; three-fourths, $\frac{3}{4}$, 0.75, 75%; one-half, $\frac{1}{2}$, 0.5, 50%; one-eighth, $\frac{1}{8}$, 0.125, 12.5%; two-fifths, $\frac{2}{5}$, 0.4, 40%; one, 1, 1.0, 100%

2–97. 0.25, 25%; 0.375, 37.5%; 0.50, 50%; 0.625, 62.5%; 0.75, 75%; 0.875, 87.5%. Explanations may vary. Each increment of $\frac{1}{8}$ equals an increment of 0.125 or 12.5%.

2–98. $66.\overline{6}\%$ replaces 66%; $\frac{3}{8}$ replaces $\frac{3}{57}$; 10% replaces 1%; $\frac{5}{6}$ replaces $\frac{3}{8}$; $0.5\overline{5}$ replaces 0.55

2–99. Explanations may vary.

2–100. No; explanations and examples may vary. All *unit* fractions whose denominators are multiples of 3 will repeat.

2–101. (a) $\dfrac{n}{238} = \dfrac{40}{100}$, $n = 95.2$ (b) $\dfrac{n}{240} = \dfrac{34}{100}$, $n = 81.6$

(c) $\dfrac{n}{150} = \dfrac{110}{100}$, $n = 165$ (d) $\dfrac{n}{100} = \dfrac{68}{100}$, $n = 68$

2–102. d is correct; (a) 4,901.52   (b) 294.84   (c) 800.4

2–103. 3.4 mg

2–104. 12; dozen

2–105. Savings, $24; recreation and entertainment, $19; extras for lunch, $14; clothing, $29; miscellaneous expenses, $10

2–106. Explanations may vary.

2–107. (a) n = 40; 40% of 70 is 28   (b) n = $36.\overline{6}$; $36\frac{2}{3}\%$ of 60 is 22   (c) n = 200; 200% of 7 is 14
(d) n = 0.5; 0.5% of 1800 is 9

2–108. 26.7%

2–109. 25%

2–110. $58\frac{1}{3}\%$, $33\frac{1}{3}\%$, $8\frac{1}{3}\%$

2–111. (a) $\dfrac{24}{n} = \dfrac{30}{100}$, n = 80   (b) $\dfrac{6}{n} = \dfrac{5}{100}$, n = 120   (c) $\dfrac{42}{n} = \dfrac{150}{100}$, n = 28

2–112. 36 feet

2–113. About 157 calories

2–114. (a) $\dfrac{n}{100} = \dfrac{49}{56}$, n = 87.5%   (b) $\dfrac{7}{100} = \dfrac{n}{56}$, n = 3.92 ≈ 4   (c) $\dfrac{7}{100} = \dfrac{56}{n}$, n = 800

2–115. Both; reasons may vary

2–116. No. Examples may vary. If the cost of a $200 item is reduced 40%, the reduced price would be $120. If this is reduced another 10%, the cost of the item would be $108. This is not the same as a 50% discount of a $200 item, which would cost $100 after the discount.

2–117. $18

2–118. $9.64

2–119. About 7 years

2–120. $4,566\frac{2}{3}\%$

2–121. 66%

2–122. Explanations may vary.

SECTION 3 MEASUREMENT

3–1. 16.5 ft., 198 in.

3–2. (a) yd., ft.   (b) yd., in.   (c) yd., ft.   (d) yd., ft., in.   (e) yd., in.

3–3. 2,000 strides; it is inaccurate because strides vary

3–4. Tom—36 in.; Lavinia—32 in.; Commodore Nutt—29 in.

3–5. 20 in. or $1\frac{2}{3}$ ft. Answers will vary

3–6. Arm is 23 ft.; leg is 15 ft.; ear is 1 ft.; chest is 60 ft.; nose is 2 ft.; height is 50 ft.

3–7. Explanations may vary.

3–8. 3 miles

3–9. (a) 1 yd., 1 ft., 6 in.   (b) 4 yd., 6 in.   (c) 4 yd., 1 ft.   (d) 2 yd., 1 ft., 8 in.

3–10. 137.5 km

3–11. (a) 200 cm   (b) 34 mm   (c) 60 mm   (d) 1.5 cm   (e) 780 mm   (f) 9.3 km

3–12. (a) 83 mm; 8 cm 3 mm   (b) 36 mm; 3.6 cm   (c) 9 cm 2 mm; 9.2 cm   (d) 25 mm; 2 cm 5 mm

3–13. 60 cm; 1,250 cm; about 21 times

3–14. Man—194.91 cm; woman—189.73 cm

3–15. 22.965 km

3–16. 1,315 mm/sec.

3–17. About 210 ft. by 420 ft.

3–18. Answers may vary.

3–19. 16 digits

3–20. 10 ft.

3–21. Explanations may vary.

3–22. $11.51

3–23. About 320 lb.; about 5 lb.; Saturn and Uranus; explanations may vary

3–24. 180 lbs.

3–25. 1 lb.; 1.25 lb.; 1 lb. 5 oz.; 1.5 lb.; 32 oz.; 200 lb.; 0.75 T; 30,000 oz.; 2,000 lb.

3–26. a, b, d; 8 lb. 11 oz.;   (c) 7 lb. 14 oz.

3–27. (a) =   (b) >   (c) >   (d) <   (e) <   (f) =

3–28. 2,000 kg

3–29. Weight—about 220 lb.; height—27.3 in.

3–30. 1, 2, 3, 4, 5, 6, 7, 8 (in grams)

3–31. 1, 2, 3, 4, 5, 6, 7, 8, 9, 10, 11 (in grams)

3–32. (a) 8   (b) 1, 8   (c) 1, 1, 24   (d) 1, 4

3–33. (a) pt.   (b) pt., qt.   (c) gal.   (d) qt., fl. oz.

3–34. 48 fl. oz. No, a quart holds 32 fl. oz.

3–35. 8 doses

3–36. 3 qt.; 7.5%

3–37. Explanations may vary.

3–38. (a) fl. oz.   (b) gal.   (c) pt.   (d) c.

3–39. (a) 3   (b) 5   (c) 4   (d) 1   (e) 2

3–40. (a) 0.0036 kL   (b) 0.00013 L   (c) 0.4 kL   (d) 23,000 mL   (e) 0.006 L   (f) 7,300,000 mL

3–41. (a) kL, mL, L   (b) L, mL, kL   (c) 9.4, kL, L   (d) 67.3, kL, mL

3–42. 16 hours, 21 minutes

3–43. 80 days

3–44. 12:30 P.M.

3–45. (a) 15   (b) 1, 30   (c) 3, 30   (d) 210   (e) 12,600   (f) 2   (g) 9   (h) 4.5
(i) 100

3–46. When the month and the day are the same numeral, both methods of recording the date are the same. For example, 2/2/99. Any date greater than 12 makes no sense in the system used in England. For example 8/13/99 is August 13 in the U.S., but this makes no sense in England.

3–47. Explanations may vary.

3–48. Students should disagree. Explanations may vary.

3–49. The letter m.

3–50. Explanations may vary.

3–51. Explanations may vary.

3–52. Yes, it's divisible by 400.

3–53. 8 A.M. on Wednesday

3–54. Words may vary; some include: biannual, twice a year; biennial, every two years; semiannual is a synonym for biannual

3–55. Canary; about 8 times. Explanations may vary. Some examples might include exercise or excitement.

3–56. There are 60 seconds in a minute. The ten-second count is more accurate than the six-second count. No. The longer the time, the more accurate the heartbeat.

3–57. (24 hours 50 minutes) ÷ 2 = 12 hours, 25 minutes. Storms, winds, and variations in coastlines will influence the timing and height of the tides. Use tide charts in nautical references.

3–58. (a) 80, 20   (b) 6   (c) 4, 9   (d) 2, 2

3–59. 1.05 seconds; 7 seconds; the period is shorter

3–60. b, e, a, c, d, f, g

3–61. Celsius; explanations may vary

3–62. Vinegar, 2° F; gasoline, –70° F; salt, 1,474° F; sugar, 300° F

3–63. –459.67° F; the second formula; explanations may vary

3–64. (a) 620.6° F   (b) 140° F   (c) 104° F   (d) 12.2° F

3–65. (a) 80° C   (b) 45° C   (c) about 0.6° C   (d) about –11° C

3–66. 72° F; about 70° F; about 66° F; chirps are less frequent

3–67. Explanations may vary.

3–68. 3 in.

3–69. $\frac{5}{36}$″ or 3.5 mm; $\frac{1}{4}$″ or 6.3 mm

3–70. (a) 655,360 bytes   (b) 1,024 kilobytes   (c) 26,624 kilobytes   (d) 976,562.5 kilobytes

3–71. 260,000 astronomical units; 24,180,000,000,000 miles

3–72. 25,200 miles per hour; about 33 times as fast

3–73. About 4.25 light years; 57,077.62 years

3–74. About 3.2 light years; about 0.3 parsecs

3–75. About 100 times

3–76. Explanations may vary.

SECTION 4   GEOMETRY

4–1. (a) line segment, $\overline{CD}$, 2   (b) line, $\overleftrightarrow{XY}$, 0   (c) ray, $\overrightarrow{EF}$, 1   (d) ray, $\overrightarrow{NM}$, 1

4–2. $\overleftrightarrow{AB}$ or $\overleftrightarrow{AC}$, $\overline{FG}$, $\overline{DB}$; $\overline{AB}$, $\overline{GE}$, $\overline{AC}$ or $\overline{AB}$; $\overline{BC}$, $\overline{BE}$, $\overline{BC}$; $\overline{CE}$, $\overline{ED}$, $\overline{CD}$; $\overline{AC}$, $\overline{DG}$, $\overrightarrow{CA}$ or $\overrightarrow{CB}$; $\overline{FE}$, $\overline{GB}$, $\overline{BA}$; $\overline{DF}$, $\overline{FA}$, $\overline{DA}$

4–3. Line a, line AB, line BA; segment AB, segment BA. A segment has two endpoints. A line has no endpoints.

4-4. b, c, d are incorrect; (b) $\overline{AB} + \overline{BC} = \overline{AC}$ or AB + BC = AC   (c) 2AB = BC   (d) AB + BC + CD = 30

4-5. The number of points in a line segment is infinite, yet the segment has a finite distance.

4-6.

E   C   A   D   B   F

4-7.

A   C   B   D

(a) $\overline{CB}$ (b) C   (c) ∅   (d) $\overleftrightarrow{AD}$ (e) $\overrightarrow{BD}$ (f) $\overline{AD}$

4-8. (a) ∠DBC or ∠DBE   (b) $\overline{AE}$ (c) $\overrightarrow{AE}$ (d) $\overline{AE}$ (e) ∠ABD or ∠DBA
(f) $\overleftrightarrow{AE}$

4-9. (a) ∠ABC, ∠B   (b) ∠1   (c) ∠b   (d) ∠BCA, ∠ACB

4-10. ∠AFE, ∠BFD, ∠AFB, ∠BFE, ∠AFC, ∠CFD, ∠AFD, ∠CFE, ∠BFC, ∠DFE

4-11. (a) acute   (b) acute, right, or obtuse, depending upon the angles   (c) right
(d) straight   (e) obtuse   (f) straight   (g) obtuse   (h) right

4-12. 35°; explanations may vary

4-13. (a) right   (b) obtuse   (c) acute   (d) obtuse   (e) acute   (f) obtuse
(g) acute   (h) obtuse

4-14. (a) 40′   (b) 42′   (c) .5°   (d) .9°

4-15. (a) complementary, 15° and 75°; supplementary, 115° and 65°   (b) complementary, 40°
and 50°; supplementary, 60° and 120°   (c) complementary, 70° and 20°; supplementary,
100° and 80°   (d) complementary, 1° and 89°; supplementary, 90° and 90°

4-16. (a) adjacent   (b) adjacent, complementary   (c) adjacent, supplementary   (d) adjacent, supplementary   (e) adjacent, supplementary   (f) vertical

4-17. a and c are linear pairs;   (b) $\overrightarrow{BC}$ and $\overrightarrow{BE}$ are not opposite rays   (d) ∠5 and ∠6 are not adjacent

4-18.

```
    3 | 1
    6 | 2
    8 | 4
    5 | 7
```

4-19. m∠1 = 95°, m∠2 = 85°, m∠3 = 95°, m∠4 = 85°, m∠6 = 85°, m∠7 = 95°, m∠8 = 85°;
m∠1 = (180 − x)°, m∠3 = (180 − x)°, m∠4 = x°, m∠5 = (180 - x)°, m∠6 = x°, m∠7 = (180 - x)°,
m∠8 = x°

4-20. (a) 90°   (b) 45°   (c) 90°   (d) 90°   (e) 180°   (f) 360°

4-21. Yes; explanations may vary

4-22. Decagon, 10; hexagon, 6; pentagon, 5; quadrilateral, 4; dodecagon, 12; n-gon, n; nonagon, 9;
triangle, 3; undecagon, 11; heptagon, 7; octagon, 8

4-23. The second and third figures are concave. $\overline{AB}$ or $\overline{CB}$ proves the second polygon is concave.
$\overline{AB}$ or $\overline{CD}$ proves that the third polygon is concave.

4-24. Drawings may vary.

4-25.  ; 3, 0; 4, 2; 5, 5; 6, 9; n, $\dfrac{n^2 - 3n}{2}$

4-26. Triangle, 3, 180°; quadrilateral, 4, 360°; pentagon, 5, 540°; hexagon, 6, 720°; heptagon, 7,
900°; octagon, 8, 1080°

4-27. (a) false; all three angles must equal 180°   (b) true; ☐ or ▭

(c) false; a quadrilateral must have four right angles   (d) true;

4–28.   (a) 3   (b) 6   (c) 4   (d) 7   (e) 8   (f) 5

4–29.   Explanations may vary.

4–30.   Heptagon; $51\frac{3}{7}°$

4–31.   Quadrilateral, 4, 90°, 360°; pentagon, 5, 72°, 360°; hexagon, 6, 60°, 360°; octagon, 8, 45°, 360°; decagon, 10, 36°, 360°; n-gon, n, $\frac{360}{n}°$, 360°; the sum of the measures of the exterior angles are equal to 360°

4–32.   (a) equilateral   (b) isosceles   (c) isosceles   (d) scalene

4–33.   (a) obtuse   (b) acute or equiangular   (c) right   (d) obtuse   (e) right   (f) acute

4–34.   (a) false; ∠E is included between $\overline{EF}$ and $\overline{ED}$ (b) true   (c) true   (d) false; $\overline{AC}$ is included between ∠A and ∠C

4–35.   (a) longest side, $\overline{AC}$; shortest side, $\overline{BC}$ (b) longest side, $\overline{FG}$; shortest side, $\overline{EG}$
           (c) longest side, $\overline{HG}$; shortest side, $\overline{HI}$

4–36.   m∠1 = 110°; m∠2 = 30°; m∠3 = 45°; m∠4= 45°; m∠5 = 45°; m∠6 = 45°; m∠7 = 90°; m∠8 = 120°; m∠9 = 60°; m∠10 = 60°

4–37.   The second and fourth diagrams could be triangles. First diagram—longest side should be less than 13. Third diagram—longest side should be less than 6.

4–38. $\overline{PG}$, perpendicular bisector; $\overline{BD}$, altitude; $\overline{BG}$, median; $\overline{EC}$, angle bisector; $\overline{AH}$, angle bisector

4–39.   (a) 5   (b) 15   (c) 13   (d) 17

4–40.   (a) $\sqrt{13}$ (b) $2\sqrt{6}$ (c) $5\sqrt{3}$ (d) $2\sqrt{11}$

4–41.   Answers may vary; an example: $5^2 = 25$, 12 + 13 = 25; the Pythagorean triple is 5, 12, 13; $13^2 = 12^2 + 5^2$; 169 = 144 + 25

4–42.   Acute—a and b; obtuse—c and d

4–43.   (a) $4\sqrt{2}$ (b) $2\sqrt{3}$ (c) 2   (d) 14

4–44.   (a) 2   (b) 1   (c) 6   (d) 5

4–45.   (a) 20   (b) 14   (c) 10   (d) 18   (e) 16   (f) 20

4–46.   15, 7.5, $7.5\sqrt{3}$; 10, 5, $5\sqrt{3}$; 6, 3, $3\sqrt{3}$; 20, 10, $10\sqrt{3}$

4–47.   (a) BC $= 12\sqrt{2}$, AC = 24   (b) DF $= 24\sqrt{3}$, EF = 36   (c) GH = 22, HI = 11   (d) JK = 1, KL $= \sqrt{2}$

4–48.   Triangles in parts a, c, d are congruent; triangles in parts b and f are congruent

4–49.   ΔABC ≅ ΔFED; ∠A ≅ ∠F, ∠B ≅ ∠E, ∠C ≅ ∠D; $\overline{AB} \cong \overline{EF}$, $\overline{BC} \cong \overline{ED}$, $\overline{AC} \cong \overline{FD}$

4–50.   (a) $\overline{ED}$ (b) $\overline{DC}$ (c) ∠E   (d) ∠CDF

4–51.   ΔABC ≅ ΔJLK, SSS; ΔDEF ≅ ΔGIH, ASA; ΔMQN ≅ ΔOQP, SAS

4–52.   ΔABD ≅ ΔCBD, HL; ΔEFI ≅ ΔGHI, AAS; ΔOPQ ≅ ΔQRO, AAS

4–53.   Sketches may vary.

4–54.   (a) no similarities   (b) SAS   (c) AA   (d) SSS

4–55.   (a) ΔABC ~ ΔEDF, 2:3   (b) several statements are possible; one is ΔGHI ~ ΔJKL, 5:3   (c) ΔMNO ~ ΔRQP, 1:1   (d) ΔSTU ~ ΔWXV, $\sqrt{3}$:3

4–56.   (a) $\frac{6}{15} = \frac{8}{y} = \frac{10}{x}$; x = 25; y = 20   (b) $\frac{3.5}{7} = \frac{1}{x} = \frac{y}{8}$; x = 2; y = 4   (c) $\frac{15}{10} = \frac{x}{12} = \frac{20}{y}$; x = 18; y = $13\frac{1}{3}$

4–57.   (a) 12 ft.   (b) 18 ft.   (c) 16 ft.

4–58.   (a) equilateral   (b) isosceles; explanations may vary

4–59.   Largest, 22 ft.; smallest, 12 ft.; sizes of individual work areas and explanations will vary

4–60.   (a) 22.5 sq. in.   (b) 20 sq. in.   (c) 4 sq. in.   (d) 600 sq. mm

4–61.   Quizzes will vary.

4–62.   The areas are the same. Explanations may vary. One is that the triangles have the same base and altitude.

4–63.   39.69 sq. units

4–64. (a) parallelogram, rectangle (b) trapezoid (c) parallelogram, rhombus (d) parallelogram (e) parallelogram, rectangle, square, rhombus (f) trapezoid

4–65. (a) parallelogram (b) square (c) trapezoid (d) rhombus (e) rectangle (f) trapezoid

4–66. 0, 0; sketches and explanations may vary

4–67. (a) true (b) true (c) false; some parallelograms are rectangles or all rectangles are parallelograms (d) false; no trapezoids are parallelograms (e) true (f) false; some rectangles are squares or all squares are rectangles

4–68. (a) ▭ (b) ◇ (c) ▱ (d) impossible (if it could have four congruent sides it would be a rhombus, which is a parallelogram; a trapezoid is not a parallelogram) (e) impossible (both squares and rectangles must have four right angles)

4–69. Total, 204; 64 1×1 squares; 49 2×2 squares; 36 3×3 squares; 25 4×4 squares; 16 5×5 squares; 9 6×6 squares; 4 7×7 squares; 1 8×8 square

4–70. 36
$1 \times 1, 1 \times 2, 1 \times 3, 1 \times 4, 1 \times 5, 1 \times 6, 1 \times 7, 1 \times 8$
$2 \times 2, 2 \times 3, 2 \times 4, 2 \times 5, 2 \times 6, 2 \times 7, 2 \times 8$
$3 \times 3, 3 \times 4, 3 \times 5, 3 \times 6, 3 \times 7, 3 \times 8$
$4 \times 4, 4 \times 5, 4 \times 6, 4 \times 7, 4 \times 8,$
$5 \times 5, 5 \times 6, 5 \times 7, 5 \times 8$
$6 \times 6, 6 \times 7, 6 \times 8$
$7 \times 7, 7 \times 8$
8×8

4–71. Both segments have the same length; isosceles

4–72. Yes, a parallelogram could be a kite if the parallelogram is a rhombus. No, a kite could be a parallelogram if all sides are congruent.

4–73. (a) all (b) all (c) all (d) square, rectangle (e) square, rhombus

4–74. (a) all (b) square, rectangle (c) square, rhombus (d) square, rhombus

4–75. 25 sq. cm

4–76. No. If the length of a side of a square is not a whole number, then the area is a mixed number. For example, if the length of a side is 1.5 units, then the area is 2.25 square units, which is not a perfect square.

4–77. A diagonal of a square equals the length of a side times $\sqrt{2}$. The area of a square whose diagonal is $s\sqrt{2}$ is $\dfrac{(s\sqrt{2})^2}{2} = \dfrac{2s^2}{2} = s^2$.

4–78. d is false; the ratio of the area of a square to its perimeter is greater than or equal to 1 if the length of the side is greater than or equal to 4

4–79. The area of bills prior to 1929 was about 23 square inches. The area of bills in circulation today is about 16 square inches. The area of the larger bills is about 1.4 times the area of the bills in circulation today.

4–80. 400 sq. ft.

4–81. 10 squares

4–82. Sketches may vary. A rectangle that measures 20 yards by 242 yards is one possible sketch.

4–83. 4,840 sq. yd.

4–84. $6'' \times 6,''$ 6 tiles are required; $12'' \times 12,''$ 24 tiles are required; 144 sq. in. or 1 sq. ft.

4–85. Smallest perimeter, $14''$ (a $3'' \times 4''$ rectangle); largest perimeter, $26''$ (a $1'' \times 12''$ rectangle)

4–86. Pedro could cut $\frac{1}{2}$ inch on each side of the diagonal of the rectangle. The remaining area is 81.5 square inches.

4–87. Area of living room and kitchen, 525 sq. ft.; area of family room, 300 sq. ft.; area of deck, 144 sq. ft.; total area, 969 sq. ft.

4–88. 12 sq. units

4–89. Explanations may vary. The height of a parallelogram is the perpendicular distance from a vertex to the base. In a rectangle, the height (or width) is perpendicular to the base.

4–90. a, b, and e, 45 sq. units; d and f, 75 sq. units; c, 175 sq. units

4–91. 60 sq. in.

4–92. Answers may vary, but may include: recycling codes, peace sign, yin and yang. Explanations may vary.

4–93. Explanations may vary.

4–94. A diameter measures through the center; sketches may vary

4–95. 10 units

4–96. Problems may vary.

4–97. (a) 62.8 in.　　(b) 47.1 in.　　(c) 56.52 mm　　(d) 6.28 cm

4–98. Explanations may vary. Circumference of rim is about 56.52 in.; circumference of basketball is about 30 in. Difference is about 26.52 in.

4–99. 2,826 sq. mi.; fog, mist, obstructions

4–100. 9,341.5 sq. mm

4–101. Area of smaller circle is $\frac{1}{25}$ of the area of the whole target

4–102. 78.57 sq. in.; 78.5 sq. in.; explanations may vary

4–103. Circle has the larger area. Area of circle is about 78.5 sq. in.; area of square equals 61.6225 sq. in.

4–104. Examples may vary; some include: a dartboard, hubcaps, ridges on plates, raindrops in a pond

4–105. About 651 sq. in.

4–106. Label each circle 1, 2, or 3. Each circle described is tangent to all three with the following circles internally tangent to the circle that is drawn: 1, 2, 3; 1, 3; 2, 3; 1, 2; 3; 2; 1; none.

4–107. An infinite amount; an infinite amount; the great circle has the larger area and circumference

4–108. Explanations may vary.

4–109. *Minor Arcs*—AB, AC, AD, AH, AG, AF, BC, BD, BE, BH, BG, CD, CE, CF, CH, DE, DF, DG, EF, EG, EH, FG, FH, GH; *semi-circles*—AE, BF, CG, DH; *major arcs*—ABF, ABG, ABH, BCG, BCH, BCA, CDH, CDA, CDB, DEA, DEB, DEC, EFB, EFC, EFD, FGC, FGD, FGE, GHD, GHE, GHF, HAE, HAF, HAG

4–110. $\angle AOD \cong \angle BOC$; $\angle DOC \cong \angle AOB$; $\angle ABD \cong \angle BAC \cong \angle ACD \cong \angle BDC$; m$\angle AOD = 60°$; m$\angle AOB = 120°$; m$\angle ABD = 30°$

4–111. Equilateral; isosceles

4–112. *Diameter*—$\overline{CD}$; *radius*—$\overline{OE}$, $\overline{OD}$, $\overline{OC}$; *chord*—$\overline{AB}$, $\overline{CD}$, $\overline{BE}$; *secant*—$\overleftrightarrow{BE}$; *tangent*—$\overleftrightarrow{AF}$

4–113. (a) 180　　(b) 200　　(c) 100　　(d) 120　　(e) 80　　(f) 60

4–114. Explanations may vary.

4–115. No. Explanations may vary.

4–116. Explanations may vary.

4–117. Explanations may vary.

4–118. Area of $\frac{1}{8}$ of the pizza is about 14.13 sq. in.; area of $\frac{1}{6}$ of the pizza is about 18.84 sq. in. Area of $\frac{1}{8}$ of the pizza is $\frac{3}{4}$ the area of $\frac{1}{6}$ of the pizza.

4–119. $(4\pi - 8)$ sq. cm

4–120. Explanations may vary.

4–121. (a) 7,776 cu. in.　　(b) 34.375 cu. ft.　　(c) 13,680 cu. cm　　(d) 4.6875 cu. ft.

4–122. 10 (3 rows of 3 boxes and 1 on its side); 870 cu. in. are wasted

4–123. 18 sq. in.

4–124. About 1.6 cu. ft.; 7.85 sq. ft.

4-125. The dish with the 5-inch diameter; the volume of the dish with the 4-inch diameter is about 21 cubic inches; the volume of the dish with the 5-inch diameter is about 26 cubic inches

4-126. Joe; John substituted the value of the diameter in the formula instead of substituting the value of the radius

4-127. V = 91,636,272 cu. ft.; SA = 1,496,880 sq. ft.

4-128. Volume of basketball is about 448.7 cubic inches; surface area of basketball is about 283.4 square inches; volume of baseball is about 14.1 cubic inches; surface area of baseball is about 28.3 square inches

4-129. The missing number in each row follows: *row 1—6, row 2—8, row 3—8, row 4—30, row 5—12*

4-130. Explanations may vary.

SECTION 5 ALGEBRA

5-1. a and c are 19; (b) 35   (d) 16

5-2. There are many possible answers; some include: $(2 + 1) - (4 - 3) = 2$; $(4 - 3) + (2 \times 1) = 3$; $(4 + 3) - (2 + 1) = 4$; $(4 + 3) - (2 \times 1) = 5$; $(4 \times 3) \div (2 \times 1) = 6$; $(4 + 3) \times (2 - 1) = 7$; $2(3 - 1) + 4 = 8$; $1 \times (4 + 3 + 2) = 9$; $4 + 3 + 2 + 1 = 10$

5-3. 665 ft.

5-4. (a) $7 \times (6 - 4) \times 4$ (b) $(18 - 8) \times 5 + 6$ (c) $8^2 - (1 \times 2^3)$ (d) $(2^2 + 3) \times (9 - 1)$

5-5. 40 ft.

5-6. 1877

5-7. 104

5-8. 451; temperature at which paper burns

5-9. $5,368,709.12

5-10. Explanations may vary.

5-11. Answers may vary; some include: positive, +; negative, −; and times, ×

5-12. (a) 2   (b) 4   (c) 5   (d) 1

5-13. (a) $.62   (b) $.72   (c) $.20   (d) $.13

5-14. 650

5-15. 1958

5-16. (a) 19 mi. per sec.   (b) 12 mi. per sec.   (c) 200 years   (d) 680 light years

5-17. 6,084

5-18. (a) 0   (b) 1, 2, 3, 4   (c) 1   (d) −3

5-19. Browning

5-20. Students should disagree; explanations will vary

5-21. Students should disagree; $|0| = 0$; $|2.5| = 2.5$; these are not positive whole numbers

5-22. (a) 0 or 1; {−3, −2, 0, 1, 7}   (b) 0; {0, −4, −5, −6, −7}   (c) −8 or −9; {−9, −8, −7, −6, −5}   (d) 6 or 8; {−4, 2, 4, 6, 8}

5-23. 20 sec.; blastoff = 0

5-24. Explanations may vary.

5-25. −15;

-2	5	0
3	1	-1
2	-3	4

5-26. Explanations will vary.

5-27. Lower temperatures require more oil; 0

5-28. Problems may vary.

5-29. (a) positive   (b) cannot be determined   (c) 0   (d) negative   (e) cannot be determined

5-30. (a) 21   (b) 14   (c) 16   (d) 25

5-31. (a) 0   (b) −16   (c) 8   (d) 16   (e) 24   (f) −8; −16, −8, 0, 8, 16, 24. The number to the right is 8 more than the number to the left.

5-32. Explanations may vary.

5-33. Explanations may vary. (a) $-6 \times -3 \times -2 \times -7$; the only product that is positive (b) $-3 \times -4 \times 0$; the only product that is 0; or $-3 \times -3 \times -1$; the only product that is less than 0 (c) $-5 \times -3 \times 9$; the only product that is not divisible by 2

5-34. (b) $-21 \div -7 = 3$ (d) $-156 \div -12 = 13$ (e) $-20 \div 0$ is undefined, or $0 \div -20 = 0$

5-35. Yes; yes; explanations will vary

5-36. (a) -14 (b) 17 (c) -24 (d) -10

5-37. Problems will vary.

5-38. $20 \times 10 - (-4) + (-2 \div -1) = 206$; $(-4 \times 20) + (10 \div -1) - (-2) = -88$

5-39. (a) $15x + 7y$ (b) $4x - 3y + 10$ (c) $4x - 3y + 10$ (d) $5x + 7y$ (e) $-x + y + 10$; b and c have the same answers

5-40. (a) $-2a, 3$ (b) $-4a, 20b, 6$ (c) $-a, c, 2b$ (d) $5a, -8$ or $8, -5a$

5-41. (a) $2a + 3b - 12c - 6$; -61 (b) $5a - 9b + 4c - 10$; -27 (c) $-4a - 3b - 4c$; -21; (d) $-4a + 8b + 3c + 10$; 57; the values are increasing

5-42. (a) $8x$ (b) $-6x$ (c) 40; 40; $13k$ (d) $2x$; 12

5-43. (a) $10x - 24$; 16 (b) $-8x - 1$; 23 (c) $32 + 21x$; -157 (d) $-3x - 11$; -23; the answers to b and d are opposites

5-44. Problems may vary.

5-45. All problems; (a) $x = -25$ (b) $x = 1$ (c) $x = -21$ (d) $x = -10$ (e) $x = 0$ (f) $x = 15$; e could also be solved by using transformation by addition

5-46. a, e; b, c, d, f; (a) $x = 23$ (b) $x = 19$ (c) $x = -20$ (d) $x = 4$ (e) $x = -7$ (f) $x = -32$

5-47. Explanations may vary; $x = 80$

5-48. (a) $x = 16$ (b) $x = 8$ (c) $x = 4$ (d) $x = -12$ (e) $x = -24$ (f) $x = -48$

5-49. (a) $3, \frac{1}{3}, 5$ (b) $\frac{1}{3}, 3, 45$

5-50. a and c, both solutions are -2; b and d, both solutions are -7

5-51. Equations and explanations may vary.

5-52. a and d are similar; (b) $7x^3, 4x^3$ or $7x^2, 4x^2$ (c) $8y^2, 8y^2$ or $8y, 8y$

5-53. $40, 30, -12, -1$

5-54. Both are correct.

5-55. a, b, and c have solutions that are even numbers; (a) $n = 8$ (b) $n = 12$ (c) $n = 4$ (d) $n = 1$

5-56. c and d have no root; a, e, and f are true for all real numbers

5-57. The symbol means "is not greater than" or "is less than or equal to." Inequalities will vary.

5-58. (a) $>, >, >$ (b) $<, <, >$ (c) $\geq, \geq, \leq$

5-59. (a) 4 (b) 1 (c) 4 (d) 2

5-60. (a) circumference of a circle; $r = \dfrac{C}{2\pi}$ (b) volume of a cone or pyramid; $h = \dfrac{3V}{B}$

(c) conversion formula for converting from degrees Fahrenheit to degrees Celsius; $F = \frac{9}{5}C + 32$ (d) perimeter of a rectangle; $l = \frac{1}{2}P - w$

5-61. a, b, and c are false; (a) It is always in the first or fourth quadrant (b) It is on the x-axis (c) It is always in the first or third quadrant (d) true

5-62. Explanations may vary.

5-63. Equations may vary.

5-64. The points in a and b are on the same line; (a) slope $= -2$ (b) slope $= 1$ (c) change $(5, -5)$ to $(5, -6)$ or change $(5, -5)$ to $(6, -5)$; slope $= 1$

5-65. Explanations may vary.

5-66. $\frac{5}{6}$; explanations may vary

5-67. (a) $y = -x$ (b) $y = 2x + 1$ (c) $y = -x + 2$ (d) $y = 2$

5-68. Both have the same y-intercept but different slopes.

5-69. (a) (1, 2)　　(b) $y = \dfrac{-4}{3}x$　　(c) $y = 2x + 5$　　(d) $y = -x - 3$

5-70. (a) first equation y, second equation x or y; x = 2, y = 10　　(b) second equation y; x = 5, y = 1
(c) first equation y; x = –4, y = –3

5-71. b is partially correct; he needs to solve for x. d is partially correct; x should equal $5\frac{3}{4}$. Since there were eight answers and he got 6 out of 8 correct, his score should be 75%.

5-72. Preferences may vary. $x = 0$; $y = \dfrac{-17}{3}$

5-73. Explanations may vary.

5-74. (a) 25　　(b) –25　　(c) 21　　(d) 2,401　　(e) –135　　(f) –3,375

5-75. (a) $15a^8$, two errors　　(b) $18x^6$, one error　　(c) $6c^2$, two errors　　(d) correct
(e) $-8c^5$, one error　　(f) $-30r^6s^7$, one error

5-76. $2\pi r^3 = \frac{4}{3}\pi r^3 + \frac{2}{3}\pi r^3$

5-77. (a) a^5　　(b) $8a^7$　　(c) $9a^2$　　(d) $4a^6b^8$

5-78. 27 times as large

5-79. Explanations may vary.

5-80. 1,000 times as large

5-81. (c) $3a^4$

5-82. (a) 4　　(b) 6　　(c) 1　　(d) 2　　(e) 5　　(f) 3

5-83. 33; answers may vary

5-84. (a) $5a + 9$　　(b) $2n + 7$　　(c) $2x^2 - xy - y^2$　　(d) $a + 2$

5-85. a and d are correct; (b) change 28 to 28x　　(c) change $-12ab$ to $+12ab$

5-86. (a) $3a - 4$　　(b) $-3b^2 + 2b + 1$　　(c) $6st^2 - 7$　　(d) $-3r^2s^2 + 5rs - 2$

5-87. (a) 3　　(b) 2　　(c) 4　　(d) 1

5-88. (a) $x^2 + 5x + 6$　　(b) $x^2 + 8x + 15$　　(c) $x^2 + 6x + 9$　　(d) $x^2 + 5x + 4$

5-89. $10^3 = 1,000$; $(-2)^3 = -8$

5-90. Explanations may vary.

5-91. $(a + b)^0 = 1$; $(a + b)^1 = 1a + 1b$; $(a + b)^2 = a^2 + 2ab + b^2$; $(a + b)^3 = a^3 + 3a^2b + 3ab^2 + b^3$;
$(a + b)^n = \left(\dfrac{n}{n}\right)a^n + \left(\dfrac{n}{1}\right)a^{n-1}b + \left(\dfrac{n}{2}\right)a^{n-2}b^2 + \ldots + \left(\dfrac{n}{n}\right)b^n$

5-92. Explanations may vary. $(3a - 5)(3a + 5)$

5-93. (a) $(a + 4)$; P = 4a + 16　　(b) $(a - 5)$; P = 4a - 20　　(c) $(7a - 4)$; P = 28a - 16
(d) $(6a^2 - b^3)$; P = 24a^2 - 4b^3

5-94. (a) 5, 1　　(b) 7, 6　　(c) 18, 3　　(d) 14x, 5

5-95. –9, $(x - 10)(x + 1)$; 9, $(x - 1)(x + 10)$; 3, $(x - 2)(x + 5)$; –3, $(x + 2)(x - 5)$

5-96. The first rectangle has the smaller perimeter. Its perimeter is $10x - 6$. The perimeter of the other rectangle is $12x + 6$.

5-97. (a) $(2 - y)$　　(b) $(1 - a)$　　(c) $(2 - x), (x - 2), (2 - x)$　　(d) $(4y - 1), (4y - 1), (4y - 1)$

5-98. (a) $m^3 - 27$　　(b) $z + 1$; $z^2 - z + 1$　　(c) $(2x - y)$; $4x^2 + 2xy + y^2$

5-99. Explanations may vary.

5-100. d, $3\sqrt{6}$

5-101. a and e are correct; (b) incorrect, $\dfrac{\sqrt{15}}{4}$　　(c) partial credit, $\dfrac{9\sqrt{2}}{4}$　　(d) partial credit, $4\sqrt{3}$;
explanations may vary

5-102. (a) $2\sqrt{17}$　　(b) $3\sqrt{3}$　　(c) $\sqrt{2}$　　(d) $-47\sqrt{3}$

5-103. Explanations may vary.

5-104. (a) 1　　(b) 3　　(c) 4　　(d) 2

5-105. (a) x = 39　　(b) x = 0　　(c) x = 49

5-106. Its degree

5-107. Explanations may vary.

5-108. b and d are partially correct; (b) x = 9, x = 4　　(d) m = 0, m = 2, m = –2

5-109. (a) x = 7, x = -7   (b) x = $\sqrt{7}$, x = $-\sqrt{7}$ (c) no real roots   (d) x = 5, x = -5

5-110. They are equal.

5-111. (a) 18, -12   (b) 12, 2   (c) $3 + 5\sqrt{2}$, $3 - 5\sqrt{2}$ (d) 3, 1   (e) 11, 5   (f) $4 + 7\sqrt{2}$, $4 - 7\sqrt{2}$

5-112. $x^2 - 2x = 20$, 1, $1 + \sqrt{21}$, $1 - \sqrt{21}$; $x^2 - 4x = 3$, 4, $2 + \sqrt{7}$, $2 - \sqrt{7}$; $x^2 + 6x - 9 = 0$, 9, $-3 + 3\sqrt{2}$, $-3 - 3\sqrt{2}$

5-113. b and d are correct; (a) c = -4   (c) b = -7, c = 4

5-114. (a) 2   (b) 4   (c) 1   (d) 3

5-115. (a) $3i\sqrt{2}$ (b) $-3i$ (c) -9   (d) -7

5-116. 1, -1, i, $-i$

5-117. Equations may vary.

5-118. Sums of roots = $\dfrac{-b}{a}$; products of roots = $\dfrac{c}{a}$

5-119. $f(x) = x^2 + 2x - 3$

5-120. The y-intercept is c.

5-121. (a) x = 0 (double root), x = $\dfrac{-b}{a}$ (b) x = 0, x = $\sqrt{\dfrac{-b}{a}}$, x = $-\sqrt{\dfrac{-b}{a}}$

5-122. 1×10^{100}; $1 \times 10^{10^{100}}$

5-123. Explanations may vary.

5-124. (a) 9×10^{-28} (b) 1.39×10^9 (c) 1.36×10^{-6} (d) 9.461×10^{12}

5-125. (a) 350,000 pages   (b) 1,500,000 light years   (c) 0.0000005 cm (d) 0.000000000000000001 gm

5-126. (a) -3   (b) -5   (c) 2   (d) 0

5-127. (a) $3x^{-1}y^{-5}$ (b) $a^{-1}b^{-7}$ (c) $8^2 \times 3^{-2}$ or $7.\overline{1}$ (d) $25a^4b^{10}$

5-128. Explanations may vary.

SECTION 6 POTPOURRI

6-1.   Problems will vary.

6-2.   6; 7

6-3.   Explanations may vary. If Mary gets a 100, her average will be 89.75, which may be rounded up to a 90. If grades are not rounded, Mary would need 101 to achieve a 90 average.

6-4.   Disagree; explanations may vary; average of two highest and two lowest equals 122.75; average of all ten equals 120.3

6-5.   .286

6-6.   .333

6-7.   3.45; the lower the ERA, the better the pitcher

6-8.   About $36.56

6-9.   48 mph

6-10. Lists will vary, but might include the following: what the average person thinks; a bowling average; the average high and low temperatures of a location

6-11. 67,663 ft.; no; explanations may vary

6-12. Individual training ranges and explanations will vary.

6-13. Explanations may vary.

6-14. E; 16

6-15. If there is an even number of data, then the data may not contain the median. Example: {1, 3, 5, 10, 11, 15}; the median is 7.5.

6-16. 1 has one factor; 4, 9, and 25 each have three factors; 16 has five factors. The median and mode each equal 3.

6-17. Median = 2,865 miles; mean is about 2,851 miles

6–18. The mode, if it exists, must be a member of the data. The mean and median may be members of the data. Examples may vary. One is {1, 3, 5, 5}. The mode is 5, the mean is 3.5, and the median is 4.

6–19. Mode = 0, 1; median = 2; mean = 7

6–20. ⌇⌇⌇⌇⌇, 5; ‖, 2; ‖, 2

6–21.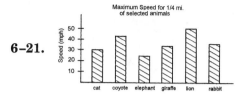

6–22. All answers are possible; explanations may vary

6–23. No. Explanations may vary.

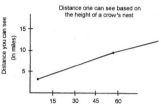

6–24.
```
0 │ 3
1 │ 0   5
2 │ 3
3 │ 3
```

6–25. (a) positive   (b) negative   (c) positive   (d) positive   (e) positive   (f) no relationship

6–26. (a) 2   (b) 1   (c) 3

6–27. Cost of 10 compasses is about $19.50; cost of 11 compasses is $19.25. The cost of 10 compasses is $.25 more than the cost of 11 compasses.

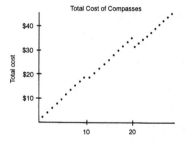

6–28.

6–29. (a) $\frac{8}{31}$ (b) $\frac{1}{31}$ (c) $\frac{11}{31}$ (d) $\frac{2}{31}$ (e) $\frac{4}{31}$ (f) $\frac{5}{31}$

6–30.

6–31. (a) $\frac{1}{2}$ (b) $\frac{1}{13}$ (c) $\frac{2}{13}$ (d) $\frac{5}{13}$ (e) $\frac{1}{52}$ (f) $\frac{3}{13}$

6–32. $.25 off next purchase, 1,000; free soft drink, 200; free sandwich, 100; "Sorry, try again," 700

6–33. No; explanations may vary. Lists of events will vary.

6–34. (a) $\frac{1}{3}$ (b) $\frac{3}{5}$ (c) $\frac{1}{1}$ (d) $\frac{1}{7}$

6–35. (a) $\frac{2}{9}$ (b) $\frac{1}{3}$ (c) $\frac{1}{18}$ (d) 0

Spinner A   Spinner B

6-36.

6-37. $\frac{1}{2}$; $\frac{1}{16}$; explanations may vary

6-38. (a) $\frac{1}{376}$ (b) $\frac{1}{2,256}$ (c) $\frac{3}{752}$ (d) $\frac{1}{564}$

6-39. $\frac{6}{1,265}$; $\frac{1}{9,765,625}$

6-40. Explanations may vary.

6-41. Explanations may vary.

6-42. (a) 162   (b) 36   (c) 18   (d) 108

6-43. $10^{13} = 10,000,000,000,000$; $\dfrac{65,000,000}{10,000,000,000,000} = \dfrac{13}{2,000,000}$

6-44. 17,576,000; explanations may vary, but might include issuing license plates consisting of a four-digit number followed by three letters

6-45. 21!

6-46. (a) 6,720   (b) 504   (c) 604,800

6-47. 7! = 5,040

6-48. (a) 20   (b) 58,905   (c) 792

6-49. Explanations may vary.

6-50. Examples may vary. Example: 11 + 22 = 33; 33 − 22 = 11. Yes. Addition and subtraction are inverse operations.

6-51. No; 2222

6-52. Answers may vary. Examples: 11 × 44 = 484; 11 × 22 = 242; 22 × 22 = 484; 33 × 121 = 3993; 11 × 424 = 4,664

6-53. Answers may vary. One solution is O = 2, N = 1, E = 6, T = 4, and W = 3

6-54. Cryptarithms will vary.

6-55. TWO IS THE ONLY EVEN PRIME

6-56. Messages will vary.

6-57. ONE IS A PERFECT SQUARE

6-58.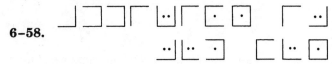

6-59. Rebuses will vary.

6-60. Problems will vary.

6-61.

10	3	8
5	7	9
6	11	4

6-62.

13	2	3	16
8	11	10	5
12	7	6	9
1	14	15	4

6–63.

17	24	1	8	15
23	5	7	14	16
4	6	13	20	22
10	12	19	21	3
11	18	25	2	9

6–64. Answers may vary; examples include: one day at a time, two peas in a pod, three's a crowd, throw to the four winds, and slap me five

6–65. Answers may vary, examples include: (a) liter   (b) line   (c) point   (d) permutations or a prime number   (e) probability of an event A   (f) Celsius   (g) hypotenuse   (h) circumference

6–66. Explanations may vary, but should note that the infinity sign was mistaken for the number 8 turned on its side.

6–67. (a) 32, 64, 128; previous number multiplied by 2   (b) 36, 49, 64; perfect squares
(c) 6.25, 3.125, 1.5625; previous number divided by 2   (d) 8, 7, 10; pattern of subtracting 1 then adding 3

6–68. Problems may vary.

6–69. The sum of the first 10 numbers is 11 times the 7th term.

6–70. (a) 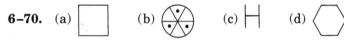   (b)   (c)   (d)

6–71. (a) 44   (b) –7   (c) 29   (d) 7.5

6–72. (a) 170   (b) 205   (c) 215   (d) –5

6–73. (a) 4   (b) 1   (c) 2   (d) 3

6–74. (a) sum does not exist   (b) sum does not exist   (c) 2   (d) $\frac{4}{9}$

6–75. 1,024

6–76. 81

6–77. $5\frac{1}{3}$ in.

6–78. 15; the fifth triangular number is five more than the fourth

6–79. 100; perfect squares

6–80. odd; odd; 1st, 2nd, odd; the sum of the first, second, third, fourth, fifth, sixth, and seventh odd number

6–81. Sketches may vary.

6–82. four ways, 2×9, 9×2, 3×6, 6×3. Yes. They are prime numbers.

6–83. 1, 10, 45, 120, 210, 252, 210, 120, 45, 10, 1

6–84. Counting numbers; triangular numbers. Yes; explanations may vary.

6–85. Several answers are possible. Example: if m = 3, $\left(\frac{10}{2}\right)^2 = \left(\frac{8}{2}\right)^2 + 3^2$; $5^2 = 4^2 + 3^2$; 3, 4, and 5 are a Pythagorean triple

6–86. Any triple that has two numbers that differ by 1 cannot be obtained by Plato's method since $m^2 + 1$ and $m^2 - 1$ differ by two. For example, 13, 12, and 5 are a Pythagorean triple that cannot be obtained by Plato's method.

6–87. 3 by 5 notecard

6–88. I, E, Y, M, and T. Examples may vary. Examples: mom, BOX, 11, 88

6–89.    A regular n-gon has n lines of symmetry.

6–90. (a) 4   (b) 2   (c) 1   (d) 6

6–91. Rectangle; area is 24 square units; perimeter is 20 units

6–92. Scalene; perimeter ≈ 22 units; area is 6 units

6–93. Answers may vary. Square or circle are two possibilities.

6–94. Midpoint of each diagonal is (1.5, –1). It appears that the diagonals are congruent and bisect each other.

6–95. (2, 1), (6, –1), (0, –3), or (4, –5).

6–96. 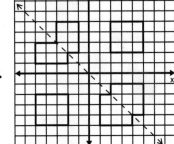 $y = -x$

6–97. Radical sign

6–98. (a) reflection or translation   (b) rotation   (c) translation

6–99. (a) 4   (b) 2   (c) 3   (d) 5   (e) 5   (f) 1

6–100. (a) x = 3, y = 7, z = 9   (b) x = 1, y = 4, z = 7   (c) x = 2, y = 6, z = 8

6–101. $\begin{pmatrix} 16 & 26 & 36 \\ 25 & 38 & 51 \\ 25 & 32 & 39 \end{pmatrix}$ No, explanations may vary.

6–102. Problems may vary.

6–103. (–2, 6) and (–1, 9)

6–104. (3, –5), (2, –8), and (0, –5)

6–105. $\begin{pmatrix} 3 & 0 \\ 0 & 3 \end{pmatrix}$ 9 times as large

6–106. The following nodes are even: A, C, E, F, G, and N; the others are odd

6–107. b and d; two odd, even

6–108. Jackson to East Brunswick; East Brunswick to Spotswood; Spotswood to East Brunswick; Spotswood to South River; South River to Jackson; Jackson to South River

6–109. 9; A defeated B; A defeated D; A defeated F; B defeated C; B defeated D; D defeated E; E defeated C; E defeated F; F defeated C. Team A won the most games; team C did not win any.

6–110. Answers may vary. Two possibilities: (1) Yes, suppose C called E, and E told the plans to L when L called. E then called H. (2) No, L could have called E before C called E. Then E called H. L was unaware of the plans.

6–111. Explanations may vary.

6–112. Personal quotes will vary.